GHOSTS OF THE AFRICAN DIASPORA

RE-MAPPING THE TRANSNATIONAL

A Dartmouth Series in American Studies

SERIES EDITOR

Donald E. Pease

Avalon Foundation Chair of Humanities

Founding Director of the Futures of American Studies Institute

Dartmouth College

The emergence of Transnational American Studies in the wake of the Cold War marks the most significant reconfiguration of American Studies since its inception. The shock waves generated by a newly globalized world order demanded an understanding of America's embeddedness within global and local processes rather than scholarly reaffirmations of its splendid isolation. The series Re-Mapping the Transnational seeks to foster the cross-national dialogues needed to sustain the vitality of this emergent field. To advance a truly comparativist understanding of this scholarly endeavor, Dartmouth College Press welcomes monographs from scholars both inside and outside the United States.

For a complete list of books available in this series, see www.upne.com.

Yael Ben-zvi, *Native Land Talk: Indigenous and Arrivant Rights Theories*

Joanne Chassot, *Ghosts of the African Diaspora: Re-Visioning History, Memory, and Identity*

Samuele F. S. Pardini, *In the Name of the Mother: Italian Americans, African Americans, and Modernity from Booker T. Washington to Bruce Springsteen*

Sonja Schillings, *Enemies of All Humankind: Fictions of Legitimate Violence*

Günter H. Lenz, edited by Reinhard Isensee, Klaus J. Milich, Donald E. Pease, John Carlos Rowe, *A Critical History of the New American Studies, 1970–1990*

Helmbrecht Breinig, *Hemispheric Imaginations: North American Fictions of Latin America*

Jimmy Fazzino, *World Beats: Beat Generation Writing and the Worlding of U.S. Literature*

Zachary McCleod Hutchins, editor, *Community without Consent: New Perspectives on the Stamp Act*

Kate A. Baldwin, *The Racial Imaginary of the Cold War Kitchen: From Sokol'niki Park to Chicago's South Side*

Yuan Shu and Donald E. Pease, *American Studies as Transnational Practice: Turning toward the Transpacific*

Melissa M. Adams-Campbell, *New World Courtships: Transatlantic Alternatives to Companionate Marriage*

JOANNE CHASSOT

GHOSTS OF THE AFRICAN DIASPORA

Re-Visioning History, Memory, and Identity

DARTMOUTH COLLEGE PRESS
HANOVER, NEW HAMPSHIRE

Dartmouth College Press
An imprint of University Press of New England
www.upne.com

Manufactured in the United States of America
Typeset in Sabon and Scala Sans by Integrated Publishing Solutions

Published with a subsidy from the Commission des publications de la Faculté des lettres de l'Université de Lausanne.

Page 237 constitutes a continuation of this copyright page.

Library of Congress Cataloging-in-Publication Data available upon request
Hardcover ISBN: 978-1-5126-0158-9
Paperback ISBN: 978-1-5126-0160-2
Ebook ISBN: 978-1-5126-0161-9

5 4 3 2 1

Everyone reads, acts, writes with *his or her* ghosts,
even when one goes after the ghosts of the other.
—Jacques Derrida, *Specters of Marx*

CONTENTS

ACKNOWLEDGMENTS

A BOOK, ACCORDING TO DAVID PUNTER, is always "only a shadow or a ghost of a book that might have been written" (6). There is—will always be—much more that I would have liked to write, and write better. But that this book exists at all is due to the help, encouragements, and support of many people I wish to thank here. Some of them played a crucial part in the thinking, writing, and revising process that resulted in this book. Others played an equally important part in keeping me strong and motivated, and in taking me out of the realm of the living dead from time to time.

I first and foremost wish to express my deepest gratitude and respect to Agnieszka Soltysik Monnet, without whose guidance and mentorship this project would never have come to life. She was often able to see what haunted a confused and not fully articulate(d) argument, and help me bring it to light. This book is also a much more coherent and carefully thought-through piece of work thanks to Teresa Goddu and Justin Edwards, whose insights and questions pushed me to re-vision some important theoretical and methodological aspects of the project. I am also very grateful to the reviewers who read the manuscript for UPNE, for their time, attention, and generosity.

Thanks to Richard Pult, my editor at UPNE, the publication process was incredibly fast and smooth, and I am grateful to him for making this first publication experience much easier than I had imagined.

I presented parts of this work and received precious feedback at various conferences and workshops, at the University of Reading, Howard University, and Southern Illinois University, at the International Gothic Association conference at the University of Heidelberg, and at the European Association for American Studies conference at Trinity College Dublin. I have greatly benefited from being a part of the PostCit community, and I am grateful to the brilliant and inspiring scholars who compose it, with special thanks to Noémi Michel. At the University of Lausanne I particularly wish to thank Christine Le Quellec Cottier and Brigitte Maire, as well as the Formation Doctorale Interdisciplinaire, and especially Jérôme Meizoz and Alberto Roncaccia.

Isis Giraldo has played a major part in my academic life and beyond, and our intellectual, political, and human bond sustained me throughout this project. I have learned much from her strength, her passion, and her unrelenting critical engagement.

Sarah Baccianti also holds a special place among the people who have inspired me. Her unwavering friendship and generosity have made academia a better place to be in.

I have been blessed to work with wonderful friends and colleagues in the English Department at the University of Lausanne, who supported and guided me through the dissertation and the publication process. I am particularly thankful to Valérie Cossy, Mary Flannery, Martine Hennard Dutheil, Roxane Hughes, Kirsten Stirling, Boris Vejdovsky, and Najat Zein, for the many ways in which they have helped me. I also wish to thank all the other people who made Lausanne such a great place to work at, in particular my ACIL friends, who helped take my mind off research and put it to more practical questions and active projects. My students throughout my years of teaching at UNIL have also been a regenerative presence. Their curiosity and enthusiasm have nourished my own.

My friends in "the real world," thank you all for supporting me and bearing with me from the beginning to the end of this long project. You didn't forget me when I became a ghost, and you brought me back to life on countless occasions.

I could never have followed this path without the love and encouragements of my parents, Dominique and Marc Etienne, who always found ways to help that only parents can, and whose interest in my work certainly made them my most careful and diligent readers. I'm also grateful to my brother Mathieu, who has taught me much about courage and perseverance in life.

Beyond words is what I owe to Cédric Cramatte. His faith, patience, and love have been a source of strength through times of doubt and weariness. The very existence of this book proves he was right on many points, and these wouldn't be acknowledgments if I didn't admit to that.

Finally, I wish to thank the Société Académique Vaudoise, the Fondation van Walsem pro Universitate, and the Commission des Publications de la Faculté des Lettres (UNIL) for their generous support, which has made this project and its publication possible.

GHOSTS OF THE AFRICAN DIASPORA

INTRODUCTION

TRACING THE GHOST

I am very happy to hear that my books haunt.
— Toni Morrison, interview with Nellie McKay

MY FIRST ENCOUNTER with a ghost was—like that of many readers of African diaspora literature—with the spiteful baby spirit at 124 Bluestone Road, on the outskirts of Cincinnati, Ohio, in the 1870s. That ghost haunted me for years.

My second ghost sighting was in the woods of Willow Springs, a Sea Island in the limbo space between Georgia and South Carolina, in the late 1990s. That apparition was far more fleeting than the house-shattering baby spirit and the fleshy ghost that named herself Beloved. In fact, were it not for that previous encounter with the ghostly, which had somehow made me more alert to such apparitions, I might not even have noticed this second ghost. While Beloved was a greedy, insatiable ghost always demanding more of everyone's attention, the discreet presence of this other ghostly woman whose name nobody remembered made itself known only in the rustle of her long woolen dress and in whispers in the wind blowing through the trees.

When, by happenstance, I landed in Jamaica in the 1950s and discovered the wilderness of the Cockpit Country, I had the uncanny sensation that this place too was haunted. Not only figuratively, by violence, racism, classism, and the specter of neocolonialism, but also quite literally by a woman warrior from the past whose struggle against the oppressive forces of her time, slavery and colonialism, seemed anything but over and whose great power and guidance were more necessary than ever.

It is that third apparition that led me to wonder about this strikingly recurring presence of ghosts in novels that were all written in the 1980s by women of the African diaspora. It is also that third ghost that made me ask myself if I was not perhaps starting to "see things." As horror film viewers as impressionable as myself have often experienced, when we have just witnessed a haunting we are likely to identify every shadow, every ripple in the air as the sign of a ghostly presence. But that is in fact, as I soon came to realize, the very nature and power of the ghost: it makes us question what we see, what we read, what we think, what we (think we) know; it makes us more attentive to what may be there even though it is not quite visible, not quite within our reach, and attentive to what really is *not* there, even though we thought it was, or wish it were. Deciding that whatever it was I had witnessed—a ghost, a figment of my imagination, something else altogether—was intriguing enough to deserve further inquiry, I set out on a ghost hunt through the literature of the African diaspora.

At the beginning of Toni Morrison's *Beloved*, when Sethe suggests to Baby Suggs that they move house to escape the rage of the baby ghost that haunts 124 Bluestone Road, the old woman replies: "What'd be the point? . . . Not a house in the country ain't packed to its rafters with some dead Negro's grief" (5). Returning to the scene of my first ghost sighting after a long journey through haunted lands, it strikes me that Baby Suggs's perceptive remark aptly describes the state of African diaspora fiction in the last thirty years. The novels of Morrison—who admitted that Beloved haunts all her early works in one form or another (Naylor, "Conversation" 217)—virtually all contain ghosts or ghostlike presences.[1] If the tremendous impact *Beloved* had on African diaspora literature might partly explain why ghosts became attractive figures, it alone certainly cannot account for their proliferation in texts as diverse—and sometimes anterior to *Beloved*—as Toni Cade Bambara's *The Salt Eaters* (1980), Paule Marshall's *Praisesong for the Widow* (1983), Wilson Harris's *The Guyana Quartet* (1985) and *The Ghost of Memory* (2007), Maryse Condé's *I, Tituba* (1986), Gloria Naylor's *Mama Day* (1988), Al Young's *Seduction by Light* (1988), Randall Kenan's *A Visitation of Spirits* (1989) and *Let the Dead Bury Their Dead* (1992), Tina Ansa's *Baby of the Family* (1989), *Ugly Ways* (1993), and *The Hand I Fan With* (1996), J. California Cooper's *Family* (1991), Charlotte Watson Sherman's *One Dark Body* (1993), H. Nigel Thomas's *Spirits in the Dark* (1993), Erna Brodber's *Louisiana* (1994), Tananarive Due's *The Between* (1995), *The Good House* (2003), and *Joplin's Ghost* (2005), Steven Barnes's *Blood Brothers* (1996), Kwadwo Agymah Kamau's *Flickering Shadows* (1996), John Edgar Wideman's *The Cattle Killing* (1996), Julie Dash's *Daughters of the Dust* (1997),[2] Nalo Hopkinson's *Brown Girl in the Ring*

(1998), Phyllis Alesia Perry's *Stigmata* (1998), Fred D'Aguiar's *Feeding the Ghosts* (1998) and *Bloodlines* (2000), or Dionne Brand's *At the Full and Change of the Moon* (1999)—to name but a few.

Of course, the ghosts that appear in these many texts take various forms and play diverse roles. Their presence does not always provoke the same reactions; and their intentions toward, and power over, the living differ in significant ways. Besides, ghosts are not new to the literature of the African diaspora. They made notable appearances in the fiction of such writers as Charles Chesnutt at the close of the nineteenth century. Nor is their proliferation in the late twentieth century unique to African diaspora literature. But if, as is conventionally thought, the dead always return for a reason, and if, as critics generally agree, the ghost always responds to specific historical and cultural conditions and anxieties, then there must be a way of explaining this overwhelming presence of ghosts in the fiction of the African diaspora of the last thirty-odd years. Accounting for this presence in that specific literature at that particular time is one purpose of this book. More precisely, the questions I pose are these: What social, political, theoretical conditions and anxieties do these ghosts address? What is their cultural specificity, and to what extent do they enter into dialogue with other ghosts outside African diaspora literature? And most importantly, beyond the poetic work that they perform as metaphors, what cultural, theoretical, and political work do these ghosts do?

Besides Morrison's *Beloved*, to which I do not devote a full chapter but which both initiates and haunts my examination of the other texts, *Ghosts of the African Diaspora* examines Fred D'Aguiar's *Feeding the Ghosts*, Gloria Naylor's *Mama Day*, Paule Marshall's *Praisesong for the Widow*, and a selection of prose and poetic works by Michelle Cliff. My aim in this book is threefold. At the level of each chapter, I analyze how these writers use the ghost trope in their texts, and what functions it serves in their respective literary and political projects. At a broader level, I argue that the trope does cultural, theoretical, and political work that is both specific to late twentieth-century African diaspora literature and related to broader theoretical developments of which the trope is an important critical resource. My discussion thus also aims to propose a more general theory of the ghost as trope, an endeavor that is particularly timely considering the fast-growing scholarly interest in ghosts and hauntings. Finally, looking at these texts through the ghost trope also enables me to propose an original reading of them, as it throws new light on aspects that have received ample critical attention and explores others that have not. Using the ghost as a guide into these texts ultimately allows me to draw new connections between them and to think about the complex ways in which the interplay of history, memory, and identity positions them as products of, and contributions to, African diaspora literature and culture. At all these levels of reading and interpretation, I relate the ghost with the notion of re-vision, a term whose various meanings and modes of interventions I will sketch in this introduction.

Situating the Ghost

Ghosts have always been with us. They have been common figures in literature across periods and genres, national and cultural boundaries. The proliferation of ghosts in late twentieth-century African diaspora literature is therefore neither a new nor a unique phenomenon. In her discussion of ghost stories in ethnic women's literature, Kathleen Brogan argues for the necessity to read what she calls "tales of cultural haunting" as "a pan-ethnic phenomenon" or a "transethnic genre" (4, 16). If her interest in ghosts was sparked by her encounter with those in African American literature, she contends that examining ghosts in this literature exclusively would obscure the similarities they share with those found in other ethnic literatures. Such cross-cultural examinations are certainly important, and *Ghosts of the African Diaspora* is largely indebted to Brogan's and other scholars' work on literary ghosts—as well as nonliterary ones. Yet this book also concurs with critics who view ghosts, despite or beyond their cross-cultural and transhistorical characteristics, as "culturally specific, behaving according to particular cultural patterns of belief and serving particular cultural (and literary) purposes" (Zamora 499). The ghosts in the texts I analyze here may have much in common with those that appear in the novels by Native American, Cuban American, or Jewish American women writers Brogan examines, in which they also serve to explore history, memory, and identity. But if the ghost trope works in ways that can to some extent be generalized, history, memory, and identity in the context of the African diaspora are also distinctive, and they intersect in specific ways that must be examined more carefully and discretely. *Ghosts of the African Diaspora* thus responds to the equally important need for a culturally focused approach that accounts for the particularities of the ghost trope in a more restricted corpus, a corpus that has as yet not received sustained and detailed attention.[3]

In order to articulate both the specificities of African diasporic ghosts and their similarities with other ghosts, I situate them in a double genealogy. On the one hand, I trace their origins to African cultures and spiritualities, origins reinvented in and through diaspora. On the other, I consider their contiguity with the theoretical and political developments that marked the last quarter of the twentieth century, which can be summarized as a radical questioning of what postmodernists would call "metanarratives of legitimation" (Lyotard) but which I will throughout this book term "master narratives." Some of the critical approaches I will draw on have often been considered as discrete or even opposed, notably by some African diasporic writers and thinkers, who have described poststructuralism and postmodernism as "a 'white' phenomenon" (K. C. Davis 244). In my view, however, not only do they share many of the same concerns and strategies, but they also have common roots. As Kimberly Chabot Davis and others remind us, the development of poststructuralism and postmodernism was very much related to the racial and sexual liberation movements of the 1960s and 1970s, as well as to the independence struggles and postcolonial contestations of universalist conceptions of culture.[4] If my analysis will draw as much on black and African diaspora studies and postcolonial studies as on poststructuralism, it is not only because all those approaches are indeed helpful for analyzing the literary texts under consideration in this book, but also because I am interested in the way these texts resonate with, build on, sometimes anticipate, and often complicate the poststructuralist challenge to traditional approaches to and definitions of reality, history, or identity. In fact, as a figure that cannot be contained in, or claimed by, any single theoretical or literary tradition, the ghost provides an interesting lens through which to explore the affinities between these approaches.

Literature, Theory, and the Spectral Turn

What cannot but strike anyone investigating the ghostly today is that the proliferation of ghosts I identified in late twentieth-century African diaspora literature is largely matched by the trope's currency in recent scholarship. While literary studies, in particular, have long been interested in the ghostly, this preoccupation has clearly grown to outstanding proportions in the last few decades. This is not merely due to the development of gothic studies and of scholarship on magic realism and the fantastic, three genres of which the ghost is a typical figure. Indeed, scholars' interest in the ghost has largely outreached the limits of genre-based studies, as they have also looked at the trope in particular literary periods (Thurston), or in corpuses delimited by gender (Carpenter and Kolmar), ethnicity (Brogan), or national culture (Goldman; Redding). Besides the studies of ghosts *in* literary texts, scholars have also used the trope as a lens *through which* to approach literature, to explore the work and influence of certain writers (Garber; Ronell), reconceptualize the concerns and contours of certain literary movements (Rabaté; Sword; Wolfreys), theorize the specificities of particular genres (E. L. Johnson; Rayner), or articulate the literary formation of cultural, ethnic, and national identities (Bergland; Edwards, *Gothic Canada*; H. B. Young). These two approaches, one that takes the ghost trope as object and one that takes the ghost as a trope through which to explore other objects, are in fact often not clearly distinguished but indeed bleed into each other—as my own approach to and through the ghost will, too. Indeed, one of the trope's particularities is its ability to always exceed the meaning one attempts to give it, and to take others that one did not even expect.

This elusive and excessive quality largely explains the fact that the ghost has also moved well beyond the realm of literary studies, its perhaps more obvious site of apparition, to invade virtually all fields of the humanities. It has been a productive trope in psychoanalysis since the birth of the discipline: Freud's concept of "the uncanny" and his discussion of repression already largely used the example and rhetoric of the ghost. But it gained prominence following Nicolas Abraham and Maria Torok's work on the "phantom," and is today commonly found in discussions of transgenerational memory and trauma. Perhaps more surprisingly, the ghost has also been claimed by anthropologists, sociologists, and political theorists, in their attempts to articulate relatedness and memory (Carsten), diasporic identity and formation (Matsuoka and Sorenson), or memorialization and international relations (Auchter). Recently, it has even made its way into the field of geography, with a special issue of *Cultural Geographies* in 2008 devoted to "spectro-geographies" (Maddern and Adey).

To situate these various studies within particular disciplines, however, does not do justice to their wide-ranging approaches and far-reaching contributions. As a trope that problematizes all boundaries, the ghost naturally calls for interdisciplinary inquiries. When introducing her own contribution to the exploration of the "ghostly matters" of the social world and imagination, Avery Gordon reminds us that interdisciplinarity is not about "choos[ing] a 'subject' (a theme) and gather[ing] around it two or three sciences" but about "creating a new object that belongs to no one." As her own book shows, the ghost has become such a new object: not only can it not "be owned by anyone" (7), but it requires us to strain the habitual limits of our fields of inquiry in productive ways. This perhaps explains the trope's prominence in cultural studies, and in collective volumes in particular: drawing together a variety of scholars and texts, such inquiries have notably identified the ghost as constitutive of North American national identity and cultural consciousness (Boyd and Thrush; Weinstock), as emblematic of the postcolonial condition (Joseph-Vilain and Misrahi-Barak), or as defining of the everyday in contemporary culture (Blanco and Peeren, *Popular Ghosts*). One may of course wonder whether the ghost might not risk losing much of its meaning and relevance by becoming such a "master trope" (Luckhurst, "Contemporary London Gothic" 527), by being "used as shorthand . . . for just about any kind of troubled or troubling relationship—physical, spiritual, emotional, literary, temporal—between one entity and another" (Sword 165). But the fact is that the ghost's ubiquity has led a number of scholars to produce work on the trope itself (Buse and Stott, *Ghosts*; C. Davis), and to identify "spectrality studies" as a new field of inquiry—one that has now achieved sufficient critical mass to justify the publication of an anthology on the subject, *The Spectralities Reader* (Blanco and Peeren).[5]

As the term chosen to identify this new field suggests, Jacques Derrida's *Specters of Marx* is usually credited as the initiator of this "spectral turn" in theory and cultural criticism. But if Derrida has certainly been extremely influential on later uses and theorizations of the ghost—mine included—this narrative traces a rather simplistic, not to say Eurocentric and patriarchal, genealogy, a genealogy that overlooks significant earlier and parallel elaborations, including in or based on literature. Gordon's *Ghostly Matters* is another important milestone and influence on later ruminations on haunting as social experience, and it seems to me much more indebted to *Beloved* than to *Specters of Marx*. In fact, Morrison's novel and in particular her evocation of "rememory," a term—as I explain below—closely related to the ghost trope, have inspired scholarly discussions of the workings of memory far beyond the literary field. More generally, the recent proliferation of ghosts in scholarship is certainly not unrelated to the development of memory and trauma studies since the 1990s, as Jeffrey Andrew Weinstock points out ("Introduction" 5). María Del Pilar Blanco and Esther Peeren also identify Terry Castle's *The Apparitional Lesbian*, which was published the same year as *Spectres de Marx* but saw in the ghost a trope of dispossession and social erasure, as an equally important book that offered not only a very different avenue for theorizing the ghost but also a significant counterpoint to poststructuralism's too often shortsighted view of instability and indeterminacy as inherently critically productive ("Introduction" 10).[6] My own discussion of African diasporic ghosts actually brings these two seemingly incompatible conceptions of the ghost together. In fact, my argument is that it is precisely the ghost's capacity to hold both meanings in tension that makes it such an effective trope for dealing with issues as complex as history, memory, and identity.

Ghosts of Diaspora

For a reader perhaps more accustomed to the ghosts of traditional gothic novels, the first thing that may be surprising in the texts of Morrison, D'Aguiar, Naylor, Marshall, and Cliff is precisely how unsurprising ghostly encounters are for the protagonists. If the baby ghost that releases its venom on the inhabitants of 124 Bluestone Road is a cause for concern, it is only because they do not know how to placate it and persuade it to "just come" so they can have a "conversation, . . . an exchange of views" (Morrison, *Beloved* 4). When, later on, Sethe realizes that the strange young woman she welcomed into her home is her daughter returned from the dead, her reaction is one of profound happiness and relief at no longer having to explain herself. As one of the survivors of a particularly murderous Middle Passage, Mintah takes as her normal duty to "feed" the ghosts of those who were thrown into the sea. When she encounters the ghosts of her ancestors in the woods, Miranda "Mama" Day does not feel fear so much as sadness for the pain they lived through. If Avey Johnson has strong reactions when spirits from her past take possession of her, at the end of her spiritual and cultural journey she is anything but surprised to see her long-dead great-aunt standing next to her as she contemplates the community she has reclaimed. As for the "duppies" that roam Cliff's homeland, the concern they may inspire comes not from their ghostly nature but from the living's awareness that they may have some responsibility in their restlessness.

The familiarity that characterizes the protagonists' relationship with ghosts is to be related to a spirituality that is rooted in many West African cultures and was then developed in various forms by the slave and free societies in the Americas.[7] This aspect of the cultural connections between African and diasporic spiritualities has received considerable attention, including as it manifests in literature, notably in *Beloved* and *Praisesong for the Widow*.[8] Many discussions of these novels' African-derived conception of the relationship between the living and the dead rely on John Mbiti's *African Religions and Philosophy*. According to Mbiti, in the African conception of time and death a person's passing does not mark a break with the community of the living: the "living-dead," as he calls them, remain "alive" in the memories of those who knew them as well as in the spirit world. The living give the dead "symbols of communion, fellowship and remembrance" (25), in the form of sacrifices, offerings, libations, and food. Should the dead not be honored through remembrance, they are cast "into a state of non-existence" (26), the worst possible fate for them. The living do all they can to avoid this, for if the dead bring support and nurturance to those who remember them, they may also bring misfortune to those who condemn them to oblivion.

Whether Mbiti's claim that "belief in the continuation of life after death is found in all African societies" (4) is correct or not, his account illuminates many aspects of the texts I examine here.[9] First, all of these texts show the dramatic consequences that a failure to maintain this continuity has on the dead, whom it condemns to eternal homelessness and restlessness or to disintegration. Refusing to be forgotten, the dead call on the living with an insistence that ranges from benevolence, through mild nuisance, to overpowering and dangerous invasion, depending on the way the living respond to their presence. Whatever effects this haunting—or, as I will read it in chapter 3, this possession—may have on the living, they are never as damaging and disabling as those that a break with the dead would produce. Without this connection and the continuity with the past that the ghosts enable, the living cannot understand, deal with, or work through their present situations, let alone envisage a future. Indeed, when they are unable to "integrate the experience of their ancestors into their lives, to inform their understanding of social reality with the inherited meanings of their natural forebears, or to anchor the living present in any conscious community of memory," the living suffer from what Orlando Patterson calls "natal alienation." Patterson identifies this form of alienation as a constitutive element of the slave condition: denied not only "all claims on, and obligations to, his parents and living blood relations but, by extension, all such claims and obligations on his more remote ancestors and on his descendants," the slave is a "genealogical isolate" (5). Of all the protagonists in the texts I examine here, only those of *Feeding the Ghosts* and *Beloved* are or used to be slaves. But even the texts set in the late twentieth century portray characters that are natally alienated and genealogically isolated. While they are not always successful, because they are not always heeded, the ghosts in these texts serve as guides in the protagonists' troubled relation with their individual and cultural history.

According to historian Elliott J. Gorn, "ghostlore" already served a sustaining function in slave culture. The slaves found support, advice, and comfort from the dead, who taught them "realistic lessons about how to survive" and gave them "a sense of their own resources" as individuals and as a people (565). But the belief in the proximity and communication between the realms of the living and the dead also "helped undermine the legitimacy of natal alienation—and by extension, of slavery itself—by affirming the importance of deep kinship ties in the daily activities of black men and women" (559). Other historians and cultural critics have also shown that "communicating with the dead" has always served not only a cultural and social function, but a political one, as African diasporic communities have used obeah, vodou, spirit possession, conjure, and other forms of ritualized performance as "resistant practices." Joseph Roach even speaks of "the revolutionary potential of the spirit-world presence" (34) in African diaspora culture and literature from colonial and slavery times through Jim Crow, a revolutionary potential that can be historically linked to the spiritual practices that often accompanied slave revolts.[10] The texts I examine here appropriate and perpetuate these social, cultural, and political functions. In reaffirming this continuity between the living and the dead, they contradict the very logic of the institution of slavery and its disruptive effects on all aspects of the lives of the slaves as much as their descendants—from the severing of the African captives from their communities by the Middle Passage, through the breaking apart of families by the exploitative and productivity-driven system of slavery, to the persistent effects of the institution's legacy on modern society. Just as spiritualities that emerged and developed from African cultures "delineate a transgenerational diasporic community of the living and the dead, the lost and the forgotten, across national borders and historical periods" (Kaplan, "Souls at the Crossroads" 515), African diaspora writers' interest in, and inclusion of, ghosts in their texts can be seen as an affirmative gesture of cultural and communal re-membering.

But ghosts also oppose the logic of slavery in another way, in slave culture as much as in contemporary literature. Through rituals and cultural practices that related them to the spirit world, slaves resisted not only their enslaved condition "but also the systems of modernity and scientific rationalism that supported slavery." As Jason R. Young points out, these systems served to control and discipline slaves first by providing slave masters with "methods of scientific management," but also by justifying the repression of "rituals, customs, and beliefs" considered as "backward (read: premodern)." Slaves' performance and perpetuation of these rituals and beliefs despite the repressive structures that would eradicate them should not be read only as evidence of their capacities of resistance, but in fact as one of the modes through which they "express[ed] their discontent with slavery's collusion with the dawn of a new era of juridical and philosophical thinking that formalized and justified the exercise of violence" (14). In affirming the continuous place of ghosts in African diasporic culture, contemporary writers thus reenact and extend this oppositional gesture against a hegemonic culture that itself keeps reenacting and extending its historical repressive and marginalizing structures. In her examination of the supernatural in ethnic women's literature, Bonnie Winsbro points to the interconnectedness of cultural traditions, alternative epistemologies, and political claims in fiction. She reads ethnic writers' use of the supernatural as a way to "assert their differences, to revitalize and reconstruct their own realities and world views" through their affirmation and representation of "alternative beliefs" (5), the very beliefs that were marginalized, denied, or silenced throughout the history of western domination of ethnic people.

This finds confirmation in Morrison's statement that the "discredited knowledge" of black people plays a particularly important role in her work; it is, in fact, because this knowledge was always discredited that the writer gives it a central place. Ghosts can be seen as integral to and representative of the "cosmology" of the African diaspora, which Morrison glosses as "the way in which Black people looked at the world," a vision that blends "a profound rootedness in the real world" with what she variously calls the supernatural, superstition, or magic, and summarizes as "another way of knowing things" ("Rootedness" 342). Cliff has also associated a certain form of discredited knowledge with an African heritage repressed by colonialism. "To write as a complete Caribbean woman, or man for that matter," she explains in one of her earliest pieces, "demands of us retracing the African part of ourselves" (*Land of Look Behind* 14). For her as much as for the protagonist of her first two novels, the historical but ghostly figure of Nanny, African warrior, obeah woman, and leader of the Maroons, appears as a guide on this cultural and political journey: "The extent to which you can believe in the powers of Nanny, that they are literal examples of her Africanness and strength, represents the extent to which you have decolonized your mind" ("Caliban's Daughter" 47).

Cliff described this decolonizing project as "'re-vision.' In the sense of re-visioning something, not in the sense of revising as in correcting it, or editing it, but in trying to see something from a different point of view" (Clawson). This notion, which interestingly echoes Morrison's association between ways of looking and alternative modes of knowing, is useful for analyzing the epistemological and political work the ghost performs, and will serve as a thread throughout this book. Important in Cliff's definition is the point that, rather than affirming the superiority of the other perspective, and thereby merely inverting the hierarchy, re-vision consists in questioning habitual, traditional, dominant ways of seeing, and therefore of knowing. Thus, while Morrison's description of black cosmology seems to rely on the categories of "the real" and "the supernatural," her point is that this cosmology actually does not distinguish between these categories but blends them. As an integral part of the character's experience and habitual order of knowledge, the ghosts in African diaspora literature blur the traditional dichotomy of natural and supernatural, rational and irrational, thereby throwing into question the very definitions and structural hierarchy of these categories and the oppressive and repressive structures and discourses they have served to justify.

While "this sense of the continuity between the natural and the supernatural" is distinctive of African diaspora literature, it is not unique to it. Even as they note that it "is often nurtured by cultural traditions other than a white Eurocentric one" (Introduction 12), Lynette Carpenter and Wendy Kolmar identify it as more generally characteristic of ghost stories written by women. While male-authored ghost stories are usually informed by a "dualistic thinking, an approach to the supernatural that seeks to confirm one side of the dichotomy by wholly denying the other," they argue that women writers tend to "portray natural and supernatural experience along a continuum, . . . so that the supernatural can be accepted, connected with, reclaimed, and can often possess a quality of familiarity" (11–12, 12). Women indeed share with nonwhite writers a distrust with the binary oppositions that underpin the hegemonic discourse and epistemology that have historically silenced and marginalized them, associating them with an irrational that must be domesticated, disciplined, mastered. This might partly explain the ghost's particular currency in texts by women of the African diaspora—a currency reflected both in the long list I offered at the beginning of this introduction and in the selection that is the focus of this book. But this questioning of the natural/supernatural dichotomy is not the only way in which women writers have used the ghost story "to critique mainstream male culture, values, and tradition" (1). Carpenter and Kolmar further argue that the genre has also served to explore female concerns in oblique ways, as the ghosts appear as "dispossessed" figures come to warn female characters about the physical and symbolic violence of patriarchy (14). Similarly noting the ghost's particularly prominent place in women's literature, Brogan proposes that "as an absence made present, the ghost can give expression to the ways in which women are rendered invisible in the public sphere" (25). This is even more true of black women, as I show in chapter 2, as well as of queer women, and queer subjects in general, whose ghosting and self-ghosting I analyze in chapter 4.[11] If all the texts I examine here to some extent use the ghost trope to represent violence and dispossession, they show that these are not merely the effect of patriarchy but also of a racist discourse deployed in and inherited from slavery and colonialism.

In the way it reveals how white, colonialist culture and discourse have marginalized and dispossessed black people, the re-visionary work African diaspora writers perform is similar to the feminist project Adrienne Rich described in her well-known 1972 essay "When We Dead Awaken: Writing as Re-Vision." In it, Rich calls for a reexamination of the assumptions patriarchal culture, and notably canonical literature, have made about women and of how these assumptions have shaped and restricted their lives, their identities, and their writing. Only by "know[ing] the writing of the past, and know[ing] it differently than we have ever known it," she claims, can we "break its hold over us" (19). For Rich, like for Cliff, re-vision is thus "the act of looking back, of seeing with fresh eyes, of entering an old text from a new critical direction" (18). I bring in Rich here not so much because she was Cliff's partner, but rather to draw attention to the broader context in which the texts I will examine were produced. As Rich's contemporaries, Morrison and Marshall were influenced as much by the critiques and demands of second-wave feminism as by its blindness with regard to racial issues; so were Cliff and Naylor, who came of age in the late 1960s. Mostly published in the 1980s, the texts I discuss in this book are exemplary not only of the interest in and emphasis on folk culture that characterized African diaspora literature in the post–civil rights and postcolonial period, but also of the proliferation of black women's voices that emerged in the 1970s and gained force in the next decade. As I point out in chapter 1, even D'Aguiar—as a male and younger writer—should be situated in this tradition of writing concerned with the particular ways in which black women have been silenced in history.

African diaspora women's double marginalization no doubt accounts for their commitment to re-visioning the historical record. Those decades were indeed also marked by a new and growing literary interest in the past, and in slavery especially. *Beloved*, *Mama Day*, *Abeng*, and *No Telephone to Heaven* in particular should be situated within the context of this turn to history, which, as I explain in more detail in chapter 2, was inspired as much by the development of slave historiography as by its gaps and shortcomings. Re-vision, as Rich's essay suggests, is not only a reading, but also a writing practice: "We all know that there is another story to be told" (25). Her call for re-vision has often been interpreted as a call for rewriting, for telling that other story that the dominant narrative has suppressed. We certainly see this impulse in several of the texts I examine here. *Beloved* and *Feeding the Ghosts* both revisit historical events and tell another story than that which appeared in legal proceedings, journalistic reports, and pro- and anti-slavery commentaries. In *Abeng* and *No Telephone to Heaven*, the colonial version of Jamaica's past is fractured and contested by the history of resistance it always tried to repress.[12]

This re-visionary approach to the past that African diaspora literature and black studies in general called for and offered in the latter part of the twentieth century is itself to be situated within a broader questioning of traditional historical narratives by those who were long absent from or silenced in them. Whether they manifested explicitly colonialist, racist, sexist, or heterosexist ideologies or whether they were a more organic part of the western, white, patriarchal philosophical and scientific tradition, these master narratives came under particularly heavy attack from the 1960s onward by not only women, as mentioned above, but also sexual and racial minorities, (de)colonized people, and otherwise oppressed and disenfranchised groups worldwide. More than a demand for marginalized people and histories to be recognized and integrated, what these various groups voiced was a radical critique of the ideological and epistemological underpinnings of the narratives that marginalized them. This assault on master narratives conversed with the poststructuralist and postmodernist challenge to conventional ways of thinking about such notions as truth, reality, meaning, power, or identity. The ghost appears as a powerful trope in this re-visionary project. As a major poststructuralist noted, "the logic of spectrality" is "inseparable from the very motif . . . of deconstruction" (Derrida 225 n. 3).[13] In Derrida's distinctive prose, the ghost "is something that one does not know, precisely, and one does not know if precisely it is, if it exists, if it responds to a name and corresponds to an essence. One does not know: not out of ignorance, but because this non-object, this non-present present, this being-there of an absent or departed one no longer belongs to knowledge. At least no longer to that which one thinks one knows by the name of knowledge" (5). The ghost destabilizes the boundaries western metaphysics and post-Enlightenment rationalism erected between the myriad categories that have traditionally served to establish and perpetuate violent hierarchies, relations of dominance, and discourses of othering: not only the natural and the supernatural, as suggested previously, but also life and death, past and present, presence and absence, body and spirit, self and other, the familiar and the strange, the knowable and the unknowable. Inhabiting the purportedly impossible space of the in-between, the ghost disturbs the "reassuring order" (48) that traditional binary oppositions secure and introduces an irreducible indeterminacy or ambivalence. In troubling the habitual order of knowledge, it requires us to re-vision—that is, to reconsider in order to completely reconceive—what we think we know and what we think knowledge itself is.

Theorizing the Ghost

As Derrida's above quote suggests, a ghost is perhaps more easily defined by what it is not or by what it troubles than by what it is. If it is generally the purpose of any introduction to define the book's key concepts and metaphors, there is something paradoxical in the very attempt at defining the ghost: to define is to establish limits, to fix definitely and definitively the form, the essential nature, and the meaning of the object; yet there is nothing definite, fixed, or essential about the ghost, a figure that has no precise outline and defies all boundaries. That is why, rather than defining what the ghost *is*, I will outline what the ghost *does* by offering in this section an overview of its functions. Because each of the chapters that follow will focus on one writer and analyze particular uses of the ghost, a more general and complete survey is useful for grasping the infinitely rich, complex, and sometimes contradictory ways in which the ghost works in African diaspora literature. In order to embody, so to speak, this "spectrography" of the ghost, I use Beloved, who perhaps best exemplifies its myriad functions, meanings, and indeterminacies. Like her footprints that continually "come and go, come and go" (275) by the river near 124 and fit anyone who steps into them, traces of *Beloved* will appear in my discussion of the other texts, and fit. Several of the writers I examine in the next chapters have identified Morrison, and *Beloved* in particular, as an influence and an inspiration, and my own understanding of the ghost trope certainly owes much to my many readings of this novel. But if *Beloved* is an inescapable text for a study of ghosts in the literature of the African diaspora, it is also perhaps too obvious a text; rather than offering yet another contribution to "the *Beloved* industry" (Sommer 164) by devoting a full chapter to it, I use it as a guide through various functions and meanings in order to produce what, for want of a better word, one could call a theory of the ghost.

Re-Visioning the Master Narrative

At the beginning of *Beloved*, the baby ghost that haunts 124 is invisible but makes its presence known in various ways, from leaving handprints in the cake and shattering mirrors to shaking the whole house or bathing it in a pool of red light that radiates sadness. After the coming of Paul D, who chases away the ghost to make room for himself in Sethe's house and life, the spirit disappears, only to return with a vengeance in the form of a flesh-and-blood young woman whose bodily features—her unmarked baby skin, the smile under her chin, her insatiable stomach, her shining—attract and hold captive every character's attention. From the moment Sethe identifies Beloved as her daughter returned from the dead, the ghost's presence becomes stronger and stronger, until it threatens to swallow everything, including a fading and exhausted Sethe. And yet, despite her overwhelming bodily presence—quite unusual for a ghost—Beloved is also always on the verge of disappearing, dissolving, or erupting into pieces whenever she does not get the attention she needs to hold herself together. When that finally happens, as Denver has finally dared walk out of the yard and Sethe has let go of her dead daughter's hand, "leaving Beloved behind. Alone. Again" (262), the ghost vanishes from everyone's view. But if it is again invisible to the people who once knew and loved her but have decided to forget her, the ghost is not gone. Returning to 124, Paul D finds a house filled with a palpable absence, "A bleak and minus nothing" (270). Not only does the ghost remain close to 124, "waiting for another chance" (263), but its presence can still be felt in "the knuckles brushing a cheek in sleep," heard in "the rustle of a skirt" (275), and even seen in the features of a familiar face in a photograph and in footprints by the stream where it used to play. Ultimately, Beloved's name, the last word of the novel as well as its title, remains a haunting presence for the reader who closes the book and, pondering the meaning of its last pages, wonders if this ghost was ever even there at all.

"We can agree, I think, that invisible things are not necessarily 'not-there'; that a void may be empty, but is not a vacuum" (Morrison, "Unspeakable Things" 11). With this statement, given in her 1988 Tanner Lecture on Human Values, Morrison was not only introducing the observation that would support her rumination on the Africanist presence in American canonical literature in *Playing in the Dark: Whiteness and the Literary Imagination*; she was also reaffirming a central function of the ghost that *Beloved*, published one year earlier, deployed in multiple ways. In troubling the boundary between the visible and the invisible, presence and absence, the ghost compels us to question what we see and feel, and, thereby, the way we approach the world and the categories and definitions that underpin our approach. To look at the ghost in the narrative is, in Gordon's words, "to start with the marginal, with what we normally exclude or banish, or, more commonly, with what we never even notice" (24–25). As a "symptom of what is missing" (63), the ghost urges us to ponder why we did not notice it right away, why it seemed invisible in the first place. It demands that we look again, not simply in the sense that we open our eyes wider, or scrutinize dark corners more carefully, but that we look beyond what we have been trained to see—and not to see. The crucial question Morrison poses in "Unspeakable Things Unspoken" and, I would argue, in *Beloved* in an oblique way, is not so much *why* African Americans have been absent from American literature, and, to extend her point, from American history; the question is, rather, *how* such a "seething" presence could be erased, "what intellectual feats" this erasure has actually required (12).[14] One of my central arguments in this book is that the ghost precisely draws attention not only to this erasure—this absence, this invisibility—but also to the ideological, epistemological, and discursive processes that have produced and perpetuated it.

As many scholars of the genre have argued, the gothic has often been a privileged mode for exploring the contradictions between a nation's ideals and its violent history by interrogating the narratives that support national identity. The coherence of these narratives depends on their exclusion or abjection of historical horrors; the return, in the gothic mode, of what these narratives repressed reveals the artifices of the foundations that sustain national identity (Goddu 10). While relying on these stories, the nation is thus always "haunted by the spectral figure of its own fabrication" (Edwards, *Gothic Canada* xix). In the United States, a nation based on the ideals of progress, freedom, and democracy, the master narrative could not accommodate the history of racial subjugation and slavery, which it either bypassed or quickly glossed over as anomaly or historical accident (Huggins xii). The ghost signifies not only those who are absent because they are dead—often, as *Beloved* shows, because they were killed, lynched, burned alive, beaten, shot, or thrown into the Atlantic—but also those who are absent from the narrative of American History itself because their presence, as well as their violent disappearance, did not fit the ideal narrative America has been telling about itself.

If the ghost is, according to Eric Savoy, so common in American gothic, it is largely because of its prosopopoetic function. Through prosopopoeia, "abstract ideas (such as the burden of historical causes) are given a 'body' in the spectral figure of the ghost" (168). Morrison's explanation for her choice of a ghost story to address the history of slavery confirms this: in order to make her reader grasp the extent and significance of the "carnage" and the "devastation" that slavery caused in black people's lives and families, she says, loss and absence could not "be abstract" but had to be given a tangible form, had to appear literally in the text (Darling 6). In a story in which absence is "a constitutive part of the characters' world" (Erickson 38), the ghost embodies—quite literally—this absence in the particular shape and meaning it takes for each character. For Sethe, Beloved is not only the daughter she killed to put her where she would "be safe" (164), but also all the people she lost because of her act: the sons who fled, the mother-in-law who let herself die, the community who rejected her. For Denver, Beloved is the sister whose blood she swallowed with her mother's milk, as well as a part of her mother's story that does not include her and that she both envies and resents. For Paul D, she is the feelings he locked long ago in the rusted tobacco tin that his heart has become and that he could not open even for Sethe, the "inside part" (116) that he must touch to allow himself to love again. For Stamp Paid, her voice is that of the "black and angry dead" (198), those absented from their family, their community, and the world by the violence of whitefolks.

That Beloved makes absence present is true not only for the characters, but also for the reader. The ghost is "not simply a dead or a missing person, but a social figure" (Gordon 8): for the reader, Beloved's presence also literalizes the absence of all the "disremembered and unaccounted for" (Morrison, *Beloved* 275) in the history of American slavery, including the "Sixty Million and more" lost to the Middle Passage whose names are not known and can therefore not be (re)called. According to Lisa K. Perdigao and Mark Pizzato, "Representations of death always already necessitate an apostrophe—from the living character's vantage point—or a prosopopoetic whereby the writer constructs the voice of the dead" (5). The ghost and prosopopoeia are in many ways equivalent tropes, insofar as they both allow the dead to speak to us, to share with us an experience that never reached us. In what is the most poetic but also the most obscure passage of the novel, Beloved voices and thus makes present for us the experience of the Middle Passage, an experience that largely remains unrecorded. The ghost's particular expressive power largely comes from its unique position, as one who has known the ultimate trauma of death and yet returned to relate it. But it also comes from its collective and timeless character, which endows its narrative with a significance that exceeds that which the account by a survivor of the transatlantic crossing would carry. Beloved's monologue is at once poignantly personal and intimate, depicting the experience of the ship's hold from an individual, probably young, female captive, and evocative of the larger experience of the millions of Africans who endured the voyage. To invoke those people—those who survived and those who did not—through numbers, as historians of slavery long did, tells us little about them beyond the magnitude of the trade and of shipboard mortality. Morrison does not only remind us that this magnitude is in fact incommensurable, as we cannot really grasp what "Sixty Million and more" represents: conjuring up their ghosts through Beloved, she also explores the "more" that quantitative descriptions cannot account for.

Beloved thus plays a crucial role in the novel's broader exploration of what Morrison has called "the unwritten interior life" of the slaves ("Site of Memory" 302). Based on the true story of Margaret Garner, *Beloved* is Morrison's attempt to do justice to the complexity of the emotional life of a woman whose perspective and subjectivity were completely absent from both anti- and pro-slavery commentaries on her act (Sale 44). The writer explained her choice of the ghost story as one that imposed itself on this story of an infanticidal mother: because nobody—neither Morrison herself, nor the reader, and certainly not those who put Garner on trial at the time—could adequately judge the mother except the child she killed, the daughter had to be brought back (Darling 5). When she comes to fully realize what she in fact always knew, that the strange young woman who one day appeared in front of her house is her dead daughter, Sethe thinks she no longer needs to remember or explain anything because Beloved knows it all. But even as she expresses her relief, in an internal monologue addressed to Beloved, the very memories of all the most painful aspects of her past that she never told anyone start to unfold. It is through Sethe's remembering—through which she also hopes to re-member her relationship with the daughter she nearly dismembered—that the reasons behind the infanticide are revealed. Serving as both a catalyst and a conduit for Sethe's subjectivity, the ghost allows for the true motives and feelings that led to such an otherwise incomprehensible act to be voiced in their full, excruciating complexity.

As prosopopoeia, the ghost thus voices that which remains unspoken in the historical narrative because it was not recorded, as well as that which remains unspoken because it was silenced, written over by other voices whose interests lay elsewhere or required that the slaves' perspectives and subjectivities be repressed. But if the ghost enables a re-vision of the master narrative, it is not only by giving a voice and "a menacing pseudo-life" (Savoy 168) to the repressed in American history but also by deconstructing the very epistemological and ideological underpinnings of traditional historiography. One of those underpinnings is a conception of time as linearity and teleology. According to Michel de Certeau, the founding gesture of modern western historiography is the separation of the present and the past; this "initial act of division" (*Writing of History* 3) is then repeated as the chronology of history is composed of periods that mark "the *decision* to become different or no longer to be such as one had been up to that time," and to consider the previous times as "dead" (4).[15] For instance, the historiography of the American South generally distinguishes between the Antebellum era and the Reconstruction era, with the Civil War marking the temporal as well as symbolic break between the two. Similarly, in the Caribbean the most important break after the European so-called discovery of the New World is generally identified as the passage from the colonial to the postcolonial period. This differentiation between successive periods is not understood merely in terms of change, but of advancement—from slavery to Emancipation, from colonialism to Independence.

Writers and scholars of the African diaspora—among others—have long contested "the linear, hierarchical vision of a single History that would run its unique course" and denounced it as "a highly functional fantasy of the West" (Glissant, *Caribbean Discourse* 66, 64).[16] Not only has the definition of History as a march of progress served to relegate some peoples to the margins, or indeed outside, of history, but in consigning things, events, or institutions to the past the "chronological delusion" (65 n. 5) also obscures their continuing effects in the present, be they symbolic, social, or material.[17] Morrison also problematizes this linear progress narrative in several ways. Set in the era of Reconstruction, *Beloved* presents a view very different from traditional historiography. The Civil War is mentioned only in passing and with an emphasis on its unimportance: its outbreak failed to "rouse" (209) a defeated Baby Suggs; when it ended, "nobody white or black seemed to know" it (52). As Brogan notes, Emancipation itself, supposedly the most important event for slaves, is reduced in the novel to a semicolon, as this so-called new era actually "only brings more of the same" (72): "Slave life; freed life—everyday was a test and a trial" (Morrison, *Beloved* 256).

But more important, the presence of the ghost itself shows that, for the formerly enslaved, there is no simple reconstruction after the horrors and terrors of slavery. Ruining Sethe's efforts to "[keep] the past at bay" (42), Beloved appears as the embodied memory of the most horrifying aspects of her life as a slave. As Morrison explains, "the purpose of making [Beloved] real is making history possible, making memory real—somebody walks in the door and sits down at the table so you have to think about it, whatever they may be" (Darling 6). As the apparition or persistence in the "present" of what has been defined as "past," the ghost dissolves the boundaries that historiography established in the continuum of time and disjoints the progress narrative they support. In his reading of *Hamlet*, Derrida calls a "spectral moment" "a moment that no longer belongs to time" (xix), a moment of "radical untimeliness" (29). "All of it is now it is always now" (210), Beloved says in a monologue that blends what would be considered as different, successive times—childhood in Africa, voyage in a slave ship's hold, sexual abuse by white men, death at Sethe's hand, the "other side," and other unidentifiable events—and breaks down the linearity of conventional language. Whereas western historiography "obtain[s] a present intelligibility" through a labor of exclusion and repression of "what must be *forgotten*" (Certeau, *Writing of History* 4), Beloved's monologue is unintelligible because it retains and collapses all times and events, offering an overwhelmingly immediate representation of experiences that are neither discrete nor situated in the past.

Telling Impossible Stories

Beloved's monologue is also unintelligible because it manifests an indeterminacy that is characteristic of the ghost itself. Beloved is unusually embodied for a ghost, yet it is impossible to identify definitely and definitively who and what she/it is. Over the last few pages, I have already read Beloved in various, sometimes contradictory ways: a presence that signifies and visibilizes an absence; an apparent absence that is actually the sign of an invisible presence; a prosopopoetics; the return of the repressed; a destabilizer of historical time, linearity, and teleology. Besides all these metaphorical and metanarrative functions, Beloved is also a character in the novel. But even as such she resists single or simple identification. Interesting as they are, the various hypotheses that the other characters and critics of the novel have formulated about Beloved's identity—she is the ghost of Sethe's daughter; a woman who was held captive and sexually abused by white men and who finds protection and a motherly figure in Sethe; a survivor of the Middle Passage; the ghost of a captive who died during the Middle Passage; the (re)incarnation of Sethe's African mother; etc.—all fail to fully satisfy. In fact, any attempt at stabilizing Beloved's meaning invariably leads to oversimplifying and impoverishing a text whose richness and complexity come from its resistance to full interpretation. A signifier with no stable signified, Beloved is all these things, and she is also, as Denver says, "—more" (266), the dash marking not so much Denver's hesitation as to who or what Beloved exactly was as her understanding of the always excessive character of the ghost.

As a figure of excess, instability, and indeterminacy, the ghost is productive for reconceptualizing the relation to "the real" and, in the context of a novel about slavery, to the past. If Beloved makes present what is absent, for Morrison and her readers as much as for her characters, she also signifies the absence that always lies at the heart of that presencing, confirming Derrida's formulation that "there is something disappeared, departed in the apparition itself as reapparition of the departed" (5). Remaining this always already absent presence, the ghost registers the elusiveness that will always characterize the past, the experiences, perspectives, and voices of the people that a text strives to recover. It therefore not only contests master narratives of history by throwing into relief their erasing gestures: it also throws into question the retrievability and representability of a past that, despite our best efforts to capture it, will always largely elude us. This may appear to be in contradiction with the prosopopoetic function I outlined earlier. And indeed, such destabilizing gestures toward history have raised considerable debate, as some critics have seen them as socially and politically disabling and at odds with African diaspora people's long-sustained efforts to not only give a voice to the victims of history but also have their own voices, as descendants of these victims, heard and recognized. Caroline Rody, for example, affirms that novels like *Beloved* "are not 'historiographic metafictions' denying the possibility of historical 'Truth.'" Rody identifies the novel's concern with historiography as the burden of "creat[ing] an authoritative voice" and "communicating an authentic truth" (21). However, her reference to historiographic metafiction fails to grasp the ambivalence that characterizes Linda Hutcheon's concept. Hutcheon's postmodernist problematization of truth and the real does not mean that the referent does not exist, but that it is accessible only through representation: as she insists, "Past events are given *meaning*, not *existence*, by their representation in history" (78). Similarly, what the ghost trope problematizes is not the reality of the (historical) referent: the person the ghost once was really did exist; in fact, that few or no traces remain to attest it or instruct us about its circumstances makes it all the more important that we recognize this existence. What the ghost problematizes, however, is our ability to access, recover, and represent that referent, as historians, writers, or readers of histories and fictions.

Against Rody's objection to critics who "would have us read *Beloved* as less a mimetic or mythic recreation of the real than an entrant into ongoing historiographic discourse" (21), my argument is that these two readings are not mutually exclusive. They are, on the contrary, both supported by the ambivalent trope of the ghost, which holds in productive tension the deconstructive and reconstructive gestures of Morrison's novel and of the other texts I examine in this book. The ghost thus functions simultaneously as prosopopoeia and as another trope that Savoy identifies as recurring in American gothic's engagement with history: catachresis. As "a figure for which there exists no precise literal referent, merely a 'something' that can appear verbally in no other way," the ghost strains toward meaning but "can at best only 'shadow forth,' to use one of Nathaniel Hawthorne's preferred expressions" (171). This is evident in Beloved's monologue, which I earlier identified—as does Morrison—as an effort to speak the unspoken experience of the Middle Passage: Beloved's attempt to "say things that are pictures" (210) is wonderfully successful, as she conveys the horror of her experience and the dissolution of her abandoned self; yet it also irremediably fails to signify, as no one will ever know "where or why she crouched, or whose was the underwater face she needed like that" (274–75). Similarly, if Beloved's return helps Sethe face her past in order to finally envisage a future, Sethe's attempts at "circling the subject" that is at the heart of her life as a slave can never "pin it down" (161, 162), no more than any writer—not even one as brilliant as Morrison—"can ever 'pin down' slavery, genocide war," or indeed "should . . . yearn for the arrogance to do so" (Morrison, "Nobel Lecture" 6). The ghost, instead, shows the novel's "deference to the uncapturability of the life it mourns." Against readings—including in some of Morrison's own formulations—that present *Beloved* as an attempt at "filling in the gaps" in the historical record, as well as the blanks in the slave narratives (Morrison, "Site of Memory" 303), I see the novel as deeply concerned with pointing out these gaps, circling them but deliberately keeping them, precisely, gaping.

As Morrison's above comment makes clear, this humility toward the (un)capturability of the past corresponds to a positioning that is epistemological (recognizing the limits of our tools for recovering and representing history) and political (opposing those narratives that claim to capture the past by speaking for the victims, silencing them in the process), as well as ethical. The preoccupation with representation and its limits is crucial not only because it concerns people who have long been silenced and invisibilized, but also because it concerns a history of violence and suffering, and therefore begs the question of how these can be adequately represented—if indeed they *should* be represented at all. The history of slavery, of racial subjection, of the Middle Passage is, in Saidiya Hartman's terms, "an impossible story," for the experience of the slaves exceeds not only the limits of the archive but also the limits of narrative ("Venus" 10). How, she asks, does one represent violence without reproducing it? How does one give a voice to the voiceless without speaking for them, thus silencing them again? Like Hartman, Morrison and the other writers in this book seem to answer that this is indeed impossible, but that it is nevertheless essential to try, and fail. As an oxymoron, a walking paradox, the ghost is crucial in this attempt to "both tell an impossible story and to amplify the impossibility of its telling" (11). It captures the epistemological and ethical tension between the necessity to narrate this history, to recover these subjects and voices, and the necessary failure to do so.

If this dilemma is metaphorically signified in *Beloved* by the ghost trope, it is also introduced in the novel's narrative form itself by the disruptive presence of the ghostly character. Trauma studies scholars have paid particular attention to the formal qualities of literary trauma narratives. Whereas the transformation of trauma into narrative is generally understood as necessary to the victim's healing, the same process in the mode of literature may impose a narrative coherence and closure that "would represent an obvious avoidance of what remains indeterminate, elusive and opaque" (Friedlander 52) in the experience of trauma.[18] The ghost's presence aptly evokes the symptoms of trauma, in its uncontrollable and repetitive occurrence and its disruptive effect on temporality and chronology, as it collapses the past in which the traumatic event occurred and the present in which the traumatized subject lives. In destabilizing narrative and meaning, in keeping an irreducible absence at the heart of its presencing, the ghost also disallows a transparent rendering of the experience of trauma that would make it too accessible and a facile assimilation that would trivialize the loss and the suffering of its original victims.

In spite—or perhaps because—of the qualities that make the ghost a productive trope for representing and not-representing trauma, to evoke a traumatic past in terms of haunting has become so common it is all but a cliché. Yet the way Morrison and the other writers I examine here use the trope is distinctive in several respects. First, they do not identify a particular event or moment as the cause of trauma. The trauma in Sethe's life is not her murder of her daughter, but her lifelong exposure and subjection to slavery, to which her desperate act was a response. While the novel relates some events as particularly violent, such as her abuse by schoolteacher's nephews when she was pregnant, or her overhearing them classify her human and animal characteristics, none of these events is identified as the one source of her trauma. *Beloved* is unconventional both as a ghost story and as a trauma narrative in the fact that the ghost is already present at the beginning of the book: if the abrupt, *in medias res* opening of the novel is meant to reproduce in the reader the slaves' feeling of being "snatched, yanked, thrown into an environment completely foreign" (Morrison, "Unspeakable Things" 32), it also establishes haunting/trauma as an almost natural part of the characters' existence.

Beloved in fact reveals the limits and inadequacy of foundational but overly general theories that identify trauma in relation to a "sudden, or catastrophic event," an event that would moreover "be outside the range of usual human experience" (Caruth 11, 130 n. 1). Such definitions fail to account for experiences like slavery or ordinary racism, forms of trauma that are neither event-based nor exceptional but continuous and part of the usual, everyday life of the victims. This is indeed a critique that has repeatedly been made in recent years against hegemonic, Eurocentric theories of trauma, whose blind assumptions about the universality of their definitions as well as prescriptions for healing can be seen as a form of cultural imperialism (Craps 22). In their tendency to focus on the individual psyche, moreover, these theories distract attention away from the social forces that caused and perpetuated the traumatic conditions and situate change in "psychological recovery" rather than in "the transformation of a wounding political, social, or economic system" (28). This is a notion Frantz Fanon, as a psychiatrist and revolutionary, contested over sixty years ago: "the effective disalienation of the black man entails an immediate recognition of social and economic realities" (*Black Skin* 12–13), and this disalienation will only be possible with the transformation of these realities, he wrote in the early 1950s, when formal decolonization was far from achieved. Writing in the postcolonial and post–civil rights era, Morrison and the other authors I discuss all emphasize the persistent legacy of these systems of oppression.

By literalizing the metaphor, by making the ghost real and, in the case of *Beloved*, physically threatening and vampiric, these texts also reinvest it with a potency that its overuse in common language as well as in theoretical discourse has somewhat deflated and neutralized. This can be seen in the juxtaposition of metaphorical haunting with literal haunting in *Beloved*. Early in the novel, shortly after Paul D has chased away the baby spirit from 124, Sethe evokes the traumatic effects of her life at Sweet Home in terms that are strikingly suggestive of haunting. In her description of "rememory," she explains to Denver her experience of time: if "some things go," other "things just stay" (35), not only in memory but "out there. Right in the place where it happened." Places, in particular, remain: Sweet Home is still present, long after Sethe escaped it, long after Emancipation—which made irrelevant the Fugitive Slave Act that allowed her master to come and claim her and her children—and even long after the place ceased to exist altogether. Sethe here seems to be speaking in metaphorical terms when associating traumatic memory with a ghost—its link to place, its persistence, its existence "outside [the] head," its constant return and even its potentially threatening character, as it will always "be there for you, waiting for you" (36). But we fully understand the truth of her description when, shortly after, the metaphor appears in bodily form, waiting for Sethe in front of 124.

Re-Membering Diaspora

Despite Sethe's repeated claim that Beloved is hers, the ghost is not hers alone. The fact that Denver—or in fact anyone else—could "bump into" one of Sethe's rememories and see it all "happen again" (36) confirms Dominick LaCapra's contention that "the after effects—the hauntingly possessive ghosts—of traumatic events are not fully owned by anyone and, in various ways, affect everyone" (*Writing History* xi). Although she did not experience slavery herself, Denver is also a victim of its effects, in a belated, mediated way that closely resembles what has been theorized as transgenerational trauma or "postmemory." Marianne Hirsch defines postmemory as a form of memory experienced by children of survivors of cultural or collective traumas who, although they did not experience the traumatic events firsthand, grew up with stories and images so powerful that they "constitute memories in their own right" (5). Slavery—and, as I discuss in chapter 1, the Middle Passage more specifically—is commonly conceived as a cultural trauma, in the sense of a primal experience that is recollected through generations and constitutes African diaspora people's individual and collective identity (Eyerman 15). Besides those I examine in this book, several writers and scholars have expressed this cultural trauma in the idiom of haunting, in their attempts to grapple with memories of slavery and racial violence that are not part of their personal history but are nevertheless constitutive of their experience and sensibility. "Being haunted," Marisa Parham writes, "means struggling with things that come to us from outside our discrete experiences of the world, but which we nonetheless experience as emerging out of our own psyches." Blurring the boundary between "self and other" and "personal and political," this haunting names an affect by which "I feel pain, but have not suffered the blow" (6). In an image reminiscent of Morrison's description of Beloved as the ghost of history, Dionne Brand describes "Black experience in any modern city or town in the Americas [as] a haunting. One enters a room and history follows; one enters a room and history precedes. History is already seated in the chair in the empty room when one arrives" (*Map* 25).[19] Theorizing through their own subjectivity as women of the diaspora, Brand and Parham both appropriate and redeploy the haunting metaphor, shifting it from a debilitating traumatic memory to a form of consciousness for living in the present.

This tension between a compulsive return to and return of historical traumas and a productive engagement with the past is what Morrison captures in her concept of rememory, in which the prefix suggests both repetition and re-vision. Revisiting her past in response to Beloved's incessant questions enables Sethe to engage with it in a (re)constructive way, to see some things in a new light and to remember others that she had simply occluded. However painful, being haunted ultimately seems a necessary condition: more than a source of suffering that binds negatively to the past, it can also be a way of poetically and politically re-visioning a traumatic history and reflecting on how it impacts diasporic identity. In its ambivalence, the ghost allows the writers I examine in the next chapters to embrace what Harvey Neptune has identified as "an abiding dualism cours[ing] through the diasporic sensibility," which oscillates between a history of loss, grief, alienation, and death, and one of resistance, hope, and survival against a suffering that shall be overcome. In its living-dead condition, the ghost holds in tension the violence and pain of a traumatic past and the imagination and creativity that resistance and resilience in the face of this tragic history inspired, without disavowing either.

If the ghost of slavery can be said to play a constitutive role in diasporic identity, then, it is not in the sense of what Hortense Spillers evoked as "some kind of genetic imprint" (Haslett), but insofar as it is mobilized in the cultural—or, within the scope of this book, literary—production of the African diaspora. I mean this last phrase in its double meaning: the ghost of slavery is produced through this literature, which conjures it again and again; but in turn the ghost of slavery contributes to producing the African diaspora as community. My choice of the term "African diaspora" to frame my discussion of the writers and texts I examine here aims to emphasize both the symbolic importance of "Africa," as point of origin, and the event that provoked the dispersion from it, namely "slavery." Following David Scott, I put "Africa" and "slavery" between quotation marks here to make clear that I am not referring to the continent of Africa and the historical fact of slavery but to tropes mobilized and deployed in the discursive constitution, development, and perpetuation of an imagined community (124)—the African diaspora.[20] It is one of this book's arguments that the ghost trope is actually useful, and is used in some of the texts, for elucidating the relationship these writers and their protagonists have not only with slavery, as suggested above, but also with Africa, a relationship that is, as Stuart Hall puts it, "always-already 'after the break'" ("Cultural Identity" 226). As I will demonstrate through my reading of Marshall's *Praisesong for the Widow* in chapter 3, Africa appears in this literature as an absent presence, what I would call a "phantom Africa."[21]

More than an example of the way elements of African cultures and spiritualities persist and are reinvented in (the literature of) diaspora, the ghost thus also serves to theorize *how* these "elements are created, imagined, and remembered" (Hartman, *Scenes of Subjection* 72) through this very process of transculturation. Indeed, Hartman proposes that these traces "function in a manner akin to a phantom limb, in that what is felt is no longer there. It is a sentient recollection of connectedness experienced at the site of rupture, where the very consciousness of disconnectedness acts as mode of testimony and memory" (73–74). Hartman's analysis of memory in slave culture can be extended to diasporic culture in general. In her view, the "sense of community" does not depend on selfsameness or on a shared condition, but on "acts of identification, restitution, and remembrance" performed "in the context of disrupted affiliations" (61, 59) and reenacting the event and memory of initial disruption. As I suggest in chapter 1, this explains why the Middle Passage, as the inaugural moment of breach, holds such an important place in African diaspora consciousness. Through their constant returns, the ghosts in African diaspora literature emphasize the centrality of both Africa and slavery in the constitution of this community; yet through their elusive quality they simultaneously convey the always-already deferred and incomplete(d) character of this literature's re-membering impulse. Beyond their specific concerns and focus, all the texts I examine in the following chapters engage with the issue of diasporic identity, with what it means to be of, and to claim identification or affiliation with, the African diaspora. Reading these texts through the ghosts that haunt them illuminates not only the similarities in, but also the complex and anything but self-evident character of, their exploration and construction of African diasporic identity.

The personal histories and trajectories of D'Aguiar, Naylor, Marshall, and Cliff in themselves make a diasporic identification more appropriate than a more strictly national one, as they navigate between the Caribbean, the United States, and England. But this framing should precisely not obfuscate the different historical, social, and political contexts their writings engage with.[22] Moreover, their uses of the ghost trope both follow the general functions I have outlined in this introduction and reveal significant singularities. This double attention to similarities and differences explains the structure of this book. Each chapter focuses on one writer—and, except in the case of Cliff, one novel—and analyzes a particular aspect of what I have summarized as the ghost's re-vision of history, memory, and identity. While they may often seem contradictory, these various functions should not be read as different conceptions of the ghost so much as illustrations of the trope's ambivalent character itself. In my view, it is precisely this ambivalence and this multivalence that ultimately explain the ghost's attractiveness for African diaspora writers.

As the long list I offered at the beginning of this introduction showed, there are many texts to choose from when examining ghosts in contemporary African diaspora literature. That Morrison, Naylor, and Cliff offered me my first experiences of ghost-sighting only partly explains why—after much wandering—I felt compelled to return to these sites. The texts I examine in the next four chapters allow me to offer both an analysis of a wide range of meanings and functions and a coherent theorization of the ghost trope. The fact that most of the texts I selected were published in the 1980s is not incidental. It reflects the particularly prominent place ghosts occupied in the literature of that period, a period that, as I noted, was marked by an affirmation of folk culture, a turn to history, and a general critique of master narratives, as well as a growing presence of women's voices in literature, a conjunction of literary, theoretical, and political projects in which the ghost is precisely a useful resource. In the following chapters I will situate each text more precisely with respect to these various projects and show how its ghosts participate in them.

As a later text and the only one by a male author, *Feeding the Ghosts* may appear doubly as the odd one out. But without contradicting the metaphorical and epistemological link I sketched earlier between ghosts and women (writers), including D'Aguiar's novel is important precisely to avoid simplistic conclusions and essentializing readings of this link. The next chapters will pay particular attention to issues of gender—the specific forms of physical and epistemic violence black women have been subjected to, their special role in cultural transmission, the constraints this role has placed upon them—but a gender-limited focus would obscure the place and role of ghosts in African diaspora literature that constitutes this book's central claim. Rather than marking a break, *Feeding the Ghosts* shows a continuity not only in its use of the ghost, but also in its narrative form and subject matter. Written in a time when the boom in slavery studies had long been under way, and when the neo–slave narrative had become not only a popular genre but an extensively theorized one, *Feeding the Ghosts* sheds light on those areas of the historical and literary fields that still remained largely unexplored at the close of the twentieth century.[23] Indeed, his novel attempts to capture the subjective experience of the Middle Passage, an experience that, despite its foundational importance and significance for the African diaspora, had until then rarely been addressed directly by fiction writers or historians.

The ghost, as well as the related figure of the living dead, is crucial in D'Aguiar's attempt. This I demonstrate in chapter 1, by coupling my analysis of *Feeding the Ghosts* with a discussion of Stephanie E. Smallwood's *Saltwater Slavery: A Middle Passage from Africa to American Diaspora*, a historical study that interestingly uses the very same tropes. Besides dramatizing the life-threatening conditions of the voyage belowdecks, the ghost and the living dead enable both texts, I argue, to explore the complexities of the liminal chronotope of the Middle Passage and its psychological, cultural, and social impact on the captives. Based on a sinister historical event that has been largely utilized by abolitionists as well as historians of the slave trade, D'Aguiar's novel also negotiates between the historical and the fictional, the particular and the general, thus posing critical questions about the issue of justice and of an ethical memorialization of the victims. I begin my discussion of African diasporic ghosts with this text because it allows me to establish the foundational place the Middle Passage occupies in African diaspora consciousness and to explore its significance as cultural trauma. Indeed, both D'Aguiar and Smallwood represent the Middle Passage as an experience that affects those who survived it well beyond the end of the voyage, thereby suggesting that diasporic condition itself is one of liminality, of living between here and there, now and then. Dealing as much with history as it does with memory and identity, this first chapter also introduces the narrative arc of the book, which the next chapters then take up and pursue.

While chapter 1 looks at how literature can supplement historiography by attempting to capture the silenced perspective of the slaves, chapter 2 examines how literature can also re-vision historiography by exposing the silencing that is constitutive of the production of history itself. Reading Naylor's *Mama Day* and the character of Sapphira Wade in parallel to historians' treatment of Sally Hemings, Thomas Jefferson's slave and alleged concubine, I analyze the ideological and epistemological processes that turned slaves into ghosts in the master narrative of American History. By analyzing the way Sally Hemings and Sapphira Wade have been written in, and indeed out of, the historical and fictional narrative of America's past, this chapter makes two major, interrelated claims. First, I read *Mama Day* as a critique of the dominant historiographical tradition, whose reliance on positivist tenets underpins the ghosting of (women) slaves in history. Second, in situating the novel in the context of the developments in slave historiography as well as of the contestation of the historical discipline by poststructuralists and postcolonial scholars and writers, I argue that the ghosts in *Mama Day* suggest an alternative epistemology for approaching the past. I propose that Naylor's novel, in reflecting the ghost's characteristics in its formal qualities, is itself a "ghostly narrative," a narrative that engages us in a more epistemologically reflexive and socially and politically accountable relation to the past.

Chapter 3 turns to Paule Marshall's *Praisesong for the Widow*. In contrast to *Mama Day*, in which the living entertain a sustaining relationship with the dead, whose ghosts help them understand and deal with their present conditions and trials, Marshall's novel explores the consequences of a life disconnected from the past. Portraying a culturally (self-)alienated protagonist, the novel traces the geographical, spiritual, and cultural journey that leads her to reclaim her African diasporic heritage and community, with ghostly figures as her guides. Reading this journey as a ritual of spirit possession, I argue that the ghosts in the novel are crucial for understanding not only the protagonist's vexed relation to cultural memory but also the novel's ambivalent conception of diasporic identity. If these ancestral figures are the link between the protagonist and the personal and collective past she repressed, their ghostly character suggests the indirect, incomplete link to Africa on which diasporic memory and identity are founded. The ghost trope thus highlights, in Marshall's novel, both the importance of cultural memory and the constructed and dynamic character of the diasporic identity that this cultural memory supports.

Moving away from history toward memory, the third chapter also marks a shift toward the issue of identity, and initiates an examination of the ghost's destabilizing effect on essentialist definitions that is pursued and developed in chapter 4. Turning to a writer whose inclusion in the African diaspora has not been self-evident, and to texts that deal with sexuality in addition to, or rather in intersection with, race, this final chapter complicates and problematizes some of the notions addressed—or, precisely, not addressed—in the previous chapters and brings an important perspective on the very definition of diaspora as a "community." A light-skinned, mixed-race, lesbian Jamaican who was educated partly in England and lived in the United States, Cliff wrote about the difficulty as well as necessity to "claim an identity" that she had not only "been taught to despise," but that she had been told was not hers to claim. Taking Cliff's own identity—as she defined it and as it has been defined by others—as a starting point for my discussion of her work, I analyze her use of the ghost as a trope that both deconstructs hegemonic and prescriptive definitions of identity and conveys the profound anxiety that such destabilization produces. Besides examining the actual ghosts that appear in Cliff's novels, in my discussion of her short stories and poetry I also use the trope as a lens for analyzing her formal and theoretical approach to queer, which is, in many ways, the ghost in her early works. This chapter thus also offers a much-needed re-vision of Cliff's work: her poetry and short stories have received little critical attention, and scholarly discussions of her early texts have tended to ghost her dealings with issues of sexuality. Reading these texts through the ghost enables me not only to draw significant links between her fiction and her poetry, but also to show how she denounces race and sexuality as intersecting master discourses that must be deconstructed together.

Rather than a conclusion, the last section of the book offers a broader and open-ended reflection on the continual—as well as future—return of the ghosts of diaspora. In a circular trajectory that is in keeping with the nonlinear structure of the texts themselves, I return to *Beloved* to explore the apparent contradiction of a literary and political project that simultaneously attempts to bury and dig up the dead. Pondering the meaning and significance of the novel's coda, I identify its central dilemma, the need to remember *and* to forget the past, as one that underlies all the texts under study and that is precisely embodied in the figure of the ghost. Summarizing the various ways in which these texts deal with this dilemma—that is, the various ways in which they deal with ghosts—I suggest that African diaspora literature invites us to live with ghosts, rather than to exorcize them or lay them to rest.

My primary aim here is of course to offer the first book-length study of ghosts in African diaspora literature. Read together, the four chapters offer a detailed and extensive—though certainly not exhaustive—analysis and theorization of the ghosts of diaspora. But each chapter can also be read for itself, and my discussion of the different texts also contributes in significant ways to the scholarship on these four writers. To look at the ghost in the narrative is to start with the marginal, with what we did not even notice in the first place. Ghosts may indeed seem to be marginal elements in some of the texts I examine here. Unlike *Beloved*, these texts have rarely been discussed with a particular attention to the ghosts that haunt and (de)structure them. Paying attention to these ghosts, ultimately, also compels us to re-vision our reading and interpretation of these texts.

[1]

"VOYAGE THROUGH DEATH / TO LIFE UPON THESE SHORES": REPRESENTING THE MIDDLE PASSAGE

The gap between Africa and Afro-America and the gap between the living and the dead and the gap between the past and the present does not exist. It's bridged for us by our assuming responsibility for people no one's ever assumed responsibility for. They are those that died en route. Nobody knows their names, and nobody thinks about them. In addition to that, they never survived in the lore; there are no songs or dances or tales of these people.
—Toni Morrison, conversation with Marsha Darling

THE FIRST THING that attracts the eye is the blindingly white sun setting in the near center. By following the explosion of color that delineates the sky and the sea, the gaze wanders slightly to the left to the ship in the midground, and is quickly absorbed into the white spray that, like ghostly hands, seems to drag the vessel toward the darkness of a storm. Leaving the ship to its fate to follow the lights and darks on the water, the eye catches among the troughs and swells small brown and black shapes in the water that it cannot immediately identify. Following their trail to the right, it suddenly stops at what is unmistakably a human leg, shackled at the ankle and emerging from the waves while the rest of the body disappears underwater. A shoal of fish of various sizes and shapes is nibbling at the flesh while, all around, more fish and other forbidding shapes and shadows appear, rushing through the waves toward the figure. Drawn back to the little dark shapes slightly to the left and looking at them more closely, the viewer now identifies them as hands and wonders at the floating chains attached to them.

Such is the sight offered by one of the most famous pictorial evocations of the Middle Passage. Despite its title, J. M. W. Turner's painting *Slavers Throwing Overboard the Dead and Dying, Typhoon Coming On*—also commonly known as *The Slave Ship*—does not show slaves in the process of being thrown overboard, but floating or drowning in the foreground while the ship, already in the distance, is sailing away toward

Joseph Mallord William Turner, *Slave Ship* (*Slavers Throwing Overboard the Dead and Dying, Typhoon Coming On*), 1840. Oil on canvas, 90.8 × 122.6 cm. Museum of Fine Arts, Boston, Henry Lillie Pierce Fund. Photograph © 2018 Museum of Fine Arts, Boston.

an ominous storm. Turner's manipulation of the viewer's gaze is crucial to the painting's impact, as it effectively guides our reaction from awe at the raw power of nature, through empathy at the vulnerability of the ship, to horror at the view of the submerged, fractured body of the slave. The force of the painting can also be said to come from the way it sublimates its theme by transposing the horror of the slave trade onto the seascape: the typhoon announced in the painting's title can be seen as a symbol of final judgment against the slavers, while the blood-colored sea evokes the violence the slave trade unleashes on its victims.

But this oblique treatment of the subject can also be seen as potentially misleading. In Cliff's third novel, *Free Enterprise*, when Alice Hooper, proud new owner of *The Slave Ship*, presents the painting to her guests, Mary Ellen Pleasant feels moved by the painting and is "grateful that the artist had portrayed it thus, indicating the horror of the thing aslant" (73). The reactions of the other—presumably white—guests, however, make Pleasant aware that they do not view the painting in the same way. One of them soon proves her fears right when he exclaims, "The thing [the slave trade] is behind us"—the year is 1874—and "surely we can enjoy the art it engendered" and appreciate Turner's "brilliance . . . with form, color" (74). While this comment fills Mrs. Hooper with shame and prompts her to write Pleasant a letter of apology and even reflect about whether her purchase of the painting might not make the art dealer profit off the slave trade, even she fails to see what Pleasant herself identifies as "the difference between [them]," the white woman and the black one: "while you focus on the background of the Turner painting," Pleasant writes back, "I cannot tear my eyes from the foreground. It is who we are" (80).

In writing these characters' fictional reactions to the painting, Cliff perhaps had in mind a particular historical response to *The Slave Ship*. In a description of Turner's work that has become as famous as the painting itself, John Ruskin presented *The Slave Ship* as being "dedicated to the most sublime of subjects and impressions . . .—the power, majesty, and deathfulness of the open, deep, illimitable sea" (377–78). His description itself conveys the light and the colors of Turner's seascape in very vivid terms. The sea seems to be taking a deep breath "after the torture of the storm" (376); in the sunset it appears "fearfully dyed" with "an awful but glorious light, the intense and lurid splendour which burns like gold and bathes like blood" (377, 376). The "dark, indefinite fantastic forms" of the fish cast "a faint and ghostly shadow" on the "desolate heave of the sepulchral waves" that "advanc[e] like the shadow of death" upon the ship. As for that "guilty ship," its mast is "written on the sky in lines of blood, girded with condemnation in that fearful hue which signs the sky with horror" (377).

This extraordinary description strikes not only by its colorful prose and gothic rhetoric, but also by its near-complete omission of one element of the painting: the drowning slaves. Ruskin's only mention of the slaves appears in a footnote glossing the phrase "guilty ship" and apparently explaining the symbolic import of the typhoon: "She is a slaver, throwing her slaves overboard. The near sea is encumbered with corpses" (377). This blatant omission has been interpreted in various ways.[1] For Marcus Wood, "Ruskin's interpretation is first and foremost a metaphorical reading." Like the painting itself, it is a brilliant example of "pathetic fallacy"—a term coined by Ruskin himself in *Modern Painters*—in which "the subject, that is the drowning of the slaves, and the horror of the slave trade, is embodied in a sky made of blood and a sea convulsed with pain" (*Blind Memory* 62). While Wood's assessment of Ruskin might be correct, other commentators—especially writers and critics of the African diaspora—have been reluctant to accept a metaphorical evocation that simply leaves the human subjects out of the picture. For Guyanese poet David Dabydeen, Ruskin's footnote "reads like an afterthought, something tossed overboard" (7). For Paul Gilroy, it reveals Ruskin's failure to "integrate this aesthetic commentary on the painting with an open acknowledgment of its 'racial' content" (*Small Acts* 83).

But, as the remark made by the unnamed guest in *Free Enterprise* suggests—a guest later identified in Mrs. Hooper's letter to Pleasant as a bishop—the very obliqueness of Turner's painting permits such (mis)readings, as the sublime may override the subject. As LaCapra points out, the sublime is a problematic mode of representation for trauma, insofar as it is a form of displacement that makes the "other" it pictures "radically transcendent, inaccessible, unrepresentable" (*Writing History* 93). Thus, while one may again agree with Wood that "the complexities of the seascape, with its contradictory effects of storm and calm, fury and dignity," successfully reflect "the difficulties in attempting to provide a dignified memorial to mass murder" (*Blind Memory* 62), Turner's *Slave Ship* and the mixed but always strong reactions it has elicited provide a good starting point to raise questions about the (un)representability of the Middle Passage: how does one adequately express the horror and terror, the violence, the trauma of the Middle Passage? How does one, to paraphrase Dabydeen, escape a representation of the victims as exotic and sublime (8)?

These difficulties might explain the particular way in which the Middle Passage has been addressed in African diaspora literature. On the one hand, its foundational importance and symbolic significance in the historical and cultural consciousness of the African diaspora make it a haunting presence in the literature, appearing in countless allusions and images and serving as a referent for ruminations on roots and rootlessness, diasporic identity, racism and violence, and even modern forms of migration. It figures prominently in poetry, from epics like Edward Kamau Brathwaite's *The Arrivants* (1973) and Derek Walcott's *Omeros* (1990), through the lyrical sequences of Dabydeen's *Turner* (1995) and Kwame Dawes's *Requiem* (1996), to M. NourbeSe Philip's experimental *Zong!* (2008). On the other hand, it is strikingly often eluded in slave narratives, and it has rarely been the direct focus of prose fiction.[2] While the reasons for this silence or oblique treatment are no doubt complex, it seems that the Middle Passage resists narrative form. As Gilroy notes, because of its traditionally mimetic quality the novel may be the genre that most seriously bears the "scepticism about the value of trying to revisit the sites of ineffable terror in the imagination" (*Black Atlantic* 218). The Middle Passage is indeed the epitome of what he calls "the slave sublime," an experience that cannot be represented but that African diaspora culture has nevertheless striven to convey. It is certainly no coincidence that the passage evoking the voyage in *Beloved*—one of Gilroy's literary examples of the slave sublime—should be the most poetic and least narrative one in the novel.[3]

The experience of the Middle Passage was also long absent from the history of the slave trade. If historians have always been centrally concerned with the transatlantic journey, only quite recently have they turned away from its economic and demographic aspects to attend to its psychological, social, and cultural dimensions and finally attempt to document the captives' experience. Though neither the first nor the only one of such endeavors, Stephanie E. Smallwood's *Saltwater Slavery: A Middle Passage from Africa to American Diaspora* (2007) is a most compelling one. Exploring the journey from the African shores through the Atlantic crossing to the American markets, it offers an unprecedented account of the captives' subjective experience. In the introduction, Smallwood announces that the aim of her book is to "[bring] the people aboard slave ships to life as subjects in American social history" (3). Paradoxically, the book largely does so through the rhetoric of death and death-in-life. One of the chapters devoted to the transatlantic voyage, titled "The Living Dead aboard the Slave Ship at Sea," particularly uses this rhetoric in order to explore not only the threat and actuality of death in the overcrowded and pestilential space of the ship's hold, but also its effects on the captives' psyches and bodies, as well as the transformations that result from this near-death experience.

Saltwater Slavery serves as a useful introduction to D'Aguiar's *Feeding the Ghosts* (1998), a novel that, though it was published ten years earlier, offers an uncannily similar representation of the Middle Passage. In this account of the fateful voyage of the slave ship *Zong*, the historical event that allegedly also inspired Turner's painting, D'Aguiar attempts to recover the voices of the victims and of the survivors. In terms reminiscent of Morrison's, D'Aguiar has described his work as an attempt "to fill in the gaps of an eradicated past and to understand history through personality, through people and their experiences rather than by a rehearsal of dates and events" (Frías 418). A literary treatment of the Middle Passage that takes us into the minds of the characters in itself allows the writer to delve into the individual, personal, intimate experience that even Smallwood, for lack of historical sources, cannot explore. But D'Aguiar's particular narrative techniques, which favor nonlinearity, polyphony, ambiguity, and contradiction—aspects he deems essential to a critical return to the past—make room for the reader to "feel and talk back to the text" (422). *Feeding the Ghosts* attempts to convey the slaves' unspeakable experience through a self-reflexive form, even as it recognizes the ineffability of slavery's terrors.

Just as the ghost in *Beloved* allows Morrison to explore the interior lives of the slaves, I argue in this chapter, the ghost and the related figure of the living dead play an important part in both D'Aguiar's and Smallwood's attempts at conveying the captives' perspective on, and experience of, the Middle Passage. Both tropes problematize "those Manichean categories of meaning" on which, according to Sara Clarke Kaplan, we too often rely in order to explain master-slave relationships and racial—as well as gendered—relations: besides black/white, passive/active, and feminine/masculine, life/death has indeed been one of those "mutually exclusive dichotomies" that "have long been integral to conceptions of American cultural politics" ("Founding (M)other" 778), with the effect of erasing the more complex meanings lodged in their interstices.[4] In Smallwood's and D'Aguiar's texts, the trope of the living dead conveys, on the one hand, the dehumanization and objectification of the Africans in a system that defines them as socially dead. On the other, as a dual, liminal figure, it powerfully captures the complex processes that take place in the Africans' bodies, minds, and cultural and social constructs.[5] The living dead is thus key to both texts' exploration of the power dynamics at work in what Gilroy described as the "living, micro-cultural, micro-political system in motion" (*Black Atlantic* 4) that is the slave ship, and of the conflicting narratives it produced.

Smallwood and D'Aguiar also problematize definitions of both life and death and previous representations of the transatlantic voyage by suggesting that, for the captives, the Middle Passage does not really come to an end with landfall in America. The state of living death continues long after the journey; it might even be a condition from which one never recovers. Ultimately, the trope poses the question that Robert Hayden's poem "Middle Passage" only intimates in its opening and closing lines:

> Middle Passage:
> voyage through death
> to life upon these shores.

What kind of life awaits those who survive the journey? Despite the sheer horror of the Middle Passage, the end of the voyage bears for those who live to see it the promise of more horrors to come. Not only does the condition of social death continue, but death itself is an inescapable part of the slaves' lives, as they remain haunted by their experience and by the memory of those who *did not* reach these shores. Smallwood and D'Aguiar both resort to the trope of haunting to describe the profound and enduring traumatic effects of the Middle Passage on the Africans' psyches and bodies. But while Smallwood, as a historian, must bring her narrative to some form of closure, D'Aguiar extends his story with an epilogue that takes the ghosts of the *Zong* into our own present. Generalizing the haunting, the novel ultimately offers a broader reflection on the Middle Passage as collective memory and cultural trauma in diasporic consciousness. Like Beloved, D'Aguiar's ghosts also embody the memory and legacy of slavery in the Atlantic world of the late twentieth century and beyond.

Contemporaneous Accounts of the Middle Passage

In order to, on the one hand, highlight the originality of *Saltwater Slavery* and *Feeding the Ghosts* and, on the other, trace their continuity with previous evocations of the Middle Passage, I begin my discussion with an overview of the treatment of the transatlantic voyage in firsthand accounts to demonstrate the way its subjective experience has traditionally resisted representation. Moving on to abolitionist propaganda, I suggest that while these texts and images, which already used the rhetoric of death and living death, to some extent successfully conveyed the violence and horror of this experience to their (white) viewers and readers, they largely did so by objectifying the Africans. For different reasons but with similar outcomes, historians of the slave trade have also traditionally approached the Middle Passage in ways that did little to give the captives the lead role and to make their subjective experience accessible. Smallwood's untraditional account thus opens up new vistas, and a discussion of her work forms a large part of the first half of this chapter.

Slave Narratives

There are very few firsthand written accounts of the Middle Passage by those who experienced it from belowdecks. In Philip Curtin's edited collection of narratives *Africa Remembered*, only two of the nine testimonies he includes mention the Atlantic crossing, and they do so only in passing. More recently, Jerome S. Handler showed that, of the fifteen autobiographical accounts in English by African-born slaves he was able to identify, only six mention the Middle Passage. In the very first slave narrative published in English, Ukawsaw Gronniosaw relates his transatlantic voyage in a single sentence: "I was exceedingly sea-sick at first; but when I became more accustom'd to the sea, it wore off" (12). Gronniosaw's experience was arguably far from representative, for his voyage seems to have been exceptionally mild. Because he was very young and the captain's pet, he apparently did not spend much time, if any at all, in the ship's hold. However, most of the other narrators who were not as lucky remain just as vague about the voyage. After a very detailed account of his trek to the African coast, Venture Smith is surprisingly euphemistic about the crossing to Barbados, which he simply describes as "an ordinary passage, except for great mortality by the small pox, which broke out on board" and left, "out of the two hundred and sixty that sailed from Africa, not more than two hundred alive" (11). For Vincent Carretta, the erasure of this experience from the narrative is "striking" and is "particularly telling" in a decade when abolitionists on both sides of the Atlantic were keen to draw attention to the horrors of the Middle Passage ("Venture Smith" 176).

Ottobah Cugoano might provide a reason for the veil that is so often drawn over this part of the slaves' accounts. After relating in great detail how he was brought to the slave ship and mentioning the "cruel bloody scene" that followed the captives' unsuccessful attempt at burning the ship before it left African shores, Cugoano interrupts his narrative and skips over the next few weeks to relate the slaves' conditions on Caribbean plantations. Of the crossing itself, he says: "It would be needless to give a description of all the horrible scenes which we saw, and the base treatment which we met with in this dreadful captive situation." The reason for this ellipsis is that "this abandoned situation may be easier conceived than described" (15). In a gesture typical of many slave narrators, Cugoano chooses to keep silent about the most violent and horrid details of his experience and calls to the reader's imagination to picture what he is, or rather is not, writing about. His silence over the details of the experience might therefore be explained by a form of censorship, which could be imposed by white editors for reasons of decorum, or self-imposed either out of a personal or cultural aversion at relating such intimate matters or out of the psychological refusal to recall events that are too painful (Diouf 41–42).

Two slave narratives devote a few pages to describing the voyage. But while both offer a rather detailed account of the material conditions of the Middle Passage, they say little about its psychological effects. Jeffrey Brace describes the lack of food and water, the sexual abuse of female captives and the brutal flogging of male captives, the many deaths and the fear, horror, and distress of the Africans; but he repeatedly notes that his feelings "def[y] language to depict" and that "language cannot describe more misery than [he] experienced" (119, 123). In what is certainly the most well-known narrative by an African-born slave,[6] Olaudah Equiano offers a very vivid description of the dire conditions of the voyage in the hold:

> The stench of the hold while we were on the coast was so intolerably loathsome, that it was dangerous to remain there for any time, and some of us had been permitted to stay on the deck for the fresh air; but now that the whole ship's cargo were confined together, it became absolutely pestilential. The closeness of the place, and the heat of the climate, added to the number in the ship, which was so crowded that each had scarcely room to turn himself, almost suffocated us. This produced copious perspirations, so that the air soon became unfit for respiration, from a variety of loathsome smells, and brought on a sickness among the slaves, of which many died, thus falling victims to the improvident avarice, as I may call it, of their purchasers. This wretched situation was again aggravated by the galling of the chains, now become insupportable; and the filth of the necessary tubs, into which the children often fell, and were almost suffocated. The shrieks of the women, and the groans of the dying, rendered the whole a scene of horror almost inconceivable. (58)

While for Cugoano the situation was more easily conceived than described, and therefore did not lend itself to description at all, for Equiano it can be, and is, described, but the horror of it is "almost inconceivable." The nauseating, graphic quality of this description—perhaps matched only in Alex Haley's *Roots*—powerfully conveys the physical sensations of the captives by invoking four senses. And yet, by focusing on the material conditions of the voyage, Equiano's account, like Brace's, says little about other, less easily accountable dimensions of the experience of the slave ship's hold. The terms used to relate the psychological impact of the voyage are much vaguer, and Equiano's distanced and slightly self-derisive evocation of the terror and wonder his younger self felt on his first encounter with white people and their maritime technology is more a means to comment on the barbarity of the slavers in a who-is-the-real-savage way than an attempt to convey his subjective experience.[7]

Abolitionist Propaganda

This limited focus on the material and physical dimensions of the experience of the Middle Passage also appears in firsthand testimonies by white people who voyaged on slave ships as members of the crew, generally as surgeons, or as passengers. These accounts similarly dwell on the stifling atmosphere and cramped space of the hold, which they identify as the cause of diseases and of great mortality among the captives. In his *Account of the Slave Trade on the Coast of Africa*, Alexander Falconbridge, who served as surgeon on several slaving voyages, writes: "The deck, that is, the floor of their rooms, was so covered with the blood and mucus which had proceeded from them in consequence of the flux, that it resembled a slaughter-house. It is not in the power of the human imagination, to picture to itself a situation more dreadful or disgusting" (25). Such testimonies were primary material for abolitionists. The Middle Passage indeed came to play an important part in their cause because the merchants of the slave trade were much more easily attacked than the American slave-owning class (Klein, *Atlantic Slave Trade* 130). Depicting the terrible conditions of the voyage was therefore a most effective way of attracting public attention to, and sympathy for, the abolitionist cause.

These texts, however, do not attempt to offer any direct description of the captives' subjective experience either. Thomas Clarkson, a founding member and major actor in the abolitionist movement in Britain, offers a telling example of this admitted and, to a certain extent, strategic failure in his monumental *History of the Rise, Progress and Accomplishment of the Abolition of the African Slave Trade by the British Parliament.* While in much of his work Clarkson uses a different strategy, inviting his readers to imagine themselves in the situations he describes at great length, when it comes to the Middle Passage he readily admits that "as far as this part of the evil is concerned," he is "at a loss to describe it":

> Where shall I find words to express properly their sorrow, as arising from the reflection of being parted for ever from their friends, their relatives, and their country? Where shall I find language to paint, in appropriate colours, the horror of mind brought on by thoughts of their future unknown destination, of which they can augur nothing but misery from all that they have yet seen? How shall I make known their situation, while labouring under painful disease, or while struggling in the suffocating holds of their prisons, like animals enclosed in an exhausted receiver? How shall I describe their feelings as exposed to all the personal indignities, which lawless appetite or brutal passion may suggest? How shall I exhibit their sufferings as determining to refuse sustenance and die, or as resolving to break their chains, and, disdaining to live as slaves, to punish their oppressors? How shall I give an idea of their agony when under various punishments and tortures for their

> reputed crimes? Indeed, every part of this subject defies my powers, and I must, therefore, satisfy myself and the reader with a general representation, or in the words of a celebrated member of Parliament, that "Never was so much human suffering condensed in so small a space." (39–40)

Clarkson here addresses the emotions and feelings of the captives more directly than any other narrative by those who actually experienced them. But his long list of rhetorical questions, while providing some elements of answer, again ultimately points to the uttermost impossibility of appropriately describing the experience of the Middle Passage.[8]

If language failed even a writer as able as Clarkson, other media could be used more effectively. Later in his *History*, the abolitionist describes a print, a "happy invention" that "was designed to give the spectator an idea of the sufferings of the Africans in the Middle Passage, and this so familiarly, that he might instantly pronounce upon the miseries experienced there" (336, 377). First published in 1788 by the Plymouth chapter of the Society for Effecting the Abolition of the Slave Trade, the original version of the print shows an overhead view of the lower deck of the slave ship *Brooks*, with 294 Africans tightly packed in four sections—for girls, women, boys, and men. Each slave wears a simple loincloth, and the men are shackled at the ankles. The text that accompanies the image of the ship details the dimensions of the space allotted to each man, woman, and child, exposes the usual conditions of a slaving voyage, and concludes with the authors' assurance that their goal is not to abolish slavery, only the slave trade. The print was later reproduced in countless versions by other abolitionist groups in Britain and the United States, with various additions and alterations to both image and text. The broadside that is today widely known as *Description of a Slave Ship* offers seven views of the lower deck of the *Brooks* instead of the single one of the original illustration, including transverse views showing the vertical arrangement of the bodies, whose number has now gone up to 482.

We are here of course far from Turner's sublime and colorful rendering of the slave ship at sea. The perfect organization of the black figures on the white page gives a deceivingly clean and ordered impression of a slave ship's hold, a very "sanitized" (Finley 16) representation of the Middle Passage that also stands in stark contrast with Equiano's graphic description. But the sobriety of the print's black-and-white, schematic design economically captures the claustrophobic atmosphere of the tightly packed hold. The paragraph detailing the dimensions of the space allotted to each slave further emphasizes the impression of confinement and

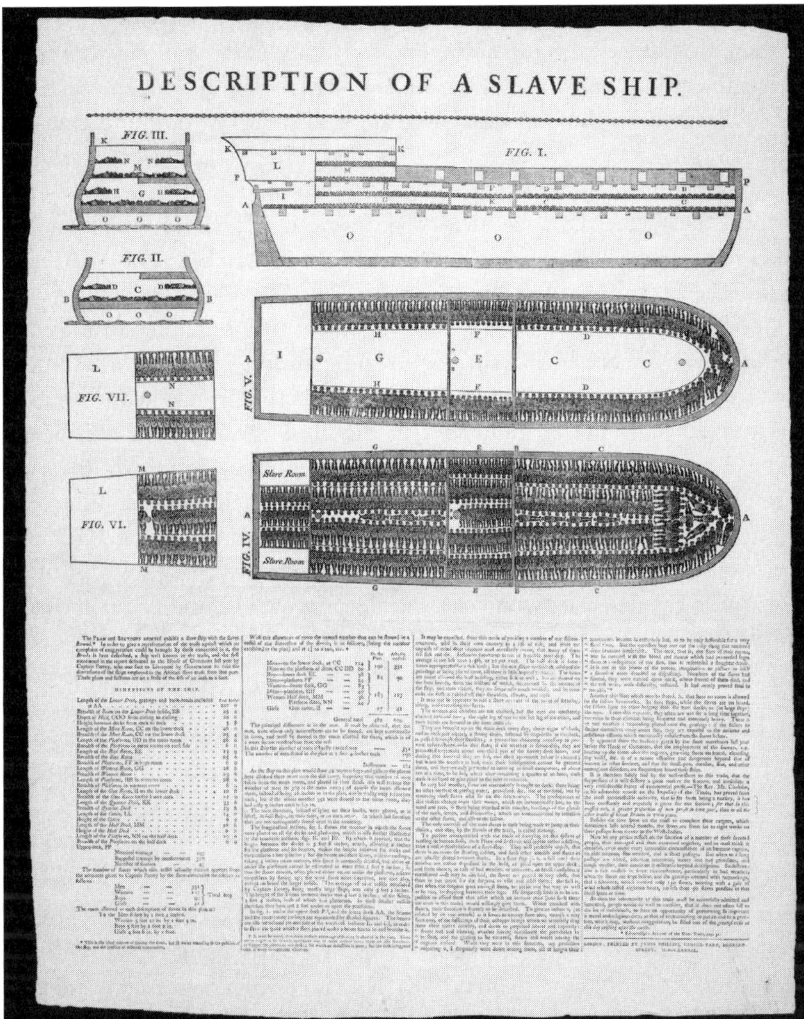

Description of a Slave Ship, 1789. Printed by James Phillips, George-yard, Lombard-street, 1789. Broadside, 63 × 50 cm. Beinecke Rare Book and Manuscript Library, Yale University.

"capture[s] the brutal logic and cold, rational mentality" (Rediker 339) that supported the slave trade. According to Clarkson, the image "seemed to make an instantaneous impression of horror upon all who saw it" (377). Yet in their attempt to imprint upon their (white) viewers' minds the horrors inflicted upon the Africans, the abolitionists in effect only further alienated the captives: drowning their individuality in a mass of hundreds of identical figures, the print visually and symbolically erases their subjectivity and locks them in the passive role of helpless victims, a role dictated by the abolitionist cultural agenda (Wood, "Imaging the Unspeakable" 212). Destined to white liberal humanists, *Description of a Slave Ship*, like Turner's *The Slave Ship*, ultimately represents less the Africans' suffering than the idea of suffering itself, before which, as Ian Baucom suggests, we stand as spectators rather than witnesses (*Specters* 292)—the very distinction dramatized in Cliff's *Free Enterprise*.

According to Wood, *Description of a Slave Ship* "is as close as the abolition movement in Britain got to the creation of a final monument to the middle passage" (*Blind Memory* 36). If the print reached its goal and proved particularly influential in the abolitionist cause, it is partly because while the other significant representations of the Middle Passage "leave the viewer firmly standing on land," this one is "the only eighteenth-century representation of the middle passage that took one not only on board, but inside the hold of, a slave ship" (38, 36). But its power also resides in its iconic potential, for which it has been borrowed, adapted, and revised in countless versions since the late eighteenth century.[9] In particular, *Description of a Slave Ship* visually conveys a reality the captives had to face during the Atlantic crossing: the omnipresence of death. Shown as it is from an overhead perspective, the hull of the *Brooks* is shaped like a coffin, and the hundreds of neatly arranged, static figures of the slaves look like so many corpses. In the American versions of the print, a paragraph added to reinforce the viewer's identification with the Africans further emphasizes this association: "Here is presented to our view, one of the most horrid spectacles—a number of human creatures, packed, side by side, almost like herrings in a barrel, and *reduced nearly to the state of being buried alive*, with just air enough to preserve a degree of life sufficient to make them sensible of all the horrors of their situation" (qtd. in Rediker 314–15, my emphasis).

This association of the slave ship with a coffin or a grave was not a mere rhetorical device created by the abolitionists. Other contemporaneous accounts of the slave trade used the same terms to emphasize the life-threatening conditions of the transatlantic voyage. In *Way of Death*, Joseph C. Miller notes that in the eighteenth century Angolan trade, Portuguese captains often referred to the slave ship with the slang term *tumbeiros*, which can be translated as "coffin" or "coffin bearer," or alternatively *túmolos fluctuantes*, literally "floating tomb" (314). Marcus Rediker similarly identifies the use of the terms "marine lazar house" and "floating bier" (274). Historians' estimates of African mortality during the Atlantic crossing have amply shown that this rhetoric of death was no hyperbole. Scholars today generally admit a mortality rate of 15 to 20 percent, with significant variations according to port and period, although the issue has been and continues to be subject to debate. In fact, the "numbers game" was long the main preoccupation of historians of the slave trade. If their work permitted a better understanding of the extent, operating processes, and demographic and economic consequences of what long remained "one of the least explored aspects of modern economic and social history" (Klein, *Middle Passage* xv), it did little to free the African captives from the role of passive and anonymous victims in which abolitionists cast them. Herbert S. Klein concluded his 1978 study of the Middle Passage with the claim that if the captives' individual experience of the voyage "cannot be recaptured," a quantitative account at least "helps to define the limits within which that experience took place" (251). Others would argue that, when dealing with historical traumas, such stark factual information as mortality rates "loses its historical weight when merely taken as data" (Friedlander 54).

In the last decade or so, however, several historians have adopted a new, more qualitative approach to the subject. Using letters, journals, and narratives—by both Africans and Europeans—instead of or in complement to ledgers and account books, these studies attempt to understand how the captives might actually have *experienced* the Middle Passage. If mortality still is an important aspect of their research, what they are interested in is not the cold facts and numbers but the live experience of the people these facts and figures long stood for. "How many people died can be answered through abstract, indeed bloodless, statistics," Rediker notes in a book that rewrites the history of the slave ship as "a human history"; but "how a few created terror and how the many experienced terror—and how they in turn resisted it—cannot" (354). In the same vein, Smallwood identifies the Africans' "trauma of death, and the inability to respond appropriately to death" as an "indirect violence [which,] arguably, was the most abject experience of the captives' Atlantic crossing." This experience and its cost for Africans, she concludes, "cannot be adequately represented by any statistics" (152). For those historians, then, the main question is not so much how many died and how many lived, but how the Africans dealt with the death of their fellow captives and the prospect of their own death, as well as how they sustained and even created life in the midst of a deathful experience. This new focus on other dimensions of slave mortality sheds very different light on both life and death and reveals the complex tensions the Middle Passage created between the two. Like Morrison, Smallwood is concerned less with the figure of sixty million than with all that is evoked in the "more" of *Beloved*'s dedication. In her discussion, death becomes a much more problematic and indefinite notion than suggested in even the most detailed account books registering mortality, which reduce it to "a simple statement of cause and effect" (Smallwood 139).

The Living Dead on the Saltwater

While the rhetoric of death and death-in-life used in abolitionist propaganda such as *Description of a Slave Ship* reduced slaves to "something less than human" (Wood, "Imaging the Unspeakable" 217), Smallwood's use of the figure of the living dead humanizes the captives, as it allows her to explore not only the material and physical conditions they endured on the voyage but also the psychological, social, and cultural journey they were forced to embark on. Appearing explicitly only in the title of one chapter but informing her entire narrative, this ambivalent, liminal figure aptly captures the in-between nature of the Middle Passage as space-time: halfway between Africa and America, freedom and slavery, subjecthood and objectification, the captives underwent profound transformations that both destroyed and created their individual and collective identities. Smallwood's work thus not only offers a deeper understanding of the Middle Passage: it also redefines the phrase itself, reviving, as it were, the primary sense of the term as "a passage that is intermediate in time or space; the middle part of a journey, a person's life, etc." and, in a figurative sense, "a course or state between extremes."[10] Referring not so much to the bottom leg of the triangular trade but rather to the captives' experience of the slave ship at sea, the Middle Passage in Smallwood—and, as we will see, in D'Aguiar as well—reminds us that in the end this story is not about the slave trade, but about those who endured it.

In Limbo

In describing the slave ship as a "limbo . . . that could sustain neither life nor death" (145), Smallwood exposes both the physical and metaphysical violence the Middle Passage inflicted upon the captives. First, death at sea produced a major social and spiritual crisis. Whereas for the slavers the death of a captive marked a simple "departure from this life," as one captain's journal phrases it, for the Africans themselves "death represented not just a discrete event but rather a shift in social relations that had wide reverberations" (139), for the dead as much as for the living. In the captives' culture, as in many cultures, consecrated ground and proper burial rites were considered essential. These rites required the support of the living, who memorialized the deceased through mourning and provided food and drink, clothing and tools so that the departed could continue their activities in the realm of the dead. All this was of course impossible on the Middle Passage, on which the dead Africans were disposed of by being simply and unceremoniously thrown overboard into the shark-infested waters. In the absence of the mourning rituals and interment that traditionally ensured the successful migration of the soul to the realm of the ancestors, the dead found themselves "trapped in a time-space regime in which they were unable fully to die" (152). The survivors who witnessed the departure and disposal of their fellow captives had to bear the burden of these wandering souls. As for the kinsmen of the deceased—whether on board the ship or in Africa—they also suffered from these unfulfilled deaths, as they were thereby deprived of "a thread of the special power and protection only ancestral members of the community could provide" (141). The trope of the living dead, in this instance, serves to explain an anomaly caused by the Atlantic slave trade in the context of cultures in which kinship and the presence of ancestors and their relationship with the living played a central role in the social and symbolic orders. The living dead translates a condition—the dead's incapacity to take their rightful and necessary place in a protective network of social relations—that poses a threat to both individuals and communities.

Smallwood's evocation of the slave ship at sea as limbo not only concerns the way the Middle Passage challenged the captives' conception of death; it also suggests its disruptive effects on their definition of life. The conditions in which the Africans endured the voyage disrupted all familiar notions of space and time. The crossing lasted a minimum of one month from the west coast of Africa to Brazil, two months to the Caribbean and North America, but it could take significantly longer in case of unfavorable weather. Thus trapped mid-Atlantic for several weeks or months, the captives were utterly disoriented. They found themselves confined on a ship that was always in motion and yet always appeared to be in the same place on the infinite sea, suspended in a time that seemed to stand still and could not be measured in any habitual way (135). The open sea itself also challenged their notion of life and death insofar as "the landless realm of the deep ocean did not figure in precolonial West African societies as a domain of human (as opposed to divine) activity" (124). Even those who were not actually thrown into its monstrous depths thus found themselves in a state of living death.

Other historians have noted that for many West African communities the Atlantic lay as a literal "boundary between the lands of the living and the domain of the dead" (Miller 4) whose crossing "represented a premature and unnatural death" (Schuler 186). For Smallwood, this explains why these communities generally explained the departures of their kin into Atlantic slavery "in the idiom of death" (58): since none of those who had been taken to the coast ever returned, they were commonly assumed to have been killed or even eaten by the Europeans. Theirs was, moreover, a dishonorable death: torn from the chain that traditionally connected the living and the dead, unable to take their proper place as ancestors, the slaves were not venerated and passed "beyond both the physical and metaphysical reach of kin" (61). Literally dead to their communities, the "saltwater slaves" also suffered the social death that was the condition of all slaves, a condition Patterson significantly describes as a form of "living death" (8). "Alienated from all 'rights' or claims of birth," he explains, the slave "ceased to belong in his own right to any legitimate social order" (5) and became a liminal being, "on the margin between community and chaos, life and death, the sacred and the secular" (51). In precolonial African societies, domestic slaves went through a ritual process that severed their ties with their kin and community, left them temporarily in a state of kinlessness, and then incorporated them into their master's lineage with a new status (53). Atlantic slavery, in contrast, secured no such assimilation into a new system of kinship and therefore condemned the slaves to "the perpetual purgatory of virtual kinlessness" (Smallwood 61).[11]

Compared to the other forms of slavery Patterson examines in his encyclopedic study, Atlantic slavery was also distinctive in that it rested on a global, capitalist system, which, before it produced "American slaves," produced commodities that were marketed, bought, and exported. The process that turned, in Smallwood's phrasing, "African captives" into "Atlantic commodities" began on African shores, when the captives were first put in fetters, kept locked in barracoons—sometimes for several months—and then sold to European slavers. Stripped of their clothes, their adornments, their names, their rights, they were divested of everything that identified them individually and socially. But it was on the slave ship itself that they were fully dehumanized and objectified, as their transportation required that they be treated as "commensurable units" (Smallwood 82) that the slavers could stow in the hold like other kinds of goods without extinguishing their lives. While the point of the trade was that the stock should reach American markets alive and in relatively good health, the ultimate goal for both investors and ship captains was to secure the highest profit. This required that the voyage be made at the smallest possible cost, notably by filling up the ship, feeding the slaves parsimoniously and, sometimes, disposing of the sick to safeguard the rest of the "cargo." In this highly rationalized enterprise, the slavers had to determine "the boundaries of the middle ground between life and death where human commodification was possible" (34). In effect redefining the boundaries between life and death, the slavers turned the captives into living dead as they treated living human beings like inanimate objects.[12]

By turning the captives into commodities, the Middle Passage produced the slavers' "desired object: an African body fully alienated and available for exploitation in the American marketplace" (Smallwood 122). Added to the disorientation and the physical and psychological agony caused by their confinement in the hold, this commodification had profound effects on the captives' ability to maintain a sense of self, as human and living beings. It "reduced [them] to an existence so physically atomized as to silence all but the most elemental bodily articulation, so socially impoverished as to threaten annihilation of the self, the complete disintegration of personhood" (125). Smallwood's description of the commodified captive as a creature reduced to its most basic bodily functions and emptied of all the social, psychological, and spiritual components that make up the self is strikingly evocative of the zombi. Of West African origin but today more generally associated with Caribbean, more particularly Haitian, culture, the zombi traditionally designates a dead person brought to "that misty zone which divides life from death" (Métraux 282) by a sorcerer or priest (a *bokor* or *houngan*), a master for whom it must work or perform certain tasks. A body without mind, personality, memory, or desire, the zombi is thus an avatar of the slave, an empty husk whose only social utility is raw labor.[13] While it seems a monstrous figure, the zombi is the result of alienation rather than the essence of otherness; its monstrosity therefore does not pertain to an intrinsic characteristic but points at the monstrosity of the forces that created it—the slavers, the slave trade, slavery. Raising crucial questions about definitions and the power dynamics that underwrite them, the trope thus allows Smallwood, paradoxically enough, to re-humanize the captives.

If the living dead and the zombi are apt tropes for the social death and the dehumanizing and commodifying processes that the Middle Passage initiates, Smallwood does not portray the Africans as the mere victims of these conditions. As Vincent Brown reminds us, Patterson's concept of social death does not "describe the lived experiences of the enslaved" but rather constitutes "a theoretical abstraction" that aims to "reveal the essence of slavery in an ideal-type slave" (1233). Therefore, from the captives' point of view, social death does not constitute an inescapable condition but rather represents "a compelling threat" that generates a "politics of survival" (1240, 1246). The living dead holds in tension—without ever resolving them—these opposite pulls. On the one hand, it seems to endorse the slavers' definition, which identifies the slaves as socially dead. On the other, it also subverts it, for it is, after all, not fully dead; the part of life it maintains suggests the possibility of resistance, the captives' relentless efforts not only to survive but also to affirm their lives as human subjects. In encapsulating both the threat of social death and the life-affirming acts and practices that this threat compels, the living dead allows Smallwood—and D'Aguiar—to navigate a middle course between what Brown identifies as an unduly pessimistic and ultimately disempowering narrative that "pathologizes" and victimizes the captives and an overly celebratory one that fails to "account for the dislocations, physical violations, and cosmic crises" that enslavement inflicted on the captives (1240, 1244).

The Tomb and the Womb

Saltwater Slavery not only demonstrates that the captives strove to retain the social and cultural life that their condition as captives and commodities threatened to dislocate; it also shows that new forms of social and cultural life actually emerged *from* this condition and that the captives, as Brown puts it, "ma[d]e their cultural practices from the stuff of death and dissolution" (1246). Smallwood explains that the slave cargo was "a novel and problematic social configuration" that "constituted the antithesis of community" (101): as the slave ship filled up in several ports according to whatever stock was available on the coast markets, it brought together individuals or small groups from very diverse social, cultural, and ethnic origins. But in the hold, such differences were toned down by the confrontation to a new Other. For most captives, their entry into the trade marked their first encounter with white people. According to Rediker, it is on the slave ship that the captives "discovered themselves to be 'black folks'" (307).[14] For Smallwood, on the other hand, the "existence and dimensions" of the community that started to take form in the hold "would become known to them only in the setting of the Americas" (120). Whatever notion of racial or cultural difference and similarity the captives might have had during the voyage, what made them a "community" is also their shared identity and experience *as captives*. And even more than this shared condition, it is the ways in which they negotiated it that created productive bonds. If the cramped space of the hold forced the captives into what Smallwood describes as "anomalous intimacies," it also generated fruitful interaction, compelling them to develop inventive means of communication and learn new languages to gather knowledge about the ship, the crew, and the best way to endure or escape their condition. The Middle Passage thus marked "the beginnings of a culture of resistance, the subversive practice of negotiation and insurrection" (Rediker 350) that would later prove useful to living on American plantations. Those who had resisted and survived violence, terror, and inhuman conditions together built new forms of kinship with those they came to call "shipmates." These bonds, as many testimonies attest, remained strong well beyond the end of the voyage. For the captives, then, the ship was also an "intermediary space" (Smallwood 120) between different social, cultural, ethnic, and racial identities.

In this last instance, the living dead captures the profoundly liminal experience of the Middle Passage, both as a space-time of the in-between and as a moment of transformation. As an oxymoron, it signifies not only the destructive, but also the creative aspects of that experience. On the one hand, Smallwood's account challenges the long-standing—but now largely rejected—view of the Middle Passage as marking a clean break, constituting such a traumatic experience that it erased all memory of Africa and all trace of African culture.[15] On the other, by exposing the disruptive nature of the Middle Passage on all aspects of the captives' lives as well as deaths, she also asks us to be wary of all-too-simple accounts of retentions and survivals of African cultures. Not only does she insist that African diaspora cultural practices emerged both from African cultural tools "carried in memory" (190) and from a need and capacity to adapt these tools to meet the demands of their new (geographical, social, ethnic) environment, but she also contends that some cultural practices were born on, or from, the Middle Passage itself. In showing how the social and cultural identities of the captives were shaped by the shared experience of the journey, she establishes the Middle Passage in very concrete ways as the foundational event of a diasporic culture.[16]

This conception of the Middle Passage as the liminal space-time that marked the beginning of a new culture is reminiscent of earlier evocations by Caribbean writers and cultural critics. Building on Brathwaite's evocation in *The Arrivants* of the limbo dance as a cultural practice born on the slave ship, Wilson Harris uses limbo as a way to theorize the development of a "new corpus of sensibility" that re-members African legacies and tribes in the New World, in a way he describes—like Hartman—as akin to a "phantom limb" ("History" 158). Reenacting the captives' resistance, this "limbo imagination" becomes a "re-creative response" (160) to symbolic and historical violence and domination in the Americas.[17] In the way it more explicitly blurs life and death, Smallwood's representation of the slave ship also echoes a recurring image in the work of Édouard Glissant, who pictures the hold as both tomb and womb: "This boat is a womb, a womb abyss. It generates the clamor of your protests; it also produces all the coming unanimity. Although you are alone in this suffering, you share in the unknown with others whom you have yet to know. This boat is your womb, a matrix, and yet it expels you" (*Poetics of Relation* 6). Like for any newborn, the delivery is painful and traumatic. But sharing the same womb, enduring together the experience of the abyss, produced a kind of knowledge, which, although unconscious, "served as the alluvium for th[e] metamorphoses" (7) that created what would come to be called the African diaspora.

Like Brathwaite's and Harris's limbo and Glissant's womb abyss, the dual figure of the living dead signifies both the destructive and the creative nature of the Middle Passage. However, instead of emphasizing the space-time of transformation, as the womb abyss and limbo both do, the living dead more forcefully conveys the impact of the experience on the people who endured it. Moreover, while limbo suggests a ritual of rebirth—as the dancers lower their body to pass under the pole and come back to their full height on the other side—the living dead also complicates the conception of the Middle Passage as a movement from life (in Africa) through death (on the Atlantic) to rebirth (in America). Like Glissant's womb abyss, which is "pregnant with as many dead as living under sentence of death" (*Poetics of Relation* 6), so inhospitable that even those it delivers alive are doomed to a life of suffering, the living dead holds life and death in constant tension rather than in sequence. The trope thus allows Smallwood to redefine the Middle Passage in yet another way. On the one hand, the dual quality of the living dead imbues the adjective "middle" with more layers of meaning, unpacking the myriad ways in which the Middle Passage constituted an intermediary space-time. On the other hand, the forever irreconcilable nature of the oxymoron recasts this liminality as perpetual. Indeed, in the last chapter of *Saltwater Slavery*, Smallwood details the many ways in which the captives' "death march continued on American soil." Not only were many of those who reached their destination "near death" (193) because of the ravages the voyage inflicted upon their bodies, but many would succumb in the first few years to overwork and infectious diseases. As for those who survived the period of seasoning, they would have to continue to endure, and find ways to counter, the social death and natal alienation that would condition their lives as American slaves, to forever forestall "further descent into an endless purgatory" (189). The slaves remained "haunted by the rhythm of untimely fatality" (193): they could never "completely escape the saltwater" (7), for it constantly reshaped their communities as the ships continued to deliver more and more captives. As the "traumatic echo" (202) of the Middle Passage—their own and those of other captives—reverberated throughout the slaves' existence, time seemed to stand still, as it had on the Atlantic itself. At the end of *Saltwater Slavery*, Smallwood comes to the conclusion that for those who survived it, the Middle Passage in fact "was perhaps the antithesis of a 'middle' passage, with all that phrase implies about a smooth, linear progression leading to a known end" (207).

As a historical study of the Middle Passage, Smallwood's book logically closes with the "American present" of the saltwater slaves (207). But the title of its concluding chapter perhaps gestures toward the future of this diasporic community founded by the survivors of the Middle Passage. Indeed, "Life and Death in Diaspora" seems to suggest that this liminal condition not only concerns those who actually endured the voyage, but might somehow characterize diasporic experience through the next generations. For Brand, to live in diaspora is to live forever in the space of the Door of No Return that literally and metaphorically marked the Africans' entry into the slave trade: "There is the sense in the mind of not being here or there, of no way out or in. . . . Caught between the two we live in the Diaspora, in the sea in between" (*Map* 20). For Brand, as for Smallwood, to live in diaspora is to be "always in the middle of the journey" (49).[18]

The Ghosts of the Zong

Ten years before Smallwood's living dead embarked on their transformative journey, D'Aguiar wrote a novel out of a similar "[interest] in the in-betweenness of a slave ship on the Atlantic for the slaves who have left home and are bound for a strange place" (Frías 422). If *Beloved* was, in Morrison's own description, "not about the institution—Slavery with a capital S," but "about these anonymous people called slaves" (Angelo 257), *Feeding the Ghosts* is not so much about the Middle Passage as about the disremembered and unaccounted for of its history. Against historians' numbers game as much as slave ship captains' cold accounting of the Africans as pieces of cargo, D'Aguiar focuses on the captives as people, exploring "their memory, their will to remember, their will to live" (Frías 422).

Feeding the Ghosts explores this experience by revisiting an infamous historical event that also inspired Turner, Dabydeen, and many other poets of the African diaspora. In 1781, the British slave ship *Zong* left the African coast headed for Jamaica with a cargo of over four hundred and fifty slaves. As it was delayed because of a navigation error, water started running short, and some of the Africans got sick. Knowing that moribund slaves would not sell well on American markets and that the ship's insurance would not cover the loss of stock that died what would be considered a "natural" death, the captain ordered that over a hundred and thirty living Africans be thrown overboard. The *Zong* eventually reached Jamaica, and the rest of the stock was sold. Upon the ship's return in England, the owners made a claim under maritime insurance law for the lost cargo, but the underwriters refused to pay, and the matter went to court. The jury, under the authority of Lord Chief Justice Mansfield, settled in favor of the owners, thereby not only confirming the necessity of the massacre but turning it into an ultimately profitable act.[19]

The details of what really happened aboard the *Zong*, who made the murderous decision, and what condition the Africans were really in are not fully known.[20] D'Aguiar's novel follows the available historical details quite closely, but he gives the captain a cold-blooded rationality he may not have had and makes rampant sickness, rather than shortage of water, the main reason for the massacre. *Feeding the Ghosts* tells the story in three parts. The first covers the three days of the systematic killing of the Africans. It is related through a third-person omniscient narrator, with focalization shifting from the crew, especially the captain and the first mate, to the captives, Mintah in particular. After she is thrown overboard with the sick for speaking out—and in English—against the massacre, Mintah is able to grab a rope and climb back on board. Hiding for two days with the help of Simon, the cook's slow-witted, kindhearted assistant, she persuades her fellow captives to plot an insurrection. Her plan fails, and she is caught, but because she is young and healthy and will fetch a good price on American markets, she is spared. This first part ends with the *Zong* approaching the shores of Jamaica. The second part relates the trial between the owners and the underwriters. Composed mostly of direct speech in the form of the various parties' testimonies and interventions, as well as of free indirect speech, these two chapters stage the ethical drama at the core of the novel by profuse use of irony. The third part returns to the voyage and the massacre, but this time relates it through the first-person narration of Mintah, starting after her return on board and including memories from Africa before her capture. It then jumps forward to her life in Jamaica after her emancipation, again including memories of the *Zong* and her subsequent life as a slave and a free woman in America. Shifting from first- to third-person narrative, the last chapter covers Mintah's last moments and her death—on the day of the abolition of slavery in the British Caribbean. The story is also framed by a prologue that introduces the major elements of the plot—the jettisoning of the slaves, Mintah's role as a "witness" (5) and her subsequent haunting—and an epilogue that both rehearses those themes and reflects on the place of the *Zong* in history and collective memory.

Feeding the Ghosts is an unusual novel not only because it is one of the very few narrative fictions that offer a detailed account of the Middle Passage, but also because it does so through the perspective of a female protagonist. As such, it offers a corrective to both contemporary novels like Haley's *Roots* and male-authored slave narratives, in which female captives' perspective and experience are even more absent. As Deborah McDowell has noted, the fact that most slave narratives were "primarily expressions of male subjectivity" and included women mainly "as victims of sexual abuse" explains the profusion of novels of slavery, or neo–slave narratives, authored by black women since the 1960s. Written in the wake of this tradition, *Feeding the Ghosts* similarly explores female subjectivity and "dramatizes not what was *done* to slave women, but what they *did* with what was done to them" ("Negotiating between Tenses" 146). As a female protagonist who is both subjected to sexual violence and the initiator and leader of resistance, Mintah indeed offers a complex portrayal of a captive woman's experience and subjectivity. D'Aguiar has explained his choice of a female protagonist by an interest in understanding the particular silencing of black women in history—or, as McDowell puts it, in "his-story." He was inspired, on the one hand, by the writings of women like Harriet Jacobs, Phillis Wheatley, and Sojourner Truth "to get a feel for the time, tone and place that black women faced," and, on the other, by the "incredibly robust grandmother" he grew up with, a figure who already featured prominently in his earlier works (Frías 422).

But D'Aguiar's portrayal of Mintah not only allows his narrative to restore black women's long-denied agency by shifting the focus "from sexual victimization to creative resistance" (D. McDowell, "Negotiating between Tenses" 146); it also enables him to explore how issues of kinship, filiation, and community are reconfigured in the context of the Middle Passage and of Atlantic slavery more generally. Over the course of the novel, Mintah appears both as a daughter desperately trying to salvage filiation through memories of her parents and home, and as a mother figure looking after the community that emerges aboard the *Zong* and in the New World, in which, as a witness and a survivor, she also serves as a memory and culture bearer. As I will show, however, the novel avoids essentializing the link between Mintah's gender and these various functions, eschewing a univocal account of her experience and its consequences. In fact, Mintah herself appears to hold life and death in tension both within her own traumatized body and in her very place within the diasporic community.

Taken Alive and Treated Like Dead

Feeding the Ghosts conveys the subjective experience of the Middle Passage in terms very similar to those of *Saltwater Slavery*, through the constant blurring of the boundaries between life and death. The ambiguity that will underlie the literary treatment of life and death throughout the novel is introduced in the prologue, which poetically evokes the jettisoning of the slaves. By referring to the victims as "bodies," the text first leaves us under the impression that we are witnessing the disposing of corpses. The bodies indeed seem lifeless and unresisting as they are first passively "receive[d]" by the sea, landing without a sound as if they have "come to rest on a cushion." But when "two hundred and sixty-four arms and 264 legs" start to "punch and kick" as they sink, the full horror of the scene before our eyes is revealed: these bodies are still alive, if only for a short while. The battle between life and death continues after the bodies have "become still" (3): the sea itself—in its traditionally ambivalent nature as both creative and destructive force—then tries to "enliven the very bod[ies] it has wrestled to a stillness in the first place," before swallowing and slowly disintegrating them. That is however not the end of these bodies, for "Sea does not stop at death." The bodies that the sea receives and consumes do not remain in this watery grave: once "dissipated," they become part of the sea, part of the wind, with which they start to "howl" (4).

What could be read as a mere extended metaphor in the poetic prologue is confirmed in the next chapters, which replay and detail the jettisoning of the one hundred and thirty two slaves. Shortly after the beginning of the massacre, the narrator notes a change in the wind:

> Now the wind intensified. Before, it was merely playing in the sails and rigging, in the sleeves, trouser-legs and shirts of the men. Now it has found a

> voice that was a hum around the mainmast and whistled through the ship's rigging and rose to a howl, drowning out rain, sea and the distress that rose from below, putting in its place those very voices locked up in the hull, up on to the deck, up into the rigging, up among the sails and all around the ship, in a chorus of lamentation from which there was no hiding place, no door to be slammed, no hatch barred and no stopper coarse enough to protect the ears. (25–26)

In this first part of the novel, D'Aguiar constantly uses the weather and its sudden changes to highlight the dramatic events taking place aboard the *Zong*. But what we see here is more than the pathetic fallacy of Turner's and Ruskin's stormy skies and raging seas. D'Aguiar is not merely attributing human characteristics to the wind by giving it a voice to mourn the loss of the first two Africans; nor is this voice the wind has found only that of the slaves locked in the hold lamenting the disappearance of those who were "taken alive and treated like dead" (27). As it soars up on the deck and into the sails and hovers around the ship, the "chorus of lamentation" also contains the voices of the dissipated, howling bodies evoked in the prologue.

This is confirmed when the narrator then describes the Africans' anguish over the fate of those who are killed and unceremoniously tossed overboard. Mintah, who was educated by Danish missionaries and therefore has some knowledge of European mores, assures the other captives that they will not be sold as meat, their bones ground to powder and used as aphrodisiac or medicine and their skin turned into clothes. But this does not assuage their concern about "what [will] become of their bones" (37): refused "the quiet of a grave in the ground," the dead will not be able to join their ancestors and will be condemned to eternally "roam the Atlantic" (4). Their spirits will follow the ship throughout its fateful voyage, and the living can but listen to their voices and wonder how their souls will "find [their] way home" (37). By turning the dead Africans into ghosts, D'Aguiar exposes, like Smallwood, the metaphysical violence that the Middle Passage and death at sea represent for the captives.[21]

While their presence is felt every time the wind howls in the rigging, the ghosts of the jettisoned slaves actually play little part during the voyage —but they will come back with a vengeance in the last two chapters of the novel. In this first part, D'Aguiar is indeed more interested in what happens to the living. By choosing to relate the particularly horrifying story of the *Zong* massacre, he offers an account of the Middle Passage in which the line between life and death is even thinner than on a more ordinary voyage. Because of the prologue, even the historically unknowledgeable reader knows from the outset what fate awaits the one hundred and thirty-two slaves, who are thus living on borrowed time. Starting *in medias res*, as the captain is pondering how to inform his crew of his plan to throw the sick but living cargo overboard in order to secure profit from the voyage, the first chapter introduces the captives as if they were already dead. "Buried deep below deck" (9), they seem to inhabit a kind of underworld clearly separated from the lively domain of the sailors bustling about on the deck. The hold is repeatedly described as a "cavern," a "dungeon" (21), a hell so dark, hot, and airless that the crew resent entering it and always drink the air avidly as they come back into the open. The Africans' cries, sounding like the wails of tormented souls, barely seep through the hatch and fail to reach the ears of the seamen. It is unclear whether the crew do not hear the sound because it is drowned in the ordinary hubbub of the creaking ship and roaring sea, or whether it has become too much a "part of the whole, all-encompassing fabric of routine" (10) for them to even notice it. In any case, the indifference that meets the distress of the captives and their relegation to another, marginal space suggests that they have "no socially recognized existence outside of [their] master." They are quite clearly, in Patterson's terms, "social non-person[s]" (5).

The captives' living death is confirmed when the sick are brought on deck for an evaluation of their state. As a more clinical description of them follows, their condition merely shifts from already dead to "as good as dead" (124). At the captain's command, First Mate Kelsal carefully inspects the first two Africans he has selected—these are the "severest cases," but he notes that "any picked at random would easily qualify as such" (20)—to estimate how much longer they have to live. Convinced that "a face doesn't lie about things like death," he takes a close look at their eyes, which are "half-closed or half-open" and "dark" (22), "like a light about to die" (145). Upon the first mate's conclusion that the two men probably will not make it beyond the next couple of days, Captain Cunningham orders that they be thrown overboard. From a legal point of view, it is crucial that the slaves be disposed of alive, rather than after they have died of sickness, in order for compensation to be claimed for their loss; from a moral point of view, it clearly does not make any difference to the captain: in the end, they are all mere strokes in his ledger. Captain Cunningham would certainly agree with Morrison's schoolteacher—another white man with a ledger who "knew the worth of everything"—that "definitions belonged to the definers—not the defined" (*Beloved* 228, 190). In showing how the slavers define the living as dead before they actually succumb to illness or are killed, D'Aguiar demonstrates that they do not only have a claim on the slaves' lives, nor do they merely have the right of life and death over those they own: they also have the power to fix and shift according to their (economic) interests the very line between life and death.

The novel takes pains to denounce Captain Cunningham and Kelsal's definition of the captives as "as good as dead" by continuously emphasizing the Africans' aliveness. Only the very first slave brought on deck does not resist, for he has no idea of what is about to happen to him. The second one, weak as he is, finds enough strength to fight for his life and make it more difficult for the crewmen to throw him over the side. Similarly, when it becomes clear to them that those who were taken on deck will never return, the other slaves, when picked as sick, fight back to show they are still strong and are anything but dead or dying. At first that is enough to convince the crew to leave them alone; but as more and more slaves must be disposed of to ensure comfortable profit, the sailors start taking away slaves randomly and must use more and more strength to force them onto the deck and into the sea. What happens to Mintah exposes the full paradox of the whole undertaking and further reveals the irrational nature, or rather, the *economically* rational nature of the ongoing events. Despite her fine health and the good price she would fetch on American markets, Kelsal has her thrown into the sea. Since his rage at her insolence toward him cannot alone justify that she be eliminated, he must base his demand on the dangerous influence her defying attitude could have on her fellow captives, namely, inciting rebellion. Whereas the other Africans are removed from the ship because they purportedly put the rest of the cargo at deadly risk, in a dramatically ironic reversal Mintah is thrown overboard because she tries to protect their lives. But even more than her desperate efforts to stop the killing, it is her surviving her own disposal that best shows her refusal to submit to the slavers' redefinition of life and death. Her first words after she has climbed back aboard the ship, "I am alive" (56), pronounced out loud although she is all alone in the storeroom, sound like a defiant contradiction to the slavers' efforts to liquidate her—as does the irrepressible laughter that then seizes her.

Mintah's alleged death makes her safe, at least for a few hours. While the other slaves locked in the hold must be reactive to show they are healthy in order to stay alive, Mintah must play dead. When she is forced to temporarily move out of the storeroom and hide in the men's section of the hold, her fellow captives first take her for "an apparition" (88). Turning the slavers' definition to her advantage, she becomes a ghost, invisible and able to move freely in the hold. The trope here briefly becomes an empowering one, as the elusive and incorporeal body of the ghost contrasts with the physicality that subjects the other captives to blows, chains, sickness, and death. Moreover, her supposed return from the dead gives her power and authority among the Africans, as what some understand as her invincibility makes her their natural leader. When she is betrayed by a woman who tells a sailor that Mintah's "spirit [is] now on board, roaming the ship" (90), it is again her status as a ghost that buys her a little time, for the captain first thinks the woman's story is mere superstition.

A Life in Abeyance

Yet her condition soon becomes ambiguous, as the reader, the other characters, and ultimately Mintah herself come to doubt that she is really alive. During her time in the storeroom, whenever she rests she falls into a sleep so "deep and dreamless" it resembles death, leaving the reader to wonder if she will ever wake up: "Her mind may have seen the shadow too late to do anything but fall silent. For suddenly she was worrying about everything and feeling every ache in her body, and as suddenly she felt nothing, not even the rice bag of another's back, nothing but emptiness, which for her was peace, was sleep" (64–65). The ominous "shadow," Mintah's falling suddenly "silent" and feeling "nothing," as well as the unexpected "peace" her bruised and tired body finds, all evoke the coming of death, until the last word, long delayed in the sentence, reassures the reader that she is only sleeping. When he finds her thus asleep in the storeroom where he came to pick up yams, Simon, the cook's assistant, similarly wonders at her condition and shakes her awake as he asks her, twice, "Are you dead?" (58). Mintah's own evocation of this episode in the third part of the novel shows more clearly the effect the idea of death has on her. Simon's question is slightly different in this second version: "Are you living or dead?" It is repeated a second time as "Are you dead or living?" But it is only when, in its third utterance, it becomes "Are you dead?" that Mintah opens her eyes. "I know what it means to be dead," she thinks. "I am only Mintah if I am living" (191). Once again, she reacts against what she perceives as another attempt at defining her condition.

But after so vehemently asserting her aliveness, Mintah herself comes to doubt that she is truly alive. All alone in the storeroom, she seems more disoriented and confused than she ever was in the hold, for she does not even have the comforting presence of her fellow captives to anchor her sense of self. Her reflections echo Smallwood's definition of the slave ship as a paradox for Africans, as a place where "life can be lived at sea" (Smallwood 124): "A life on water was no life to live, just an in-between life, a suspended life, a life in abeyance, until land presented itself and enabled that life to resume" (61). On this ship that is "going nowhere," time itself has stopped, as it "runs on the spot, neither backwards nor forwards" (199).[22] In a desperate effort to disable the devastating power of the sea, she tries to give it the familiar features of her African homeland, seeing on its waves and troughs the benign shapes of hills and valleys, but it constantly shifts shape and conspires with the slavers to keep her doubly captive. This spatial and temporal disorientation is reinforced by her sense of natal alienation on this sea that has a "limitless capacity to swallow love, slaves, ships, memories" (27). Unable to foresee an end to the voyage, Mintah starts to believe "that the land was the past and the sea was the present; that there was no future. The sea was the beginning and end of everything" (112). As she finds herself thus trapped in limbo, "*between* [her] life" (199), the question that Simon asked and that made her jump awake has now become her own: "Am I living or dead?" (196). D'Aguiar's portrayal of Mintah as a living dead and a ghost effectively translates her subjective experience of the sea—both of nearly dying in the sea and of living at sea—and the way this experience shatters her definitions of life, death, and her own condition.

Her sense of self is further disrupted by her growing dispossession of her own body. If the sea has utterly disoriented her senses, slavery has deprived her of all control over her own body:

> My body already belongs to the sea. . . . My body belongs to the *Zong*. . . . And the captain of the *Zong*. . . . Kelsal too thinks I belong to him. . . . The crew know they can do whatever they please with it since it is theirs too before it is mine. My body belongs to everyone but me. I move in it like a thief. I do not belong to it. All this journey it is trying to separate itself from me, to be rid of me once and for all. My body seems to think that if it dies it will kill me, the intruder in it. (200)

At the hands of the crew—Kelsal beat her, the boatswain tried to rape her, the crew kept her in fetters—Mintah's body has been alienated from her. Not only does she not possess and control it anymore, but it has become her enemy, an instrument of torture that can be used against her. She is fully aware of what is happening to her, and of where this process will lead her if she cannot stop it. As she pictures herself as a slave in America, she expresses her future condition in terms that evoke zombification: "My body will set foot on land, and I will be inside unable to see this land since I will have died inside that body, killed by it" (200–201). When Mintah's mind and soul have been killed by what is already the slavers' instrument, what will be left of her is this commodified body that will senselessly and subserviently work on a plantation or in a cane field.

Simon's gentle treatment of both her body and her mind acts as a temporary remedy against zombification. By hearing him call her name, she sees it "attach itself to [her] body" again (202), while his kisses and caresses allow her to reclaim her body, a body now weightless that cannot be hurt or held in chains. This brief moment of solace evokes what Hartman theorizes as "redressive action": a re-membering of the captive body that reconfigures it as "a site of pleasure, eros, and sociality" through the attention it directs toward meeting the subject's needs and desires.[23] As "an exercise of agency," redress is also "a re-membering of the social body," a process that links subject and community through "the reconstitution of violated natality, and the remembrance of breach" (*Scenes of Subjection* 77). Indeed, as she experiences the release of her body, Mintah thinks of her fellow captives in the hold, who "must benefit from this lightness, this bodilessness in the body," but also of their homeland, their ancestors and their gods, which they all carry "in [their] bodies." Suddenly free and "unburdened" (202), she imagines their bodies can fly over the Atlantic, back to Africa.

If the chapter ends on this optimistic note, we know from the account of the voyage in the first part of the novel that Mintah's reunion with her body lasts only as long as her union with Simon. As Hartman makes clear, redress, however necessary, is always limited and incomplete, as long as the conditions it seeks to counter have not been superseded. Mintah's brief moment of redress does play a significant part in her attempt to change her and her companions' condition. Shortly after this episode, she makes her presence known to the other captives and persuades the men to revolt. But they are caught, and she ends up tied on the deck, her body chained and subjected to blows again. As she is forced to watch the incessant jettisoning of her fellow captives, she desperately asks for their names before they disappear over the side, promising that they will be remembered. Some of them call out her name, as if it could help them find the strength to vanquish the sea as she did. However, voiced in "their last breath," her own name sounds to Mintah like "an accusation. A bad omen. A sentence" (213). Instead of the strokes in the captain's ledger, it is now her name that ticks the beat and punctuates the death of each slave. After so desperately trying to keep her name attached to herself, she now recoils from a name that has become Death itself.

In an attempt to escape being irretrievably turned into a living dead and hoping to find peace in death, she asks Kelsal to throw her overboard again, but instead finds herself returned in chains to the hold. The state of numbness she then falls into has all appearances of living death. But the process is not actually one of zombification, for her transformation does not occur in the idiom of death but of wood, an element that has been her ally throughout the voyage, literally saving her from the sea and giving her a sense of stability and a point of reference against disorientation. This suggests that although it is a consequence of the psychological and physical abuse she was subjected to, her transformation is somehow voluntary: it is a way for her to temporarily escape the pain and the horror of the ongoing events and to protect herself from her body until she can "get it back to land," where it "will recognise [her] again as a part of it" (200). This is indeed what happens as the *Zong* approaches Jamaican shores: slowly emerging from her torpor, she first recovers her body, then her subjectivity, and, finally, her name, as she slowly transforms back from a "plank of wood" to "bendable wood," to "living wood. Wood breathing," and to, finally, "Mintah" (134).

"Life" upon These Shores

The first part of the novel ends with Mintah affirming her life again by saying her name aloud. In part 2, however, she becomes a ghost again as she completely disappears from the narrative. The Africans indeed have no role to play in the trial, in which the deliberation concerns only the financial consequences of the recent events. Mintah's name comes up during the proceedings, as the underwriters' counsel produces a notebook in which she related the massacre aboard the *Zong* while she was hiding in the storeroom, and which she entrusted to Simon with the promise that he would make sure people knew what happened on the *Zong*. Her account, however, is presented as unreliable by the counsel for the investors, on the ground that "a slave could not have written it" (168): first because she could not in all likelihood have procured the necessary material to write it and then kept it hidden from the crew, and second because the absence from the court of the supposed author proves that the book was "penned by a ghost" (169). "Which are we to believe?" the counsel asks, "the captain's account or the ghost-written musings of a mind prone to invention?" (170). The question is, indeed, merely rhetorical. Like all slave narratives, the authenticity and authorship of her account are considered essentially doubtful. In rejecting her testimony, the court confirms that Mintah and her fellow captives—whether they survived the massacre or not—legally still are nonpersons. And in ruling in favor of the investors, that is, in recognizing the captain's extreme measure as justified by necessity, it symbolically kills the victims a second time.

As a direct counterpoint to this reaffirmed definition of the slaves as socially dead, D'Aguiar gives the third part of the novel to Mintah. In making her the narrator of and agent in her own story, D'Aguiar works against the silencing and objectifying gestures and discourses that are intrinsic to the institution of slavery; but he thereby also exposes their inevitable and long-lasting effects on the slaves. Eschewing heroism as well as victimhood, the story of Mintah in America is one of sustained life-affirming acts in an existence marred by death, bearing the physical and psychological marks of a traumatic experience. We thus learn how, against the prediction that she "would die and be buried" on the Maryland plantation to which she was auctioned, she was in fact able to buy her own freedom with money she earned by teaching poor white children. Yet despite her claim that she "ha[s] always been free" (205), she remains a slave to the past and is never able to fully enjoy her freedom. Her emancipation does not bring her long-awaited peace, but a responsibility toward both the living and the dead. In Maryland, she helps slaves escape North; in her mind, the fugitives merge with the dead of the *Zong*, for whose each and every death she multiplies by two the number of people she guides toward freedom. While her efforts to redeem the lives of the lost by securing freedom and education for the next generations demonstrate her struggle against natal alienation, she pays a bitter price for her actions: when rumors about her participation in the Underground Railroad start spreading, she is forced to abandon her home, friends, and lover, and to be alone and isolated again. Moving to Jamaica "to put slavery behind [her] once and for all" (207), she finds herself surrounded by the sea, a sea that was "spoiled" and "ruined" for her and that only brings up painful memories (219). To protect herself and the dead from a sea that "possesses and never relinquishes," that "destroys but does not remember" (210), she naturally turns to wood, her old ally. She buys land and plants "one tree for each soul lost on the *Zong*" (219), and starts carving little wooden figures to give a refuge to the spirits of the dead—just as grain was her own refuge aboard the *Zong*.

Her story does not lead to the happy ending of many classic slave narratives: like Harriet Jacobs's, it does not end "in the usual way, with marriage" (Jacobs 201); unlike Jacobs, however, she has no children to be reunited with at the end of the story, for her traumatic experience on the *Zong* has made her body infertile and will not allow her to "be made into newer shapes of people" (210). Mintah's infertility is presented as profoundly ambivalent. On the one hand, it allows her to escape "the African female's reproductive uses within the diasporic enterprise of enslavement and the genetic reproduction of the enslaved" (Spillers 74). This was foreshadowed through her performance of the "death of fertility dance" on the *Zong*. Forced to dance for the crew as punishment for her repeated calls on Kelsal, she chooses this particular dance as a way to reclaim possession of her body, erase the slave ship's arrested temporality by resituating herself within the familiar cycles of the moon, and counter the slavers' definition of the captives as living dead by symbolically performing "fertility's temporal death and rebirth" (31). Yet not only did her act lead to her brutal beating and near-rape—which she escaped thanks to the menstrual blood released by her dance—but it also appeared to her as vain and shameful after the murder of young children, leading her to wish her womb would be barren forever. While the fulfillment of her dramatic vow exempts her from participating in the reproductive system of New World slavery, it also prevents her from fully participating in the founding of diaspora, and turning a destructive event into a productive one. On the other hand, she also transfigures her ruined reproductive capacity through the wooden figures she creates, thereby aligning herself with her wood-carving father rather than her mother.[24] Giving birth to the past instead of the future, Mintah illustrates the shift Brogan identifies in narratives of cultural haunting from traditional "metaphors of blood descent to ghostly inheritances" (25).

As her "progeny" (210), the wooden figures stand for the descending lines broken by the Middle Passage. But they also become her kin, in the absence of her shipmates. While she is very active in her community, Mintah appears as always isolated, as if her experience would keep her forever apart from those who did not share it. She lives in the past, reliving every night in her dreams the moment of creation of her community. Indeed, her ordeal on the *Zong*, and in particular her acts of resistance, have created a bond between her and the men who fought with her. Tied together on the deck after the revolt failed, they spontaneously intone "a song of their own," a song of comfort and hope that soon becomes an "anthem" (111), suggesting the formation of a collective identity. Despite their situation, the comfort Mintah finds in the men's presence and the proximity of their bodies leaning on one another and keeping each other warm turns this night into a moment of redress. The memory of that moment is tied in Mintah's mind to the hope that slavery will one day come to an end, that Africa and America will finally be united in freedom, just as she then felt united with these men.

But full redress remains again impossible, as long as the conditions that broke their physical and social bodies have not been superseded. As Hartman puts it, only "an event of epic and revolutionary proportions—the abolition of slavery, the destruction of a racist social order, and the actualization of equality" could permit the full redress of the (ex-)slave's pained condition (*Scenes of Subjection* 77). When slavery is abolished in Jamaica, the sense of joy is mitigated by the bitter recognition that for so many, freedom came much too late, and by the fact that "in Maryland they are still slaves" (205). Moreover, the dead remain forever captive of their enslaved condition. For a moment, Mintah allows herself to believe that abolition will set things right for the dead, that the ghosts of the *Zong* "now, today, . . . are free men, women and children" too (211). At the parade, she thinks she recognizes them in the people dancing and celebrating around her; she reconsiders the meaning of the figures she carved, and revises their story:

> I thought the shapes were trying to rise from the sea, but now I know they were dances. Each figure made by me was in this square. A man, woman or child in some movement to the music. Not movements to the music of the sea, as I had thought. These were dances of freedom. The faces were not scared on those figures but excited. I had made them then read them wrong. Now they were here before me showing me their meaning, and I had helped to shape it. They were dancing not struggling. Ecstatic not terrified. (218)

The souls of the victims of the *Zong* have taken human form; instead of wood and grain, they are now "sweat, flesh, blood, breath and on land" (219). But just as the loss of the one hundred and thirty-one dead could not be made up for by Mintah's helping twice as many fugitive slaves across the Mason-Dixon line, these deaths "cannot be undone" (230) by Emancipation. Her aestheticization of the figures as dancing instead of drowning, ecstatic rather than terrified, suggests a problematic and, as soon becomes clear, illusory rewriting of a painful past. Her association of a young woman's movements with the memory of her own dance on the deck of the *Zong* casts a shadow on the joyous scene, as it links dancing with violence and death. Her romantic reunion with a white-haired Simon, who has spent his life looking for her and has succeeded in making her notebook "famous in England" (220), throws her into an emotional state that is uncannily evocative of drowning. And indeed, Mintah soon wakes from her dream, to find herself sitting alone, with her ghosts as sole company.

The *Zong* and the Politics of Memory

In refusing his protagonist this happy ending, D'Aguiar not only mitigates the creative dimension of the Middle Passage outlined earlier, as Mintah's community remains a ghostly one; he also resists a facile representation of working through that would trivialize trauma. These two aspects are in fact intimately related, and go against what LaCapra identifies as a tendency in modern culture to transcend trauma through its valorization as a basis for individual and collective identity (*Writing History* 23). While D'Aguiar's work certainly participates in a diasporic project of memory and identity, *Feeding the Ghosts* is deeply concerned with the forms and modes of such a project. What would constitute productive and nonproductive modes for a politics of memory is suggested in Mintah's own dealing with the ghosts. When Mintah wakes up from her dream, she realizes that her efforts to "assuage their hunger" (222) have been misguided, for she did not feed them what they really want. The novel's epilogue spells out what sort of food ghosts need: "the story of themselves" (230). Telling that story, however, is the one thing that Mintah has not really been able to do.

She tried to tell it in the notebook, but it was dismissed in court and disappeared forever when Simon, appalled by the outcome of the trial, embarked with it on a ship for an unknown destination. She also somehow tried to tell the story through her wood carving. Like the notebook, the wooden figures are designed as both memorial and counternarrative: if the notebook's capacity to "contain the worst things" enabled Mintah to "forget on paper" (196) and thereby bear the horrors of the present even as she recorded them, the figures help her "f[i]ght against forgetting with wood as [her] guide" (210). Against the anonymizing and dehumanizing narrative of Captain Cunningham's ledger—as well as the uniform pattern of *Description of a Slave Ship*—each of the one hundred and thirty-one figures has a name, an age, and a favorite position. Like the notebook, however, the figures ultimately turn out to be useless in both their memorializing and re-visionary functions. Although Mintah's visitors "love" the figures and correctly identify them as "some kind of man, woman or child reaching up out of the depths" (208–9), they find them too disturbing to have them in their own homes, and they do not know what they really represent.[25] "Her life of feeding the ghosts," she realizes, is "hers alone" (222). So when fire destroys both the figures and Mintah herself, no one and nothing is left to tell that story, and the ghosts are released to go back and eternally roam the sea.

If the story of the victims of the *Zong* died with Mintah in the fictive world of the novel, it did survive and become famous not only in England but throughout the Atlantic world. Because of the trial that followed, and of abolitionist Granville Sharpe's vain efforts to have the crew prosecuted for murder, the story became a cause célèbre. It was then quickly absorbed into abolitionist propaganda, where it took a prominent place as a "murder site" and a "powerful political referent" (Rupprecht 267). If for the abolitionists the Middle Passage effectively epitomized the horror of the slave trade, the *Zong* just as effectively epitomized the horrors of the Middle Passage itself. But in order to fully work as an example of the inhumanity of the slave trade, the story had to be stripped of its singularity, as Baucom argues in his discussion of abolitionist William Wilberforce's treatment of the story: "If Wilberforce was to inspire in his audience anything but melancholy, anything but a paralyzed regret before the absolute specificity of a scene of irreversible human damage," Baucom explains, the story "had to become generic" ("Specters" 65). Anita Rupprecht similarly describes how the abolitionists turned the event into "a generalised story of ineffable loss, passive victimhood and redemptive tragedy" (266).

This move, as useful as it may have been for the abolitionist cause, can also be seen as detrimental to the actuality of the original event and to the integrity of its historical victims. Evoked in "a serialized, dematerialized relation to itself" (Baucom, "Specters" 65), the story of the *Zong* has paradoxically been deprived of part of its horrifying content. This is also evident in the way the story was later treated by historians. Although the *Zong* often appears in histories of the slave trade, it is usually mentioned only in passing. Like abolitionists, historians use it as a stock example of the horrors of the Middle Passage, and more particularly of the commodification and objectification of the Africans, who could be simply tossed overboard alive in the name of profit. But a survey of those accounts quickly shows that they all relate the event in terms so similar that those reading broadly about the Middle Passage or the slave trade more generally might quickly find themselves tired of a story that has become all too familiar. In such narratives, where the simple fact of the Africans' death overshadows the complex realities of their lives, and where the horrifying nature of the number of victims comes at the expense of their individual significance, the story of the *Zong* itself might run the risk of becoming a soulless, empty husk.

Although *Feeding the Ghosts* is also largely based on "reiterativity" (Baucom, "Specters" 80), insofar as it retells the same events in each of its five parts, each utterance is not merely a repetition but a significantly —sometimes dramatically, sometimes ironically—different version presented from another perspective and narrated in a distinctive voice. This repetitive structure is thus very different from other, negative or nonproductive forms of repetitions we see in the novel, such as Captain Cunningham's nauseatingly mechanical strokes in the ledger or Mintah's compulsive tree planting and wood carving. While D'Aguiar associates simple repetition with mass murder and trauma, he presents the polyvocal, pluralistic re-vision of the event as a strategy against the "exclusive and exclusionary" (Frías 422) nature of a narrative related through "a single consciousness" or "a single authorial voice" (423). The novel also negotiates between the two directions outlined above, directions that are opposite but that, eventually, lead to the same dead end: minimizing the impact of the story by locking it in its own singularity, and possibly making it anecdotal; or emptying it of its significance and stripping it of its human, deeply personal dimension by using it as an urtext for the history of the Middle Passage. Although *Feeding the Ghosts* is first and foremost about "the *Zong*"—these are the first two words of the first chapter—and its victims, the novel as a whole also goes far beyond an account relating a particular historical event. Opening with the very epigrammatic statement, "The sea is slavery"—an echo of Walcott's poem "The Sea Is History"—the prologue does not mention the name of the ship. And if it repeats in various forms the exact number of slaves who were thrown overboard, it is not so much to indicate to a potentially knowledgeable reader that this is indeed the story of the *Zong* and its one hundred and thirty-one victims, but to convey the extent of the horror and prepare the reader for the announced jettisoning of those live human beings. In the epilogue, the *Zong* is mentioned nominally, but it is also given a more universal, indeed generic value. The description of the sea as being "accustomed to rehearsal, to repeats and returns" (229) reinscribes the particular story of the *Zong* in a centuries-long history of violence and death.[26] Horrible as it was, the *Zong* "incident" was certainly not unique, or even exceptional, as Cliff also suggests in *Free Enterprise*: when Mrs. Hooper asks Mary Ellen Pleasant if she can "instruct the company about the incident the painter was illustrating" in *The Slave Ship*, Pleasant thinks to herself, "I wasn't at all sure. What incident had Turner chosen? Which of the hundreds that came to light?" (72).

Whereas Cliff shows the gap that separates Mrs. Hooper's guests along color lines in their reaction to Turner's painting and the relevance of its subject, D'Aguiar calls on all of us to take responsibility for the horrors the painting and the novel evoke. The narrator's sudden shift to the collective pronoun "we" in the epilogue blurs the identities of those involved, as *we* are all dead and *we* all committed cruelties: "One of them is me. One of them is you. One of them is doing the throwing, the other is being thrown. I'm not sure who is who, you or I" (229–30). In thus obscuring the roles and problematizing the responsibilities that otherwise appeared obvious in the story, the epilogue engages us to think about our own position as readers in the late twentieth century and beyond. Remembering and commemorating slavery have often been done through what Barnor Hesse describes as "a historically positioned racialized embodiment," so that "the black subject remembers slavery through trauma and the white subject remembers it through guilt" (164). In contrast, by placing us all aboard the *Zong*, D'Aguiar suggests that as far as this memory and this history are concerned we are, indeed, all in the same boat.

The change in the pronouns, accompanied by a shift from past to present tense, also involves us in a history that is anything but over. D'Aguiar places aboard the *Zong* not only all the other victims of the Middle Passage, but also all their descendants who have endured slavery and its legacy, up to the present. The *Zong* is on an "unending voyage"; the death it symbolizes "remains unfinished because it recurs" (230) in other forms, other places, and other times. Other evocations of the Middle Passage give us examples of this recurrence. At the close of Guy Deslauriers's film *Passage du milieu*, the living-dead narrator reminds us that it all happened again as recently as 1992, a few weeks after the five-hundredth anniversary celebration of America's "discovery," when the crew of a cargo ship threw eight African stowaways into the Atlantic, adding their bodies to the road of bones that paves the bottom of the sea.[27] In her meditations on "blackness and being," Christina Sharpe shows how the slave ship, and the *Zong* in particular, haunt contemporary diasporic condition: "The *Zong* repeats; it repeats and repeats through the logics and the calculus of dehumaning started long ago and still operative" (*In the Wake* 73). Poignantly asking if "*the sentence*" for the "*crime* [of] *blackness*" is forever to be "*the circuit between ship and shore*" (57), Sharpe shows how the narratives that frame the innumerable deaths that have occurred on the sea between Haiti and Florida, and more recently on what she calls the "Black Mediterranean," only perpetuate "the ghosting these ships do of transatlantic slavery or the afterlives of slavery or the afterlives of property" (55). D'Aguiar's ghosts are thus not only the haunting memory of "the interminable grief engendered by slavery and its aftermath"; they are also the living-dead reminders that "the time of slavery" is not over and done with (Hartman, "Time of Slavery" 758). If the "revolutionary" event of abolition occurred long ago—though not everywhere—the other conditions Hartman identified as necessary for redress, the end of racism and inequality, have yet to happen. D'Aguiar's next work, *Bloodlines* (2000), makes this point more explicitly than *Feeding the Ghosts*. This novel in verse explores the intimacies and difficulties of a nineteenth-century mixed-race romance through the voice of the son who was born from it, a living dead who traverses centuries, condemned to live eternally until slavery and its afterlife have finally been overcome. Poised at the dawn of the new millennium, he does not seem any closer to his final rest.

"The past is laid to rest when it is told" (230). These are the last words of *Feeding the Ghosts*, but certainly not the end of the story. D'Aguiar's telling of the story of the *Zong* in the late 1990s clearly shows that, to him, that past had not been told yet, at least not in any satisfactory way. In a piece published one year before *Feeding the Ghosts*, he explains that he once imagined himself writing "a last poem, a last play, a last novel, a last song, about slavery." He understood this impulse as "a call for slavery to be confined to the past once and for all; for slavery's relevance to present anxieties about race to come to an end; to kill slavery off" ("Last Essay" 125). But this, he soon realized, is impossible not only because of slavery's bearing on modern race relations, but also because, just as the ghosts of the *Zong* voraciously and insatiably feed on the story of themselves, the present always "hungers" for more stories about the past. Each generation of writers re-visions this history because they "need their own versions of the past, to see the past in their own images, words. To have slavery nuanced in their way" (126). But rather than viewing the profusion of slave novels as a "compulsive need to revisit slavery" (Craps 69), a form of acting out that would merely reenact past violence and trauma, D'Aguiar invites us—both explicitly in "The Last Essay about Slavery" and implicitly in the narrative structure of his polyvocal novels—to see in this very profusion the sign of a productive and necessary engagement with the past. As he reminds us, "we are talking about slavery, a 400-year old institution. How many books are enough?" (Frías 419).

As I further argue in chapter 2, however, re-visioning history through the ghost is not about "us[ing] literature to tell the other side of history and to refashion the narrative so that history comes out right this time" (Peterson 183), as if it could be said once and for all, and in the right way. If a novel can serve as the "suitable memorial" that Morrison laments she could not find anywhere and whose absence compelled her to write *Beloved* ("Bench by the Road" 44), it should not petrify that history into a static, definitive narrative that serves as a mere gravestone, a monument to death rather than life. This might be, ultimately, what distinguishes literary from historical writing. For Certeau, historiography effects "a labor of separation" from the other, its object. The project of historiography "aims at calming the dead who still haunt the present, and at offering them scriptural tombs" (*Writing of History* 2). If historiography can be seen as a form of exorcism (Toews), literature, on the other hand, allows us to bridge the gap—as Morrison suggests in this chapter's epigraph—between the past and the present, the dead and the living.

[2]

DUSKY SALLYS: RE-VISIONING THE SILENCES OF HISTORY

It's not that we haven't always been here, since there was a here. It is that the letters of our names have been scrambled when they were not totally erased, and our fingerprints upon the handles of history have been called the random brushings of birds. —Audre Lorde, foreword to *Wild Women in the Whirlwind*

WHEN HE PUBLISHED HIS (in)famous article in the *Richmond Recorder* in 1802, revealing Thomas Jefferson's liaison with his slave Sally Hemings, James Callender opened the door to over two hundred years of controversy. When commentators nicknamed Hemings "Dusky Sally," they certainly meant to evoke more than the color of her skin: they also pointed to the mystery in which, despite her instant fame, she remained shrouded. But this nickname proves fitting in other respects as well. Ever since the first national outburst of the scandal, Sally Hemings has been, in every sense of the word, a shadow. She is the shadow behind Jefferson, ever following the great man and tainting his public image. She is a ghost haunting American collective consciousness and memory, an absent presence that, like slavery itself, many would like to forget and some have tried to erase. She is, finally, a shadow in the sense that in over two centuries and a considerable number of apparitions in scholarly works, she has hardly ever been approached as an actual and complete person. Her name may be at the center of the debates, but her life always remains at their periphery, and her subjectivity lies far beyond the scope of the discussions. For historian and law professor Annette Gordon-Reed, whose engagement with this "American controversy" has largely contributed to finally bringing Hemings center stage, the silence that has surrounded her is strategic: "Historians, primarily interested in proving Callender's charges false, had no interest in attempting to discover who this woman was," Gordon Reed explains, "because writing about her would draw more attention to the underlying allegation. The project of defeating the notion of a relationship between Jefferson and Hemings demanded that

Hemings herself be kept invisible" (159). Historians and biographers thus merely viewed and presented Hemings as the instrument through which a muckraking and vengeful journalist tried to harm Jefferson's reputation and political career. If they mentioned her at all, they did so only to reject the idea that she could have been the great man's concubine, let alone his beloved, and to put her back in her place—that of a mere slave woman.

The story of Sally Hemings is in many ways uncommon. From what we can infer based on the few sources available, her life and condition as a slave woman were not those of field slaves, and she did not endure the kind of physical and sexual violence so many others were subjected to—the kind of violence we see exerted against Sethe or Mintah. But as Hartman and others remind us, the violence of slavery is not to be located only in scenes of extreme brutality, such as those that inspired *Beloved* and *Feeding the Ghosts*: it also appears in "the terror of the mundane and quotidian" (*Scenes of Subjection* 4), and more particularly in the complex relations between masters and slaves, or what Christina Sharpe terms the "monstrous intimacies" of the slave system. Whether she was Jefferson's mistress or not, whether their sexual relations were physically coerced or not, Hemings was in any case subjected to a system in which her body was not hers to use and grant or refuse access to, and in which the distinction between "consent and coercion, feeling and submission, intimacy and domination" was anything but clear (Hartman, *Scenes of Subjection* 81). My interest in this chapter, however, is not in this form of violence, any more than it is in the actual nature of Hemings's relationship with Jefferson. Rather, I am interested in another form of violence that is of course only an extension of the legal, physical, and sexual subjugation of slave women: the epistemic violence that has erased them and silenced their subjectivity in the narratives about the past.

Indeed, while Hemings's story is also uncommon insofar as her name—unlike most slave women's—actually reached us, it offers fascinating insights into the way slaves, and slave women in particular, have been ghosted in the master narrative of American History.[1] As Nathan Huggins points out in *Black Odyssey*, until the 1960s the social death that made the slave a nonperson "was carried over into the writing of American history," as this history "was written as if blacks did not exist and their experience was of no consequence" (xvii). Even in the historiography of slavery their role remained marginal, for "the habit was to write about it as an abstract social or economic institution, to see it as provocative of sectionalism and as an element in the cause of the Civil War" (xviii). Following the framework established by Ulrich B. Phillips at the beginning of the twentieth century, who depicted the plantation as a school where slaves were educated and civilized by benevolent masters, the first generations of historians who did show interest in the slaves cast them mainly in the role of objects, whether of benign attention or of abuse by a lucrative economic system. It is only in the late 1950s that a productive debate centered on the slave began, as "phrases such as 'the slave personality,' 'the slave community,' and 'slave culture'" (Parish 8) finally entered the scholarship. With the institutionalization of black studies in the wake of the civil rights and black power movements, scholarship on slavery exploded in the fields of history, sociology, and anthropology and profoundly remapped the terrain of American slavery, moving from "'what was done for slaves' (the paternalistic approach), to 'what was done to them' (the protest approach), and finally to 'what was done by them' (the focus on black agency and subjectivity)" (Sollors 167–68).

Yet this "renaissance in African-American Studies," as Deborah Gray White called it, was primarily concerned with "restor[ing] to black men the masculinity Americans had denied them" (3). When White first published *Ar'n't I a Woman? Female Slaves in the Plantation South*, in 1985, slave women were still largely neglected in the scholarship. This silence about slave women in historiography is largely due to their triple burden as black, female, and poor, which positions them at the intersection of three traditionally neglected topics in the field of history. As White concludes, "few historians saw [slave women] as important contributors to America's social, economic, or political development, and few publishers identified an audience for books that connected black women's thoughts and experiences to the history of other Americans" (3–4). As a result, the slave woman is particularly invisible in the history of slavery, appearing "solely in terms of her service, or lack thereof, to her mate, her children, her master or mistress" (Wallace 137).

It is both the tremendous progress made in slave historiography and scholars' persistent failure, inability, or unwillingness to engage seriously and satisfactorily with the lives and circumstances of the slave woman that account for the central place she has come to occupy in African diaspora literature. As I noted previously, since the 1960s, writers of the diaspora, and women writers in particular, have persistently used fiction to rescue the slave woman from historical, cultural, and academic invisibility. From Margaret Walker's *Jubilee* (1966) to Sherley Anne Williams's *Dessa Rose* (1986) and Morrison's *Beloved*, the neo–slave narrative has been a favorite genre for exploring her suppressed subjectivity and giving flesh to the ghosts in and of history. Hemings herself finally became the protagonist in her own story in Barbara Chase-Riboud's *Sally Hemings* (1979), while Chase-Riboud's later novel *The President's Daughter* (1994) imagines the life of Jefferson and Hemings's daughter Harriet.

A number of writers, however, have been less concerned with imaginatively reconstructing the slave woman's experience than with assessing and criticizing the ways in which this experience was long (mis)represented or simply silenced in traditional historiography. Read against the backdrop of the historiographical developments outlined above, as well as within the broader context of postcolonialism and poststructuralism's joint assault on scientific orthodoxies, Naylor's *Mama Day* (1988) can be considered as such a critique. Mostly set in the 1980s, the novel follows the lives and relationship of Ophelia "Cocoa" Day and her husband George Andrews, largely in the form of a conversation between the two protagonists. The main narrative, however, is haunted by the memory of the slave past of the island of Willow Springs, where Cocoa was born and raised and where the major part of the action takes place. This past is embodied in Sapphira, the Days' ancestor and the founder of the community of Willow Springs, a slave woman who bears uncanny resemblance to Sally Hemings. Everybody knows about Sapphira, yet her life and circumstances remain shrouded in mystery, particularly the nature of her relationship with her master, Bascombe Wade. She is not a protagonist in the narrative, and her subjectivity is therefore never directly accessible, but always mediated through the interpretation of the people who try to uncover her story. While Sally Hemings is a shadow that metaphorically haunts America's collective consciousness, Sapphira Wade literally appears in the story as a ghost whose absent presence points to the persistence and importance of her heritage in collective memory as much as the silence and oblivion to which traditional—that is, white, patriarchal—history relegates her.

This chapter begins with a parallel examination of these two slave women, the historical figure and the fictional character, and of the way they are ghosted in master narratives. By following George on his visit to Willow Springs and drawing on examples from the Jefferson-Hemings controversy, I first demonstrate how George's approach to the past mirrors the traditional historiography of slavery. Drawing on Haitian scholar Michel-Rolph Trouillot's analysis of the various moments at which silences enter the production of history, I explore the ideological, epistemological, and discursive processes that turn slave women into ghosts in the historical narrative of America's past and in the fictional narrative of *Mama Day*. In my analysis, the ghostly figures of Sapphira Wade and Sally Hemings signify the repressed of historiography, the excess that cannot be absorbed but must be policed and expelled by the science of history in order to keep its claim to the facticity that is "its special truth" (Gordon 26).

But the ghost is not only "a symptom of what is missing" (Gordon 63), the passive and powerless victim of an erasure; its haunting presence also marks the return of the repressed: its intrusion "indicates that, beneath the surface of received history, there lurks another narrative, an untold story that calls into question the veracity of the authorized version of events" (Weinstock, "Introduction" 5). By drawing our attention to what Morrison described as those invisible things that are nevertheless there, those voids that are not actually vacuums ("Unspeakable Things" 11)—the black presence in the American literary canon, the slave woman in history—the ghost provokes an epistemological shift that undermines master narratives. In the second part of the chapter, I thus show how the ghosts in *Mama Day* enable a re-vision of the past, not only by introducing silenced perspectives but also, through their elusive quality, by destabilizing received notions of historical "truth." Wandering in and out of the text, disrupting the narrative and fracturing authoritative views into a kaleidoscope of voices and perspectives, the ghost ultimately questions the notion of a coherent, complete, and exhaustive history.

While the presence of ghosts in *Mama Day* suggests that our knowledge of the past is necessarily fragmented, subjective, and provisional, the novel does not promote simple relativism, an "anything goes" type of view that is as intellectually limiting as it is politically sterile—especially at a time when African diaspora people, and women in particular, were claiming subject positions for themselves and their slave predecessors.[2] Rather, the liminal figure of the ghost offers a middle ground "between the mechanically 'realist' and naively 'constructivist' extremes" and partakes of what Trouillot describes as "the more serious task of determining not what history is . . . but how history works" (*Silencing the Past* 25). Through *Mama Day*, Naylor does not suggest that historiography has no epistemic value; but she denounces those histories that present themselves as the objective, authoritative, and definitive representation of the past even as they silence or distort the experience and subjectivity of women like Sapphira Wade and Sally Hemings. Read as a call to historiography to recognize its constructive and interpretive processes, *Mama Day* confirms Harris's belief that "a philosophy of history may well lie buried in the arts of the imagination" ("History" 156).

Silencing the Past, Ghosting Slave Women

As soon as he sets foot on the Sea Island of Willow Springs, New York born-and-bred George Andrews is struck by the pervasive presence of the past. "Something about this place," he remarks, "call[s] up old, old memories" (Naylor, *Mama Day* 184). Unlike his wife Cocoa, who grew up listening to stories and plans to go back to college to get a degree in history, George has no family or cultural inheritance to claim for himself: the son of a fifteen-year-old prostitute and one of her anonymous clients, he was raised as an orphan at the Wallace P. Andrews Shelter for Boys, where the mottos were "Keep it in the now, fellas" and "Only the present has potential, *sir*" (22–23, 23). He is ill-equipped to understand the history of Willow Springs and the place the past occupies in the life of the community. He is particularly bemused by the story of Sapphira, the slave woman who somehow took her freedom from her master after bearing him seven children and who persuaded or forced him to deed the island to their descendants. "The whole thing was so intriguing," he reflects, "I wondered if that woman had lived at all. Places like this island were ripe for myths, but if she had really existed, there must be some record. Maybe in Bascombe Wade's papers: deeds of sale for his slaves" (218). Despite his genuine interest in the stories Cocoa and her great-aunt Miranda "Mama" Day tell him about their ancestor, George is not satisfied with, let alone convinced by, those accounts. Dismissing their stories as mere "myth," he looks instead for material evidence, tangible traces of Sapphira's existence. These, he thinks, will provide him with her "true" story.

This passage is central for what I argue is the novel's engagement with historiography. As I will show, it reveals the processes that have permitted and perpetuated the absence of women like Sally Hemings in the master narrative of American History. My analysis follows Trouillot's compelling demonstration in *Silencing the Past* that power is involved at all stages of the production of history. Through his critical re-vision of the Haitian Revolution and of the West's persistent failure to acknowledge it as a revolution, Trouillot identifies four moments at which "silences enter the process of historical production . . . : the moment of fact creation (the making of *sources*); the moment of fact assembly (the making of *archives*); the moment of fact retrieval (the making of *narratives*); and the moment of retrospective significance (the making of *history* in the final instance)" (*Silencing the Past* 26). His insights are particularly helpful for analyzing, on the one hand, how George's attempt at recovering the story of Sapphira actually silences her, and, on the other, how historians and biographers of Jefferson have consistently silenced Hemings.

The Making of Sources

Although he does not get to see it, the document George hopes to find, Sapphira's bill of sale, appears in the course of the novel. Miranda finds it in Bascombe's ledger at "the other place," the Days' old family house in the woods, where she often goes to tend the garden and connect with her ancestors. But the piece of paper has been badly damaged and is largely illegible. It would in fact not have allowed George to ascertain the truth of Sapphira's existence, for her name itself has been almost completely erased. Moreover, the few remaining words would certainly have led him to erroneous conclusions, as Naylor suggests by providing us with a complete version of the bill of sale in the novel's paratext.[3] The first line, which is the most legible, is already incorrectly read by Miranda as "*Tuesday, 3rd Day August*, then a 1 and half of what must be an 8, with the rest of the date faded away." As we know from the complete transcript, "what must be an 8" is actually a 9.[4] That a fact as basic and supposedly transparent as a date can be misread predicts more important problems for the rest of the document, as Miranda is forced to reconstitute whole sentences from a few isolated words: "*Law . . . knowledge . . . witness . . . inflicted . . . nurse*. It's all she can pick out until she gets to the bottom for the final words: *Conditions . . . tender . . . kind*" (280, ellipses in original). What those words evoke when considered individually and out of context is strikingly different from their actual meaning in the complete version of the document. The passage containing the words "law," "knowledge," and "witness" actually warns Sapphira's new owner against her "vices." The negatively connoted adjective "inflicted" points to her resistance to her enslaved status, for she is in fact "inflicted with sullenness." While the word "nurse" suggests that Sapphira had skills in tending children, this incomplete version of the bill leaves the reader unaware that she served as such "not without extreme mischief and suspicions of delving in witchcraft." Finally, the last words, "Conditions . . . tender . . . kind," do not refer to Sapphira's humane qualities, but, ironically, to the conditions of her sale, "one-half gold tender, one-half goods in kind."

As a historical source, Sapphira's bill of sale contains many silences. These are first the result of the passing of time and too many storms, which have literally erased large parts of the information originally recorded in it. Had it remained intact, however, the document would still have contained silences because, as Trouillot points out, silences are "inherent in the creation of sources" (*Silencing the Past* 51). The very moment at which sources are created in fact marks the first moment of silencing in the production of history insofar as "sources imply choices": some events are recorded, while others are not. Far from being "neutral or natural," "the presences and absences embodied in sources" are therefore "not mere presences and absences, but mentions or silences of various kinds and degrees" (48). As a case in point, Trouillot reminds us that Caribbean plantation records usually silenced slave births, not by negligence or manipulation of facts but for practical reasons: in a context where infant mortality was very high, it made more sense to *not* register these births and to later correct the omission if the child reached a certain age (51). While deliberate, such instances of silencing were not ideologically motivated. Other examples, however, such as the presence and absence of Hemings and her children in the historical record, might betray other motivations. Gordon-Reed thus surmises that the absence of Hemings's first son Tom from the farm book that recorded the births and deaths of the slaves and the expenses devoted to their maintenance is strategic. While she admits that Jefferson did not consistently keep his farm book during those years in which his service as secretary of state often kept him away from Monticello, she argues that "he would have had a reason not to list the birth of the child" (67): according to Callender's revelations, "President Tom," as he called him, was born a few months after Hemings returned from Paris, where she was sent to serve as a maid and companion to Jefferson's daughter during his time as American envoy to France; had Tom's birth appeared in the farm book, it would have left little doubt that he was conceived during Hemings's time in Paris with her master—far from the other residents of or visitors to Monticello who have since then been considered as more plausible genitors.[5] It is Gordon-Reed's more general contention that someone like Jefferson, who knew that he would be remembered as a great man and that historians would look for sources to inscribe him in American history, could certainly deliberately silence some facts to control "the image he wanted to project to posterity" (127).

Whether they respond to practical or to ideological motivations, ultimately silences are also "inherent in history because any single event enters history with some of its constituting parts missing. Something is always left out while something else is recorded" (Trouillot, *Silencing the Past* 49). The existence of Sally Hemings and Sapphira Wade, and their status as slaves, were recorded, and thereby became historical facts. What was silenced, on the other hand, is virtually everything else about them. The sources that attest the "event" of their existence and of their status as chattel—Jefferson's farm book and Bascombe's ledger—certainly created "facts." But these facts were created only at the expense of—that is, by the silencing of—other facts, notably these women's subjectivity. This owes to the fact that historical sources "are not created equal" (47). Insofar as historical actors experience inequalities, Trouillot explains, they have uneven power in the inscription of the traces upon which sources are built: some actors leave traces, others simply do not. The history of slavery is of course a prime example of this uneven historical power and of the consequently unequal traces its actors left. Slaveholders produced the vast majority of the available sources; among the few sources produced by slaves and ex-slaves, even fewer were produced by women. As George's dismissal of Cocoa and Miranda's stories in favor of the bill of sale suggests, however, what counts as a source is not so obvious in the first place, and actually brings us to the second moment of silencing.

The Making of Archives

Trouillot's analysis of "the moment of fact creation" demonstrates that silencing occurs in the production of history long before historians actually enter the scene. Their silencing role becomes central, however, at the second moment: the making of archives. Archives are not simple repositories of facts that would be neutrally and exhaustively collected, but institutions that "condition the possibility of existence of historical statements" (*Silencing the Past* 52) by selecting and organizing facts and sources according to the rules established by the "guild." These rules were largely established at the time of the institutionalization and professionalization of the historical discipline in the nineteenth century, when history distanced itself from the fields of literature and rhetoric and moved closer to the natural and social sciences. As Georg Iggers explains, "The historians shared the optimism of the professionalized sciences generally that methodologically controlled research makes objective knowledge possible. For them as for other scientists truth consisted in the correspondence of knowledge to an objective reality that, for the historian, constituted the past 'as it had actually occurred'" (2). Conceived as the neutral and objective recovery of the past, the historian's task was thus defined in clear opposition to the writer's imaginative creation of it.[6] The ideal of objectivity had important consequences on the making of archives, as it determined what constituted a historical source by distinguishing between reliable and unreliable traces of the past. This distinction notably concerned documentary and oral sources: the former were considered to guarantee a necessary distance between the historian and his or her object, as well as a stable record of the past and a direct window onto it; the latter were viewed as necessarily biased by the personal implication of the historian-interviewer in the recording of the past, and as being subject to the failings and distortions of memory.[7] The making of archives thus marks a second moment of silencing because, rather than a simple act of collection, the work of "fact assembly" is really one of selection, of evidence as well as procedures, "which means, at best the differential ranking and, at worst, the exclusion" of some evidence and some procedures (Trouillot, *Silencing the Past* 53).

By privileging a documentary source (Sapphira's bill of sale) over an oral one (Cocoa and Miranda's stories, and more generally the oral tradition of Willow Springs), George merely follows the methodological principles of traditional historiography. That he should endorse the guild's ideal of objectivity is fully consistent with his portrayal throughout the novel as a very rational man. As he says himself, the shelter where he grew up "wasn't the kind of place that turned out many poets or artists," because it did not encourage the children to "dream big" (26, 27). As a young man he logically pursued his education to become an engineer, confirming he fully integrated the lesson he learned throughout his childhood that there are "only rules and facts" (24). He became the kind of man who, recently married, buys books with the hope to find "a totally objective guide to what [is] going on inside of females" (142), and uses a slide rule and graph paper to measure the space he and Cocoa will need to fit all their clothes in the same closet when she moves into his apartment. Thus, when Cocoa tells him the story of Sapphira, he does not take her account at face value: he treats it not only as a story but as a "legend" and a "myth" (218). In contrast, a document like a bill of sale would furnish, he thinks, not only unquestionable evidence of Sapphira's existence, but also a reliable account of it.

George's definition of the Willow Springs oral tradition about Sapphira as "myth" finds an interesting echo in some scholars' treatment of the primary source attesting to an intimate relationship between Hemings and Jefferson. Indeed, besides Callender's intervention in the *Richmond Recorder*, the main source supporting the allegation is the oral testimony Hemings's son Madison dictated to the editor of the *Pike County (Ohio) Republican* in 1873, in which he claimed that he and all his siblings were the children of Thomas Jefferson. Jefferson scholars have fiercely contested Madison's memoir, judging it suspect and unreliable. In this respect, they follow not only traditional historiography's general suspicion toward oral sources but more specifically the premise established by Phillips that such "reminiscences should be disregarded, for the reason that the lapse of decades has impaired inevitably the memories of men" and that such testimonies are therefore "generally unsafe even in supplement" (xxiv). They indeed invoke the fact that the testimony was recorded when Madison was already an old man and is therefore based on what can only be vague memories of the events—some of which, moreover, he could not even have seen or known firsthand, like his own conception. After reminding his readers that "the historian must recognize that oral tradition is not established fact," Jefferson biographer Dumas Malone concludes that the oral tradition handed down by the Hemings family is "material for the tragedian" (497). Much more recently, David Mayer—a member of the "Scholars Commission on the Jefferson-Hemings Matter"[8]—similarly denounced the use of oral sources as an "assault on standards" (294) that leads to the corruption of historiography. Even more than oral tradition, he adds, "family oral tradition" is particularly unreliable because of "the high probability of errors creeping into stories that are told and retold from one generation to the next, as well as the tendency 'to embellish the family legacy to instill pride and confidence in the next generation.'" Echoing George, he therefore concludes that "family oral traditions really ought not to be called 'history' at all, for they are rather, quite literally, *myth*" (292).

The historiography on the Jefferson-Hemings controversy, and the historiography of slavery more generally, demonstrate Trouillot's point that the moment of the making of archives silences not only some sources but also some producers of sources. Oral sources have historically been produced mostly by marginalized communities and people. As far as the historiography of slavery is concerned, given that most slaves were illiterate or did not have the means to leave documentary traces, excluding oral sources virtually means excluding sources produced by slaves and ex-slaves. But scholars' treatment of Madison's memoir provides an interesting case to test the limits and blind spots of the methodological principles linked to the tradition of the historical discipline. In her discussion of the controversy, Gordon-Reed denounces the use of double standards in the treatment of oral sources: she points out that the suspicion toward the oral accounts of black people does not seem to be matched by a similar caution toward the white oral sources that contradict Jefferson's alleged paternity—such as the oral testimony of Jefferson's overseer or those of the Jefferson-Randolph family. These double standards, according to Owen Whooley, should not be attributed so much to individual historians' racism as to the racial prejudice that was incorporated in the ideal of objectivity as the historical discipline was constituted and consolidated: from the Reconstruction era through most of the twentieth century, "the professionalization of history occurred against the backdrop of increasing racism in American society," so that "historians incorporated (consciously and unconsciously) some of these racist ideas in their theoretical and methodological frameworks, especially in regards to what sources of documentation could be trusted for objectivity" (1376). In this framework, blacks—as well as, Whooley points out, women—were not considered as valid sources. From this perspective, Madison's memoir might thus have been rejected not only, or mostly, because it was originally an oral testimony, but because it was the testimony of a black man and a former slave.

The Making of Narratives

In Gordon-Reed's opinion, most of the arguments used to reject Madison's testimony are in fact based on stereotypes about black people: he lied about the identity of his father because it is "a well known peculiarity of the colored race" to "lay claim to illustrious parentage" (John A. Jones, qtd. in Gordon-Reed 12); his memoir cannot be authentic because "the stilted overblown 'literary' language in which the 'interview' is couched" (John C. Miller, qtd. in Gordon-Reed 20) is too sophisticated for a slave, even one of Madison's education, and, as Gordon-Reed summarizes, it "just does not sound right" (19); that this inconsistency is seen as betraying the hand of the editor is, moreover, a sign that Madison played the stock character of "the feebleminded black person as pawn to a white man" (11). If these arguments have allowed historians to reject the main source supporting the allegation, Gordon-Reed continues, other preconceptions have been used to dismiss the very possibility of a sexual or romantic relationship between Jefferson and Hemings as simply preposterous. These preconceptions, she explains, are first based on general and unquestioned assumptions about the nature of relationships between masters and slaves: while historians have had no difficulty accepting the possibility of maternal love between slave women and the white children in their charge—a notion based on the "Mammy" stereotype—"they view the possibility of romantic and sexual love between a black slave woman and a white man during the same era as absurd and perhaps slightly alarming." The reason, she hypothesizes, is the unacceptable "possibility of reciprocation" this view would entail: while it would not be unthinkable that a white child should return a slave woman's affection, it would be inconceivable that a master should reciprocate his slave's love, for that would jeopardize the harmony and purity of the white slaveholding family (167).[9]

In the particular case of Jefferson, this assumption is reinforced by the received knowledge about the man. If the nature of a relationship that allegedly produced seven children was not romantic, Gordon-Reed points out, then it could only take the form either of rape, or of a purely sexual and loveless affair. Both scenarios, however, are equally implausible, according to most Jefferson scholars. While historians cannot deny that some masters abused their female slaves, this cannot hold true for Jefferson because "[he] was not known as an 'abusive' individual" (Gordon-Reed 108). Nor would he have engaged in a consenting but morally reprehensible relationship with a slave: he was too devoted "to beauty and refinement" to mingle with "the squalor and horror of the slavery that existed below him on the mountain top" (Garry Wills, qtd. in Gordon-Reed 169), and/or he was too dedicated to reason and philosophy to have romantic or sexual yearnings. As Malone concludes, echoing the argument made by many other biographers, the charges against Jefferson are "distinctly out of character, being virtually unthinkable in a man of Jefferson's moral standards and habitual conduct" (214).

Malone's words are interestingly reminiscent of Trouillot's analysis of the Haitian Revolution as an "unthinkable" event. This was, Trouillot claims, the general conception among white contemporaries, a conception that made them incapable of predicting the uprising and prolonged struggle and then of understanding the event as a revolution even as it was happening (*Silencing the Past* 73). But this was also the enduring view among western historians, who until at least the 1960s did not identify it as a revolution.[10] The fact that a black revolution—and *a fortiori* a successful one—was unthinkable has been key to the silencing of this event in historiography, a silencing that occurs at the "moment of fact retrieval" through the "making of narratives." According to Trouillot, "Historical narratives are premised on previous understandings" (55), which "prepar[e] facts for historical intelligibility" by "set[ting] up both the substantive and formal elements of the narrative" (52) constructed by the historian. Like all narratives, historical narratives follow certain plots and tropes based on a limited number of conventional structures available in the discipline. Following these preestablished understandings and structures thus effectively silences other potential narratives.

According to Gordon-Reed, in order to determine the nature of the relationship between Jefferson and Hemings, historians and biographers have tested the plausibility of various configurations against plots and models based on predefined, limited, and often stereotypical conceptions of the protagonists. Similarly, in order to understand Sapphira and Bascombe's relationship, George tries out several narratives based on previous plots and scripts. First, the very fact that George should look for Sapphira's bill of sale, a document that defines her as an object that can be sold and bought, already suggests he approaches her through a predefined and limited category. His repeated references to her as a "slave woman" contrast with the way Cocoa and Miranda more often identify her as a woman, an ancestor, or a conjure woman.[11] Having locked Sapphira in this role that denies her agency, George cannot understand Cocoa's contradicting evocation of her power: "You told me that woman had been your grandmother's great-grandmother. But it was odd again the way you said it—she was the great, great, grand, Mother—as if you were listing the attributes of a goddess" (218). While he senses that his wife's use of the adjectives "great" and "grand" signify more than her genealogical link to Sapphira, he is unable to take them seriously as markers of her actual power and treats them as mere hyperbole—a trope that logically leads him to identify the whole story as a legend. Because Cocoa's account does not correspond to the traditional narrative about slave women, the facts as she relates them are unthinkable, or, more precisely, they are unthinkable as history and only thinkable as myth.

Dismissing this "version of history and the tale of a female slave that subvert white historical [narratives]" (Meisenhelder 409), George turns to more familiar scripts to reconstruct Sapphira's relationship with Bascombe. When Cocoa takes him to the other place, he imagines that Bascombe built the house so he could come here with Sapphira. He pictures them, the white master sitting on the verandah and the black slave woman tending the garden under his benevolent gaze. The whole scene, as Susan Meisenhelder notes, seems to come straight out of *Gone with the Wind* (410).[12] And indeed George's fantasies about Willow Springs, which appears to him as a quaint piece of "paradise," and about the South more generally, which "conjure[s] up images of jasmine-scented nights" (222, 33), clearly betray the influence of white narratives and motifs. If he ultimately rejects the vision, it is not so much because "he senses the absurdity of casting Sapphira Wade as a demure Southern belle" (Meisenhelder 410), but rather because he perceptively concludes that this "nice image" (225) does not fit with the pain and loss that he feels still pervade the other place—a hint at another, silenced narrative he will eventually become a part of.

Later on, he tries another script that casts Sapphira and Bascombe in different roles. Visiting Bascombe's grave again as the winds are slowly building up to a hurricane, he feels particularly sympathetic to what he imagines the man—"that poor slob" who "gave her a whole island" (247) and whose heart she broke anyway—endured because of his love for Sapphira: "There had to have been some days like this, I thought, when he stood here and waited for her. . . . Bascombe Wade's tombstone was barely visible in the clearing as the oak branches swished even louder in the building wind. *Waste. Waste.* Yes, I looked at his monument; those leaves could easily be crying that" (248). Although this version of the story grants Sapphira the agency George earlier denied her, in relinquishing the image of the slave to recast her in the role of the heartbreaker he merely reduces her to another stereotype, this time relying on the well-worn narrative plot of the tragic romance. While George's narratives change, depending on the plots and tropes he unconsciously—and, at times, consciously—follows, what they have in common is that they all rely on a white male script (Meisenhelder 410). Indeed, in their various versions, these narratives confirm that the previous understandings on which historical narratives are premised "are themselves premised on the distribution of archival power" (Trouillot, *Silencing the Past* 55), a power that is, as suggested earlier, distributed unequally: a guild that was long restricted to, and then largely dominated by, white men would logically produce historical narratives that reflect their authors' limited perspective and interests. While it might seem odd to associate George, as a black man, with this guild, he is actually in many ways a good example of those people Miranda calls "honorary whitefolks" (38). As a "cultural orphan" (Meisenhelder 407), he has a limited number of plots to choose from.[13] Not only cannot his white male script but fail to account for the complexity of Sapphira's relationship with Bascombe, it limits her to a mere supporting role in her master's story.

The Making of History

This script is in fact the very same one that underpins his narrative about his relationship with Cocoa, culminating with his approach to the strange illness that strikes her. As Miranda sympathetically observes, George "believes in himself—deep within himself—'cause he ain't never had a choice" (285): as an orphan, he learned early on to rely on himself alone, and therefore undertook and pursued everything "with the knowledge that [he] was all [he] had" (291). When he met Cocoa, she became "all he had," and, when she falls ill, he in turn believes he can only be all she needs to survive. As Meisenhelder analyzes, George follows till the end the white male script of "the traditional romantic hero, trying to 'single-handedly' save 'his woman' from evil forces" (411). He gives himself the leading role in this plot, rejecting the help of both the Willow Springs men, whom he sees as "fools" and whose "acute madness" (286) almost leads him to violence, and Miranda, that "crazy old woman" (296) who offers only "mumbo jumbo" (295) against Cocoa's illness. He thereby unwittingly reproduces a script that men—both white and black—have played with Day women throughout generations, in which men firmly believed "that the work of their hands could wipe away all that had gone before": Bascombe used his hands to build a house in which he could keep Sapphira; after the accidental death of their child, John-Paul used his hands to carve little wooden animals and flowers to keep his wife Ophelia's mind occupied and, when he realized it would not be enough, to cover the well in which little Peace died so her mother would not try to follow after her. Like Bascombe and John-Paul, who "*believed* . . . in the power of themselves, in what they were feeling" (285), George relies only on himself, on his love for Cocoa, and on the power of his own hands, which he obsessively uses to rebuild the bridge that was destroyed by the hurricane, cutting off Willow Springs from the mainland and what he sees as real medical help. His inability to integrate other perspectives into the narrative he has constructed about the events, in particular perspectives that recognize the agency and power of black women—Sapphira, Miranda, and Cocoa herself—eventually leads him to the same end as his predecessors, death from a broken heart.

I will return to the notion that the past informs the present—as the same script is played out across generations, like transgenerational haunting—in the second part of this chapter, when I examine how Miranda's recovery of her family past allows her to understand the events in the present. What this quick flash forward was meant to introduce is not so much the fact that the past shapes the present as the fact that the present shapes the past. George's experience of life and love inevitably affects his interpretation not only of what is happening—Cocoa's illness and the way to save her—but also of what happened in the past. For example, the narrative that casts Sapphira in the role of the heartbreaker and Bascombe as the tragic victim of his love for her is clearly tainted by George's own state of mind on the night of the hurricane—weather conditions that are "perfect for [his] mood, bleak and awful"—namely his frustration with Cocoa after their "worst fight ever" (247, 230). Similarly, the scene he pictures at the other place is only a mirror image of what he would like to do with his own wife, as the latter perceptively notes: "You wanted to sit in the rocking chair and play southern gentleman with me on your lap" (224), she accuses him, irritated by his naïve views about the South, and about life in a place like Willow Springs. The parallel ways in which George views his relationship with Cocoa and Bascombe's relationship with Sapphira reveal his own personal and ideological investment in his reconstruction of the past.

Many commentators have charged Jefferson scholars with similarly problematic "political and personal investments in the historical record" (Pollard 128). The outraged reactions the allegation of an intimate relationship between Jefferson and Hemings has often provoked among historians suggest that there may be more at stake in this story than a concern with historical truth. Joseph J. Ellis, who first rejected the liaison as unlikely in his biography *American Sphinx* and then revised his judgment a year later after DNA tests proved a genetic link between the descendants of the Hemingses and of the Jeffersons, humbly admitted that "although we [historians] are the official custodians of the past, Jefferson has escaped the past and our control over his place in it. All discussions of his legacy, even those conducted by professional historians, end up being less about him than about us" ("Jefferson" 138).[14] What Ellis's comment points out here is the place Jefferson has come to occupy in American collective consciousness. He has often been considered as a synecdoche for the American nation (Lewis and Onuf)—a view best summarized by James Parton's famous aphorism, "If Jefferson was wrong, America is wrong. If America is right, Jefferson was right" (iii). Accepting the liaison as historical fact would mean revising the biography of a Founding Father and, thereby, the history of the United States of America.

The Jefferson-Hemings story is indeed based on another, broader narrative. As Huggins noted—in 1989, one year after the publication of *Mama Day*—all American history is written against the backdrop of a master narrative that starts with the Pilgrim Fathers, moves through the establishment of a "more perfect union," and continues to this day with the image of a free and democratic nation that presents itself as an example for the world (xlvi).[15] In order to keep up this image of America, historians long produced narratives that silenced the fact of slavery: they either relegated it to a discrete field of inquiry in which it was "studied in and of itself, apart from general American history," or they marginalized it as "a curious nuisance, complicating and temporarily drawing attention away from the central American story" (xxxii, xxxiii) but having no bearing on our understanding of the birth and development of America, up to our present society. This illustrates what Trouillot identifies as the fourth and last moment of silencing, "the moment of retrospective significance (the making of *history* in the final instance)" (*Silencing the Past* 26): the importance historians grant specific events and the way they write those events into the grand narrative of History determine how the past will be remembered. By turning Hemings into a ghost, Jefferson scholars wrote a whitewashed history that leaves the image of the great man, and thereby of the nation, unscathed. The result of George's silencing of Sapphira is a story in which the white man plays the main role and the black woman remains a mere shadow.

Trouillot's analysis of power and the production of history is not only helpful for unraveling the various ways in which "any historical narrative is a particular bundle of silences" (*Silencing the Past* 27); it also demonstrates what kind of work is necessary, at each moment of silencing, in order to write alternative histories. The unearthing of neglected historical subjects, facts, or events requires "extra labour not so much in the production of new facts as in their transformation by way of new positioning" ("Silencing the Past" 46). That is precisely what Trouillot's unconventional study of the Haitian Revolution attempts to do. Similarly, Gordon-Reed's *American Controversy* does not base its argument on hitherto inaccessible or unknown material, but looks at the available material in a new way—and its conclusions have largely been contested for that very reason.[16] As I show in the second part of this chapter, in *Mama Day* the ghost is precisely what enables a new positioning. Drawing attention to silenced facts, compelling the protagonists to re-vision their narratives, and calling into question traditional modes of representing the past, the ghosts in Willow Springs signify an alternative epistemology at all four moments of historical production.

Mama Day *as Ghost (Hi)story*

"It ain't about right or wrong, truth or lie," the collective voice of Willow Springs tells us at the beginning of *Mama Day*; "it's about a slave woman who brought a whole new meaning to both them words, soon as you cross over here from beyond the bridge" (3). By crossing the bridge to Willow Springs, one does not enter a different world, a magical world of sorts, but a place whose liminal position—like a ghost, it occupies the space between two states—throws into relief the limitations of predefined categories and binary thinking. The narrator illustrates its initial point through the cautionary tale of Reema's Boy. Born and raised in Willow Springs and later college-educated "beyond the bridge," Reema's

Boy returned to the island to conduct anthropological research and tried to make sense and trace the origins of the expression "18 & 23." Instead of simply listening to people, he "rattled on about 'ethnography,' 'unique speech patterns,' 'cultural preservation,' and whatever else he seemed to be getting so much pleasure out of" (7) and used textbook formulas like "asserting cultural identity" and "inverting hostile social and political parameters" (8), which he indiscriminately applied to the culture under study. Having come "determined to put Willow Springs on the map," he left with a logical answer to the meaning of "18 & 23": these are the inverted coordinates of the island. When the collective voice of Willow Springs mocks Reema's Boy's claim that he did "extensive field work" by noting that he "ain't never picked a boll of cotton or head of lettuce in his life" (7), what it really emphasizes is the limited and limiting character of predefined categories and the arrogance of those who uncritically use them.

In his need to find a single and stable answer to his question about the meaning of "18 & 23," Reema's Boy is what Derrida calls a "scholar": "There has never been a scholar who, as such, does not believe in the sharp distinction between the real and the unreal, the actual and the inactual, the living and the non-living, being and non-being ('to be or not to be,' in the conventional reading), in the opposition between what is present and what is not, for example in the form of objectivity" (12).[17] Derrida's scholar believes only in the binary oppositions of ontology—something is or is not; what is and what is not can be determined objectively. As a scholar, Reema's Boy cannot take in the answers the people of Willow Springs offer him about "18 & 23," an unstable and equivocal phrase that is used as a noun, adjective, adverb, and verb and signifies differently depending on the context and the speaker. George also acts as a scholar through most of the novel, in his professed interest in the "true story" of Sapphira. Like Derrida's scholar, Reema's Boy and George would "not believe in ghosts—nor in all that could be called the virtual space of spectrality" (12). The ghost escapes the inquiry of Derrida's scholar because it cannot be approached in objectivist, binary terms, cannot be interrogated through ontology but requires a different mode of interrogation—one Derrida terms "hauntology."

George demonstrates his inability to "deal with ghosts" in his reaction to the ceremony of the "standing forth," after the death of Little Caesar the night of the hurricane. As an outsider to Willow Springs, George looks for familiar elements in the ceremony, which he interprets as "concessions . . . to a Christian ritual" (269): the people assembled for the occasion, the coffin, the minister, the church. But he also comments on the aspects that do not conform to what he, following his predefined categories, decidedly wants to call "a funeral": there is no music, no sermon, no flowers, no tears; people speak in a voice that is strikingly "matter of fact"; and, most puzzling to George, people do not wear "special clothes" but "whatever they were wearing when they knew the time had come" (268), appearing in tar-covered overalls or with a towel around their freshly shampooed hair. At the end of the ceremony, while those who had gathered calmly return to whatever they were doing before, George lingers by Little Caesar's grave, "trying to sort out the meaning of all this" (269).

As a scholar, George "believe[s] that looking is sufficient" (Derrida 11). He sees, however, only what he has been trained to see. What he fails to see—what he witnesses yet is unable to register—is the nature of the relationship between the living and the dead that the standing forth manifests. For the community of Willow Springs, death does not fundamentally and irremediably sever all ties with the deceased. George is particularly confused by the fact that Bernice, Little Caesar's mother, apologizes to her son for forgetting for a moment that, even though he died, he is "still here" (269). With its ritual mode of address, "when I first saw you" / "when I see you again," the standing forth is not only a way of paying respects to the dead and sharing memories with the living; it also rests on the notion of an actual exchange between the living and the dead. When the people gathered around the coffin address the deceased, they are not, as George thinks, merely "acting as if they expected an answer back" (268): they really do expect a response, for they know the dead listen, and speak. The novel's narrative form is precisely based on this idea, as the dialogue between Cocoa and George that composes the major part of the novel is itself a standing forth: it begins with Cocoa addressing George, telling him what he was doing the first time she saw him, and closes with her vision of what will happen when she sees him again. And George, in his turn, answers.

George will go a long way, from his misunderstanding of the standing forth to Cocoa's standing forth for him. Unlike Reema's Boy, he will learn to listen and to open himself to other narratives, as his ongoing conversation with Cocoa demonstrates. But it is only through death, and through becoming a ghost himself, that he will learn to re-vision his approach.[18] "You can only start seeing," Jacqueline Rose notes, "when you know that your vision is troubled, fallible, off-key"; the only way of seeing differently is therefore to "disorient oneself" (144). If in George's case becoming a ghost is necessary to effect such disorientation, for other characters interaction with ghosts is sufficient. After following George, I now turn to follow Miranda, whose various encounters with the ghosts in Willow Springs deeply affect her view of both the past and the present.

To Let the Ghost Speak

Miranda deals with ghosts on a daily basis. When she goes to the Days' graveyard, she does so not only to tend to her ancestors' graves, but also to spend time with them and listen to their stories. When she puts moss in her shoes to soften her steps, she can hear the voices of her kin. Those who do not have a grave, like Sapphira, who "left by wind," and Miranda's mother Ophelia, who "left by water" (152), speak in the breeze coming from the Sound. The spirit voices that fill Willow Springs are as much a part of its life as the surrounding presence of water. To hear them, however, requires not some supernatural power but a willingness to listen to what they have to say.[19] Yet even as open and perceptive a person as Miranda—who anticipates people's visits and defections, feels the presence of impending death, and foresees the coming of the hurricane and its devastating force—can also at times remain deaf to the voices around her. Miranda is of course no scholar; and yet, like George, she sometimes commits acts of silencing of her own and fails "to do what is necessary" (Derrida 11): to speak of the ghost, and especially to let the ghost speak.

Her failings often betray her fear, reluctance, or simple refusal to face a painful past. As she walks through the woods near the other place on a Candle Walk night, thinking about her mother Ophelia and her tragic end, she feels a ghostly presence and is suddenly afraid:

> She tries to listen under the wind. The sound of a long wool skirt passing. Then the tread of heavy leather boots, heading straight for the main road, heading on toward the east bluff over the ocean. It couldn't be Mother, she died in The Sound. Miranda's head feels like it's gonna burst. The candles, food, and slivers of ginger, lining the main road. A long wool skirt passing. Heavy leather boots. And the humming—humming of some lost and ancient song. Quiet tears start rolling down Miranda's face. Oh, precious Jesus, the light wasn't for her—it was for him. The tombstone out by Chevy's Pass. How long did he search for her? Up and down this path. (118)

As she hears Sapphira's ghost passing, closely followed by Bascombe's, she gets a faint sense of something she had never considered before: she feels, for the first time, the pain of her forefather. This leads her to reconsider the meaning and origin of Candle Walk, the ritual that brings all the people of Willow Springs together on the road with lights in their hands every December twenty-second. The tradition might not symbolize the light Sapphira used in her walk across the ocean back to Africa, or the lightning bolt in which another story has her escape Willow Springs. Nor does it represent the "army of stars" (110) that fell to the earth when God created the island and which Sapphira used to guide her people. Candle Walk might in fact be about the light Bascombe used in his heartbroken search for his beloved across the island. Miranda is not able to make more of it at this point, because she cannot remember what her father told her about Candle Walk. She now knows that it has to do with men "somehow" dying of broken hearts, but the "how" still eludes her. Telling herself it might "come to her" when she spends more time at the other place and "listen[s] to the wind from The Sound" (118) for answers, she deliberately delays facing the past.

But the ghosts soon return to haunt her, another night on which she ruminates on the past. As she is patiently working on a quilt made of pieces of cloth that belonged to her kin, Miranda acknowledges that even those pieces that bring painful memories—such as her mother's suicide—must be included, for they are indeed "too precious to lose." Yet she deliberately "forgets" to include a piece of Bascombe in the family quilt (137). While stitching in a piece of homespun that belonged to Sapphira, she is suddenly possessed by the same partial memory about her ancestors. Only this time she further senses that their past is somehow tied to Cocoa and George's present and future: the link between Sapphira's relationship with Bascombe, which led to his broken heart, the meaning of Candle Walk, and the lives of her grandniece and her new husband, whom she has yet to meet, is unclear but undeniable. Feeling the pain in that old story, she is tempted to take the piece of homespun out of the quilt, but she knows it is too late, "and it didn't matter no way. Could she take herself out? Could she take out Abigail? Could she take 'em all out and start again?" While she realizes that, whether she likes it or not, they are all part of the family history and therefore all belong in the quilt, she nevertheless decides to fight back the past by convincing herself that it is "gone, just as gone as it could be." Shutting herself against the voice and the feeling that tell her otherwise, she leaves the memory of Bascombe out of the quilt of her family's history because, simply, "She doesn't want to know" (138).

It is George's long-awaited coming to Willow Springs that brings about both her third encounter with Bascombe's ghost and her third act of silencing. As they stop by Bascombe's solitary grave at Chevy's Pass on their walk together across the island, she again refuses to hear, and especially to let George hear, about men dying of broken hearts. As George bends over Bascombe's gravestone to read the inscription, Miranda sees the "heart-shaped ginger leaves twine around his knuckles, as if they were pulling him closer to listen, willing to hold him there until he does." Here and throughout the novel, George and Bascombe are connected through the heart-shaped wild ginger leaves, which symbolize their similar fate. Had she listened, Miranda would have heard Bascombe warning them about what Cocoa will later hear when she and George return to the family graveyard: that she will break his heart. But Miranda is still "afraid to remember": "Ain't *nothing* he needs to hear around here" (207), she thinks, as she quickly leads George away from the grave and talks and talks about other things to drown the ghosts' whispers.

It is only when she is faced with something more frightening than this past that Miranda resolves to open herself fully to it. When her grandniece falls ill, she can no longer pretend that the past is gone and can just be ignored, for she knows that what is happening to Cocoa is linked to the history of the Days. And so, therefore, must be the way to save her. She finally goes to seek for answers at the other place, because "all that [Cocoa] is was made by the people who walked these oak floors, sat and dreamed out on that balcony" (278). She tries to conjure good memories, which are hard to find in a place where so much was lost. When she finds the bill of sale in Bascombe's ledger, she quickly dismisses it, not so much because it is hardly legible but because "the paper, itself, means nothing to [her]. All Willow Springs knows that this woman was nobody's slave." Yet the half-absent name of her foremother on the stained and faded paper provokes in her a feeling of loss that she knows is the "missing key" to saving Cocoa. Trying to remember her ancestor's name and seeing only "a vast gray wall" (280), she stops looking and conjures the ghost of Sapphira in her sleep.

Her ancestor meets her in her dreams and leads her through door after door to make her understand the necessity to "look past the pain" (283), starting with her own pain at the tragic death of her mother, whose memory Sapphira's haunting presence brought back, and of her young sister. When she awakens, Miranda knows she must go to the well in the garden, which her father sealed up after little Peace fell in it, driving Ophelia mad with sorrow. When the lid finally comes off and Miranda looks down into the darkness of the well, the voices of the ghosts strike her in "circles and circles of screaming." The voices are those of the Day women who begged their men to "let them go with peace": Sapphira, asking Bascombe to free her and let her go back to Africa, and Ophelia, asking John-Paul to let her follow her dead daughter. Looking down at her own hands that "refus[e] to let go of the edge" of the well, just as Bascombe's hands refused to let Sapphira "go with peace" and John-Paul's would not let Ophelia "go with Peace" (284), Miranda finally understands what "looking past the pain" means: it is to "feel for the[se] m[e]n" (285) and their belief in their own hands. It means, in other words, to see things from *their* perspective. That is something, she realizes, she has never done before.

Finally including these silenced perspectives into her narrative also enables her to understand George's perspective, and therefore what he will need to do to give Cocoa peace. If he is to avoid Bascombe and John-Paul's fate, George will have to willfully relinquish his faith in the single power of his own hands and consent to write a new narrative with Miranda, one that acknowledges the pain as well as power of both men and women. She sends him off to her chicken coop with Bascombe's ledger and John-Paul's walking cane—two symbols of male power, two objects that belonged to men who refused to let go—on a quest to find only his own empty hands. Refusing in his turn to let go, George cannot *see* what he has found and uses the cane and ledger to fight the hen that attacks him.[20] But his death ultimately opens another memory for Miranda, adding yet another meaning to Candle Walk: in this new narrative, the ritual does not symbolize Bascombe's pain, which compelled him to obsessively chase after the love he lost, but his faith and hope, which elevated him to "the highest place" (308).

The Ghost as Alternative Epistemology

As this overview of Miranda's successive encounters with her ancestors has shown, the ghost intervenes at the first two moments of historical production. It introduces unrecorded facts and expands the archive to new historical voices by drawing attention to neglected sources. Ghosts in *Mama Day* bring in other perspectives, those that did not make it into the official record. If the scholar, or traditional historian, believes only in what he or she can see in the documentary archive of slavery, it is significant that Naylor's ghosts—unlike Morrison's Beloved or Marshall's spirits—do not *appear*, in visual terms, but rather make their presence known through another mode. This mode is to some extent aural, as the characters hear them if they are able, or willing, to listen; but if they can be said to tell stories, ghosts do not speak in the usual sense in *Mama Day*. When Cocoa converses with George's ghost on the rise by the Sound, it all happens with "neither one saying a word" (10). When

Miranda encounters her great-grandparents on Candle Walk, it is the rustle of Sapphira's wool skirt, the heavy tread of Bascombe's boots, and the "humming of some lost and ancient song" (118) that lead her to re-vision their story. And when she conjures Sapphira in her dream, Miranda "can't really hear" her voice "'cause she's got no ears" (283). An apparent exception is when the ghosts in the Days' graveyard, John-Paul, Jonah, and Grace, take turns telling their stories when Miranda and Cocoa visit them, for they speak in the first person and their voice is reported in free direct speech. Miranda and Cocoa "know [they are] there, 'cause they listen" (151). But when Cocoa silently asks about the two missing graves, those of Sapphira and Ophelia, the response is not spoken but, as often, voiced through the wind, as "the breeze coming up from The Sound swirls the answer around her feet" (152).

While the ghosts play a crucial role in the protagonists' efforts to recover the past, they do not provide them with direct answers. The way in which Miranda is progressively led to re-vision her family history rather suggests an affective mode. Her successive encounters with ghosts provoke in her various feelings: fear, pain, loss, but also wholeness and "the sense of being" when Sapphira helps her remember that, long before she became "Mama Day," she was "Daughter" (283). The ghosts not only expand the limits of the archive by bringing new kinds of sources: they also signify another way of knowing, an alternative epistemological mode that strikingly resembles what Gordon describes as "haunting." Taking her cue from Beloved, whose presence, in Denver's phrasing, provides access to and knowledge of "the things behind things" (Morrison, *Beloved* 37), Gordon defines haunting as "a very particular way of knowing what has happened or is happening," as it "draws us affectively, sometimes against our own will and always a bit magically, into the structure of feeling of a reality we come to experience, not as cold knowledge, but as a transformative recognition" (8). Like Derrida, Gordon proposes that paying attention to ghosts radically challenges and changes what we know and how we produce knowledge.[21]

In mediating the past through the protagonist's subjectivity, the affective mode that characterizes the ghost's epistemology seems to contrast with the ideal of objectivity professed by traditional historiography. As a presence from the past that intervenes in the protagonists' present, the ghost also collapses the distinction between "historical process and historical knowledge" (Trouillot, *Silencing the Past* 5), between the subject (the historian) and the object (the past) of knowledge—the very distinction that has traditionally been seen as the guarantee of the historian's objectivity and of history's scientificity. But rather than serving as a contrast to the scientific mode, the ghost's epistemology throws into relief historiography's own myths. As we saw, George may believe his rational approach and his status as an outsider to Willow Springs put him in a better position to uncover the truth about Sapphira, to unravel historical fact from myth, but he is actually just as implicated in the past as Miranda. Both approach and give meaning to the past through the prism of the present; what distinguishes them is her ability, and his failure, to admit to the biases and limitations of their views and to re-vision them accordingly.

Against the historicist approach, which rests on the principle of an "imagined correspondence between the linguistic text, and the non-verbal, referential, categories outside it," *Mama Day*'s ghosts thus foreground "the fact that the sense of the past has been summoned through an iteration that takes place in the context of the present" (Buse and Stott, "Introduction" 15). If the ghost is a productive and much-used deconstructivist trope, it is because it highlights "the linguistic mediation of history," thereby debunking the notion of "the existence of a historical field outside of language." But it is not only the ghost's "anachronistic" character that "serves to destabilize any neat compartmentalization of the past as a secure and fixed entity" (14). Its defining elusiveness, or what Daniel Erickson calls its "underdetermination," also signifies the interpretive work that any attempt at recovering the past necessarily entails. In his close analysis of the metaphor of spectrality — and of the similarities between spectrality and metaphor itself — Erickson argues that the ghost's underdetermination, in producing an excess of signification, a lack of direct referentiality, requires a process of interpretive supplementation on both the characters' and the readers' parts (110). In *Beloved*, which is the focus of his analysis, the ghost's underdetermined presence demands that the other characters use their own experience and knowledge to "*work* at her interpretation" (111); this, as I pointed out in the introduction to this book, partly explains why Beloved signifies differently to each character. This interpretive process is also crucial to how the text is experienced by the reader, who must similarly supplement meaning by filling in the "holes and spaces" (Morrison, qtd. in Erickson 112) that the writer leaves in the text and thereby participate in the construction of its meaning. This is particularly important for a novel dealing with the history of slavery, a history that is also underdetermined, full of holes and spaces that "deficient, reductively materialist historical conceptions of slavery" (Erickson 104) fail to fill in or even address, and that therefore requires the reader's active exploration and supplementation. Like Beloved, the ghosts in *Mama Day* thus also more generally suggest the ever-elusive nature of the past and the difficulties with which its representation is fraught.

The ghost's intervention therefore also has important consequences on the third and fourth moments of historical production, for it profoundly affects the mode of narration and redefines the significance the past is given in the final instance. According to Peter Buse and Andrew Stott, "a negotiation of the spectral effects of historicity as they appear in the text" can offer a welcome "alternative to traditional historicism" ("Introduction" 16). Instead of rejecting anachronism as antithetical to the historical project, historiography would gain from recognizing it as its "hidden trope," as it "selects its objects and makes them available in a fashion that can only be incomplete and out of time" (16–17). "An awareness of the motif of spectrality" (15) would therefore enable a more self-critical and honest historiography that admits to its interpretive and reconstructive gestures rather than obscuring them, thereby highlighting the facts, events, and people it silenced. But, as Gordon pertinently asks, if "we are part of the story, for better or worse," and consent to admit it, "What methods and forms of writing can foreground the conditions under which the facts and the real story are produced?" (24). What form of narrative could not only take into consideration and visibilize the ghosts and silences in and of historical discourse but also draw attention to these very processes of silencing?[22]

If Gordon found inspiration for the form of her own narrative in Morrison's *Beloved*, it is not merely because it is a literary work. Certainly, like many before her who have used literature to debunk history's claim to scientificity by demonstrating the proximity of historical and literary narratives, Gordon "hoped to find in writing that knows it is writing as such lessons for a mode of inscription that can critically question the limits of institutional discourse" (26). But if, of all literary texts, she turned to *Beloved*, it is because she also found in it an apt trope for "communicat[ing] the depth, density, and intricacies of the dialectic of subjection and subjectivity . . . , of domination and freedom, of critique and utopian longing" (8). As she explains in her introduction to *Ghostly Matters*,

> It seemed to me that radical scholars and intellectuals knew a great deal about the world capitalist system and repressive states and yet insisted on distinctions—between subject and object of knowledge, between fact and fiction, between presence and absence, between past and present, between present and future, between knowing and not-knowing—whose tenuous-

> ness and manipulation seemed precisely to me in need of comprehension and articulation, being themselves modalities of the exercise of unwanted power. (xvii)

For Gordon, the ghost offers a new grammar against the limitations of the categories, vocabulary, and modes of inquiry traditionally available to scholars trying to think and articulate the dynamics of power, domination and subjection, freedom and resistance at work in the social world and the way people experience them and are affected by them. Gordon's "radical scholars" are as limited as Derrida's scholar because their predefined, binary categories do not allow them to see, and therefore to make visible, "what is elusive, fantastic, contingent, and often barely there." In what remains of this chapter, I examine how *Mama Day*, as a narrative, manifests the form of writing Gordon said she hoped to find, writing that "acknowledge[s] . . . just those twists and turns, forgettings and re-memberings, just those ghostly haunts that a normal . . . scientific account routinely attempts to minimize" (26). Whereas traditional historiography obscures its "rhetorical movements" (Certeau, "History" 214) through a unified, coherent, monological, and linear narrative that presents itself as the one authoritative and definitive representation of the past, *Mama Day* foregrounds its constructed, fragmentary, tentative, and incomplete character.

Mama Day as Ghostly Narrative

The ghostly plays a major role in the narrative structure of *Mama Day*. The greater part of the novel is a conversation between the living and the dead, taking place years after George's death, or perhaps piece by piece through the years as Cocoa visits Willow Springs and stops on the rise by the Sound to "meet up with her first husband" (10). We are unlikely to realize this until late in the novel, however, because the hints about George's death are rather subtly given in the prologue, with the twice-repeated euphemism that Cocoa "left, and he stayed" in Willow Springs (9, 10). Because Cocoa's opening description of what George was doing the first time she saw him is not preceded by the opening formula of the standing forth, we might also not understand that this is what their conversation actually is until George dies, or even until Cocoa closes her narrative with the traditional "when I see you again." More than a clever narrative strategy, this structure foregrounds the fact that the narrators-protagonists, Cocoa and George, do not so much relate the events as reconstruct them, through dialogue, as they both attempt to figure out "what really happened to us" (311).

Starting with Cocoa and George's first encounter, moving through their dates and life as newlyweds, and leading up to their visit to Willow Springs, which ends with George's death, the story seems to follow the linear, chronological structure of traditional historical narratives. Western historiography rests on the primary epistemological principle—which is of course also, as I noted previously, an ideological principle—that history follows a linear course. Chronology is not only the logical structure for narratives based on this principle, but also "a method [that] allows events to be located at a point in time" and thereby grants these events a "'real' or factual" character (L. T. Smith 30): as a mode through which a coherent narrative is produced, chronology "suggests that we can assemble all the facts in an ordered way so that they tell us the truth or give us a very good idea of what really did happen in the past" (31). While chronology largely seems to organize *Mama Day*, it is also broken right from the start by the prologue that introduces the main narrative. The prologue situates us in Willow Springs some fifteen years after Cocoa and George's visit. But it also takes us immediately into a distinctly dated past, 1823, with the foundational story of the community. Proceeding by associations, it then meanders through diverse temporalities, from various natural and human disasters, including the visits of greedy real estate developers, up to the return of Reema's Boy, even taking a detour through the conditional mode by telling us what would have happened, had the boy only listened. More than acknowledging its own role in "the narrativization of history, the transformation of what happened into that which is said to have happened" (Trouillot, *Silencing the Past* 113), the collective narrator playfully foregrounds this role by directly addressing the reader, which it locates in yet another temporality: "Think about it: ain't nobody really talking to you. We're sitting here in Willow Springs, and you're God-knows-where. It's August 1999—ain't but a slim chance it's the same season where you are" (10). The narrator here deconstructs its very existence and reveals itself for what it is: a mere narrative device.

Mama Day also opposes traditional historiography through the multiple, polyvocal quality of its narration. Because the guild's ideal of objectivity cannot accommodate any notion of point of view but, on the contrary, presupposes the absence of a viewing subject in favor of a preexisting, independent reality, "the historian's position is officially unmarked: it is that of the nonhistorical observer" (Trouillot, *Silencing the Past* 151). The narrative produced by the historian therefore reflects the absence of a narrator through an impersonal, disembodied, "voiceless" voice (LaCapra, *History and Criticism* 117). Against the "univocity" of historiographical language (Certeau, "History" 202), *Mama Day* shares out the narrative between several narrators that not only speak in distinctive voices but, more often than not, offer contrasting and contradictory accounts of the same event.[23] Closely following Miranda's point that "everything got four sides: his side, her side, an outside, and an inside" (230), George, Cocoa, a third-person omniscient narrator, and the collective voice of Willow Springs all contribute to the reconstruction of the past. The novel thus draws our attention not only to the biased and limited character of the protagonists' conceptions, but also to the silences each narrative produces. Whereas traditional historiography—putatively deprived of a narrative voice and, thereby, of a particular point of view—presents an authoritative account of the events, the plurality of perspectives in *Mama Day* calls into question received notions of historical truth: there is no simple answer to "what really happened" because, as Cocoa realizes through her conversation with George's ghost, "there are just too many sides to the whole story" (311).

Yet the approach to the past *Mama Day* proposes is not tantamount to what Hayden White would qualify as "debilitating relativism," following which everything is "a matter of opinion" (76), or to an extreme form of constructivism that views "a historical narrative as one fiction among others" (Trouillot, *Silencing the Past* 6). This is what the prologue may first seem to suggest, as the people of Willow Springs disagree on the color of Sapphira's skin, which ranges from "satin black, biscuit cream, red as Georgia clay: depending upon which of us takes a mind to her." The story of her relationship with Bascombe, the narrator proceeds to tell us, also exists in myriad versions:

> And somehow, some way, it happened in 1823: she smothered Bascombe Wade in his very bed and lived to tell the story for a thousand days. 1823: married Bascombe Wade, bore him seven sons in just a thousand days, to put a dagger through his kidney and escape the hangman's noose, laughing in a burst of flames. 1823: persuaded Bascombe Wade in a thousand days to deed all his slaves every inch of land in Willow Springs, poisoned him for his trouble, to go on and bear seven sons—by person or persons unknown. (3)

If what exactly happened between Sapphira and Bascombe has spawned various narratives—a variety reflected in the unstable, fluid expression "18 & 23"—there are facts upon which everyone will agree: even though its circumstances remain obscure, Bascombe's death is attested by the presence of his tombstone at Chevy's Pass; whatever it took Sapphira to get Bascombe to give the land of Willow Springs to her/their descendants, the deeds, "all marked back to the very year" (3), are sources that prove he did; and while Bascombe may or may not have fathered them, the fact that Sapphira had seven sons is proved in the flesh by the existence of these sons' own granddaughters, Abigail and Miranda. But rather than transcending or synthesizing the various perspectives by silencing one or the other and imposing a univocal, authoritative account of the past, the narrator acknowledges what cannot be known and allows the different narratives to coexist.

Against western history's totalizing discourse, which "assumes the possibility and the desirability of being able to include absolutely all known knowledge into a coherent whole" (L. T. Smith 30), *Mama Day* emphasizes its gaps and silences and reminds us, in the blanks that signal each section break and mark the shift from one narrator to another, that there is more in those interstices that remains inaccessible. As Gordon reminds us, "The whole story is always a working fiction that satisfies the need to deliver what cannot possibly be available" (174). But if the novel does not offer "the whole story," it is also in the sense that the narrative is never complete(d). The novel ends—for want of a better word—with a glimpse into the future, with the "things [that] are yet to be" (312): Cocoa, now an older woman, is only at the beginning of a new journey into the past, as she is "ready to go in search for answers" about her family history. Her great-aunt predicted that it would come down to her to "learn about the beginning of the Days" (308), by walking through the doors Miranda could only open. It is through her conversations with George's ghost that Cocoa will learn to re-vision her narrative about what happened to them. When she tells George, in the closing formula of the standing forth, "when I see you again, our versions will be different still" (310–11), what she refers to is not only their habit of disagreeing about just everything, so that the next time she comes to visit him on the rise by the Sound her version will again be different from his, and his from hers. What she means also is that as they engage in more conversations together, reconstructing and re-visioning the past through their narratives, their versions, hers and his, individually and together, will be different from what they have been in the novel we are about to finish.

Mama Day succeeds in mirroring this dynamic character within the constraints of a fixed text. If we read the novel again, we will likely experience it very differently. We will no doubt notice what we did not in our first reading: the meaning of the narrator's twice-repeated hint in the prologue that Cocoa left Willow Springs while George stayed. We will also pay more attention throughout the novel to all the clues foreshadowing the tragic ending. And if we read the novel yet a third time, we will maybe read the ending as not so tragic after all. Our relationship with *Mama Day* is thus similar to Cocoa's conversation with George: "each time I go back over what happened, there's some new development, some forgotten corner that puts you in a slightly different light." The past is not like a photograph, always the same, fixed, immutable, dead. That is why Miranda burns all the pictures of George after his death and why Cocoa understands, after the first shock and sense of loss her great-aunt's initiative causes her, that "it's a lot better this way": not only does George "change as [she] change[s]" (310), but she is certain that when she thinks about the past she will not be tempted to settle for prescripted narratives. The voice of Willow Springs warns us against the risks of relegating history to the past: telling the story of Cocoa and George "ain't about chalking up 1985, just jotting it down in a ledger to be tallied with the times before and the times after" (305). Against master narratives' impulse to cast history as "an irrevocably interpreted past" (Eva-Marie Kröller, qtd. in Tiffin 176), Naylor presents it as a living, always redefinable story of the present.

According to a well-known aphorism, those who neglect the study of the past are condemned to repeat it. Hayden White qualified this idea by adding: "It is not so much the study of the past itself that assures against its repetition as it is how one studies it, to what aim, interest, or purpose. Nothing is better suited to lead to a repetition of the past than a study of it that is either reverential or convincingly objective in the way that conventional historical studies tend to be" (82). Walter Benjamin took a similar position when he famously argued that "to articulate the past historically does not mean to recognize it 'the way it really was' (Ranke). It means to seize hold of a memory as it flashes up at a moment of danger" (247). The past that is not recognized as a concern for the present will "disappear irretrievably"; the danger, then, lies in leaving history in the hands of conformists and conquerors, who will seize the past only as it concerns them. The dead will not be safe; they will be ghosted, disappeared, made invisible like Dusky Sally. For Gordon, "To write stories concerning exclusions and invisibilities is to write ghost stories" (17). But to write ghost stories is not only to write stories concerning exclusions and invisibilities, or even contesting exclusions and invisibilities: to write ghost stories is also to investigate the processes of exclusion and invisibilization, the ideological, but also epistemological and discursive processes that make people ghosts in history and in society.

When Barbara Chase-Riboud published *Sally Hemings*, a historical novel that relates the liaison from Hemings's point of view, historians and biographers of Jefferson generally gave the novel the same reception many have more recently given Gordon-Reed's scholarly work. In *The Jefferson Scandals: A Rebuttal*, a book he wrote to denounce "fiction masquerading as fact" in texts like Chase-Riboud's, Virginius Dabney expressed his concern about "the manner in which myths concerning Sally Hemings have been accepted as truth and disseminated to countless readers" (121). This reaction puzzled Chase-Riboud, who "f[ou]nd it extraordinary that certified historians are rebutting a novel" (E. McDowell). Yet the concerns Dabney and his peers manifested proved true: not only did the novel rekindle the controversy by raising fresh interest in Hemings, but it also gave the liaison a new plausibility in America's collective imagination. With over a million and a half copies sold worldwide in the early 1980s, Chase-Riboud's novel, in Gordon-Reed's opinion, "probably has been the single greatest influence shaping the public's attitude about the Jefferson-Hemings story" (4). From a shadow behind Jefferson, Hemings suddenly turned into a full human being who could love and be loved. Her incarnation no doubt gained even more force when she became a flesh-and-blood woman in the Franco-American drama film *Jefferson in Paris* (1995) and in the CBS miniseries *Sally Hemings: An American Scandal* (2000)—significantly retitled for worldwide distribution as *Sally Hemings: An American Love Story*.[24] Paradoxically, Hemings became a real woman when she became a character in works of fiction.

For many, Sally Hemings has become a metaphor for the condition of black people, and of black women in particular, in American society. The social death of black people under slavery did not end with Emancipation, or even with the demise of segregation in the United States, or of colonialism in the Caribbean. "Some subjects," Sharon Patricia Holland points out, "*never* achieve, in the eyes of others, the status of the 'living'" but "merely haunt the periphery of the encountering person's vision, remaining, like the past and the ancestors who inhabit it, at one with the dead" (15). This explains the persistence of Hemings's story and its importance for many African Americans. Whether the story of her liaison with Jefferson is true or not matters little; as Huggins notes, it is "*symbolically* true" (xlvii) insofar as, if it maybe did not happen to them, it did happen to countless other slave women and masters. When the 1998 DNA tests brought some definite answer to this "210-year-old paternity suit," Ashraf Rushdy points out, it marked a significant moment in "the struggle of not only the particular descendants of this specific line of Jeffersons but all African Americans to get recognized as *kin* in America" (*Remembering Generations* 166). This also explains the place the slave woman has come to occupy in African diaspora literature. By writing about those slave women history has silenced, all the Dusky Sallys of the past, and by moving them out of the shadow, African diaspora writers have also been moving themselves out of the margins to which society relegated them, and have been affirming their existence and central position as artists and as persons. When she was asked in an interview, "What is it that comes from the pens of black women?" Naylor replied, "It's a real simple answer: themselves, their lives, the announcement that 'I am here' and 'I am to be reckoned with'" (Rowell 190).

[3]

"YOU BEST REMEMBER THEM!": REPOSSESSING THE SPIRIT OF DIASPORA

There's a thought . . . a recollection . . . something somebody remembers. We carry these memories inside of us. Do you think that hundreds and hundreds of Africans brought here on this other side would forget everything they once knew? We don't know where the recollections come from. Sometimes we dream them. But we carry these memories inside of us. —Nana Peazant, in *Daughters of the Dust*

IN A BRIEF HEADNOTE to "To Da-Duh: In Memoriam," a largely autobiographical short story evoking her first visit to her parents' native Barbados, Marshall explains that her maternal grandmother made such a strong impression on her that the old woman appears throughout her works. "She's an ancestor figure," the writer comments, "symbolic for me of the long line of black women and men—African and New World—who made my being possible, and whose spirit I believe continues to animate my life and work. I wish to acknowledge and celebrate them. I am, in a word, an unabashed ancestor worshipper" (95).

Marshall is of course not alone among writers of the African diaspora to give ancestral figures an important place in her writing. As I noted in chapter 1, D'Aguiar's grandmother features prominently in several of his works, which were also inspired by other strong historical women. By the end of *Feeding the Ghosts*, Mintah herself appears as an ancestral figure, playing an important part in the protection and education of her community, as do Miranda and Sapphira in Naylor's *Mama Day*, and Nanny in Cliff's *Abeng* and *No Telephone to Heaven*. Morrison, whose own work is also full of such figures, has commented on the importance of "the ancestor as foundation" in African diaspora literature and culture: "There is always an elder there," she writes, "a grandfather as in Ralph Ellison, or a grandmother as in Toni Cade Bambara, or a healer as in Bambara or Henry Dumas." What interested her as a reader, and later as a writer, was how "the presence or absence of that figure determined the success or the happiness of the character" ("Rootedness" 343)—as Milkman's restorative journey in *Song of Solomon* or Jadine's cultural and spiritual isolation in *Tar Baby* indeed confirm. Associating the presence of an ancestor with a sense of historical and cultural continuity, Morrison concludes that "if we don't keep in touch with the ancestor . . . we are, in fact, lost" (344).

These ancestral figures are the guardians of what Morrison refers to as the "discredited knowledge" of black people, a knowledge that, as I pointed out in the introduction to this book, is part of a way of looking at the world that productively blends an acceptance of, and reliance on, the "supernatural" with practicality and "shrewdness." This knowledge, Morrison notes, is not only discredited by the dominant white culture because black people are discredited: it is also often discredited by black people themselves "because the press toward upward social mobility would mean to get as far away from that kind of knowledge as possible" ("Rootedness" 342). Morrison's assessment could not more aptly describe Marshall's *Praisesong for the Widow* (1983). Indeed, Marshall's third novel—which she dedicated to her grandmother, Da-Duh—is the very illustration of what Morrison points out as the "dangers" of losing the ancestor. The story proves that "nice things don't always happen to the totally self-reliant if there is no conscious historical connection" (344). At sixty-something, the novel's protagonist Avey Johnson is, in Marshall's own words, a woman who "has made it," who "would be referred to . . . as a CTTR, a Credit To The Race" (Baer 24). After years lived in poverty, enduring racial discrimination and injustice, working themselves out just to make ends meet and send their three daughters to school, Avey and her husband Jay finally secured a materially comfortable situation and a house in the suburbs. Now, a few years after her husband's death, free from financial concerns thanks to the funds he secured for her, Avey seems to feel at home in the middle class, as we meet her on her third cruise in the Caribbean. And yet, as we soon learn, this material success came at a high price, as it was acquired at the expense of the sense of rootedness that Morrison claims is essential to the life and future of both individuals and communities. Estranged from her culture, her people, Jay, and ultimately herself, Avey suffers from what Jayne O. Ifekwunigwe calls an "orphan consciousness" (146). Her cultural isolation is similar to George's in *Mama Day*, except that while George, as an actual orphan, was brought up without any connection to African diasporic culture, Avey has abandoned hers, surreptitiously and not fully consciously. In her struggle to survive and overcome the realities of mid-twentieth-century urban life in a racist society that locks black people in debilitating and exploitative work conditions, Avey has in fact condemned herself to natal alienation. "When you kill the ancestor you kill yourself," Morrison claims ("Rootedness" 344). Jay's spirit died long before he actually passed away from exhaustion at working too hard for too many years; and Avey herself is only the shadow of the vibrant, lively woman she used to be.

Praisesong for the Widow traces Avey's physical, spiritual, and cultural journey of recovery. This journey is first of all one through memory, for "in order to regain her 'soul,'" as G. Thomas Couser puts it, "Avey not only needs to remember what she has forgotten, but also needs to forget much of what she remembers" (109–10). The novel repeatedly collapses temporal boundaries, using various narrative devices and tropes to bring the past and the present in the same space. As figures from her personal history as well as from a larger cultural history, ghosts play a key role in this process, compelling her to re-vision her past and her relation to it. The ghost of her great-aunt, who first appears to her in a dream, opens a breach in the wall Avey has erected around her complacent life. The visitation of her dead husband sends her into a trancelike state in which she reconsiders the last thirty years of her life, and sees how far she has come and how much she has lost. For Avey, remembering also involves re-membering her body, reconnecting with the sensations and sensuality of her personal and cultural past, as well as re-membering the collective body of diaspora. After encountering other haunting figures on the way, which bring back more memories and annihilate the distance she has put between herself and her former life and the people and culture she once claimed as hers, she is finally drawn back into the community when she accepts the presence of the dead in her life.

Rather than haunting, the presence of ghosts in *Praisesong for the Widow* takes the form of possession. By making this distinction I do not follow critics who understand haunting and possession as fundamentally different or even opposite processes or conditions, conceiving haunting as positive and constructive and possession as "a destructive form of haunting" (Clewell 137) or "a dangerous incorporation of the dead" (Brogan 10) leading to the compulsive acting out of a traumatic past. Possession, in my reading, has effects in many ways similar to those I have described in the previous chapters; but it is also distinctive in the way it refers to a particular cultural and spiritual practice of the African diaspora. Instead of the word "ghost," in this chapter I will therefore generally use the word "spirit" in order to emphasize the link these ghostly manifestations have with African diasporic spiritualities. An instance of discredited knowledge, spirit possession partakes in what I have identified, following Morrison, as "another way of knowing things" ("Rootedness" 342).

By using the word "spirit," or "spirituality," I do not mean to mark an opposition between the spiritual and the material. In my view, the novel does not posit an incompatibility between material security, or even materialism, and spirituality or spirit possession. It is a common view that material security inevitably comes at the expense of spirituality, and that holding on to one's ancestral culture necessarily means renouncing the materialism that seems to be the appendage of modern society. However, not only would such a view bear the mark of a dubious primitivism, a perspective Marshall does not adopt toward African diaspora culture; it would also go against a notion the writer identifies as a fundamental one in the culture she grew up in, which posits that "a thing is at the same time its opposite, and that these opposites, these contradictions make up the whole" ("From the Poets" 631).[1] The crucial question, which Avey ponders in a central moment of the novel, is whether it is possible to "do both": achieve material comfort and security while "safeguarding, treasuring . . . the most valuable part of themselves" (139).

In positing an essential link, rather than a break, between the material and the spiritual, the body and the soul or mind, *Praisesong for the Widow* also contrasts with the western, notably Christian, philosophical tradition. Christian worship is "characterized by humility, effacement, and the silence of the body" as its "activity . . . is suspended in conformity to the dualistic metaphysic which separates mind and body and condemns the body to effacement as the mind communes with God." In contrast, possession involves the "total participation of the devotees" (S. Walker 6), to the extent that in Haitian vodou the ritual is commonly referred to as spirits "riding" the initiate's body like a horse. Ultimately, the novel's rejection of the body/mind split also opposes the rationalism that situates knowledge in the mind rather than in bodily experience, a rationalism, as I pointed out earlier, that has been largely complicit with the racial terror that supported slavery and continues to feed discrimination against black people and cultures. As the most extreme incarnation of the rationalist construction of the slave as a soulless working body, the figure of the zombi appears in *Praisesong for the Widow*, as Jay works himself out of his mind to survive in a society ruled by injustice, racism, and physical and symbolic violence. The trope of zombification is one among other narrative devices the novel uses to blur temporal boundaries and suggest continuity between a condition of slavery supposed to belong in the past and the condition of black people in the present. Significantly, as

Joan Dayan and others have shown, the "dispossession" effected by slavery is precisely what is reconfigured through rituals of possession, in which the possessing spirit guides the possessed "back to the self, to an identity lost, submerged, and denigrated."[2] While zombification is "the ultimate sign of loss and dispossession" (Dayan 37), possession is strengthening and enhancing, actually providing "greater freedom" (S. Walker 84); whereas zombification separates the mind or soul from the body, possession affirms the importance not only of spiritual life, but also of an embodied spirituality. Far from the common—western, colonial—view of possession as a disabling condition, in *Praisesong for the Widow*, as in African diasporic traditions more generally, possession is therefore empowering and liberating: being possessed by spirits ultimately enables Avey to repossess her own spirit, and her own identity. In this context, my use of the term "possession" also plays on the movement from commodity (the master's possession) to free self (self-possession) that the novel traces through Avey's journey.

Several critics have noted the similarities this journey bears with a ritual. Yet most have not read it through the particular patterns and modalities of spirit possession.[3] Approaching the novel in those terms, however, not only allows for a better understanding of some of the cultural references the text makes only in passing, but it also reinforces the importance such cultural elements have in Marshall's literary project. Marshall has described her first three novels as a trilogy that traces a "spiritual return to [her] sources" (J. Williams 52), by which she means primarily her African sources but also the diasporic culture that developed from it. Possession is not a direct remnant of African culture, but rather a good example of a cultural, social, and spiritual practice of African origins that has been adapted in the American context by the diaspora. A profoundly syncretic cultural practice, Marshall's version of possession and the rituals associated with it borrows from various traditions: Haitian vodou, with its pantheon of figures whose avatars appear across cultures in West Africa, South America, the Caribbean, and the United States; but also dance ceremonies performed in distinctive forms in Carriacou and in the Sea Islands off the coast of South Carolina, which emerged from the fusion of Christian worship and slave dances. All these cultural elements cannot be identified with a single culture but rather testify to the creativity of African diasporic cultures and to the dynamic relationship between an African origin—itself already diverse—and its New World developments.

Marshall's approach to African diaspora culture and tradition is largely visible not only in her representation of possession, but also in her use of the ghost, or spirit. Although most discussions of *Praisesong for the Widow* point out the importance of ancestors in the novel, few comment on the particular form these ancestors take.[4] Whereas the figure of the ancestor suggests a direct connection with a cultural past, the more elusive figure of the ghost troubles this relation. As in the other novels I have discussed, the ghosts in *Praisesong for the Widow* first signify the persistence or, in this case, the return of a (cultural) past that refuses to be forgotten; but they also destabilize the notion of an unmediated access to the past and suggest the dynamic and creative nature of any act of historical or cultural recovery. When asked about the importance of a return to African sources, Marshall explained that to her Africa is both "a concrete destination and a spiritual homeland" that black people must "reinvent" (J. Williams 52–53). This tension between recovery and reinvention, actual cultural reference and phantasm, runs through the novel and accounts for some of its inherent and, I will argue, deliberately unresolved contradictions. Reading *Praisesong for the Widow* through the tropes of the ghost and of spirit possession will demonstrate that the novel deals with the issues of cultural memory and diasporic identity in a more complex way than has often been recognized.

Marshall addresses in *Praisesong for the Widow* a question Stuart Hall poses in his essay "Cultural Identity and Diaspora," when he asks what exactly is the nature of the project in which so many writers and thinkers of the African diaspora are engaged with respect to history, culture, and identity: "Is [this project] only a matter of unearthing that which the colonial experience buried and overlaid, bringing to light the hidden continuities it suppressed? Or is a quite different practice entailed—not the rediscovery but the *production* of identity. Not an identity grounded in the archaeology, but in the *re-telling* of the past?" (224). The novel's answer is, as I will show, ambivalent, and testifies to the complexities entailed in the notion of (diasporic) identity, which oscillates between the rallying and sustaining potential of an essentialist view and the critically valuable caution of a constructivist one. This apparent hesitation is not surprising in a novel written in the early 1980s, a time of transition between "the essentialist identity politics . . . and insidious nationalist orthodoxies" of the 1970s and the "commitment to contingent, ambiguous definitions of self" of the theories of the "post-" of the 1980s and 1990s (Hirsch and Miller 3–4). Building on critical examinations of the notions of diaspora and cultural identity, this chapter ultimately also aims to situate *Praisesong for the Widow* in its historical and theoretical context and to relate it to Marshall's own political sensibilities.

From Spirit Possession to Repossessing the Spirit: Avey Johnson's Initiation

We meet the protagonist of *Praisesong for the Widow* in the middle of the night, and in the middle of a packing frenzy. Resolute to leave the ship *Bianca Pride* only a few days into her cruise in the Caribbean, Avey knows that her two companions, Thomasina and Clarice, will not understand her decision. How could they? She cannot account for it herself. The two reasons—if they can be called that—she gives herself are a disturbing dream featuring her great-aunt and a peach parfait she had trouble digesting even though she did not even eat it. In his analysis of the novel, Keith Sandiford comments that "Avey's sudden and unexplained emotional disturbance is inarguably the single most delicate contingency in Marshall's overall design of this novel." What, he asks, could drive the rational and self-controlled Avey to behave so out of character? And does it not "strain the limits of credulity" to give the dream of Cuney, or to give Cuney herself, so much power? This, he concludes, "would hardly pass the scrutiny of Western rationalist logic or even a moderate dose of secularist scepticism" (375).

In his comment, Sandiford does not so much explain Marshall's plot decision as suggest the irrelevance of such an explanation. He reads Marshall's choice as one that "remove[s] her heroine from the linear, causative environment of the *Bianca Pride* . . . and place[s] her in a cosmos whose rules are determined by a radically different mythology" (375), a mythology derived from African cosmology. Without substantially disagreeing with Sandiford's reading, I will argue that Marshall does not "remove" Avey from a western environment and put her in an African cosmology so much as bring this African—or rather, African diasporic—cosmology, which used to be part of her life years earlier, back into her present. Even more significant is the process through which this conflation of different times and places is produced: spirit possession. Although the trope of possession is close to that of haunting in many ways, it also differs from it in the way the visiting spirit not only brings the past into the present, but also takes the possessed into the past, in a double and, quite interestingly, not necessarily simultaneous movement. The effects possession induces in Avey are translated at times as a ghost from the past irrupting into her present and immediate space, sometimes as her being suddenly transported into another time and space, and at other times as both at once, so that we cannot tell if what is described is reality, memory, fantasy, or something else altogether.

Sandiford's comment also points to the strange, foreign, and ultimately supernatural character that possession has from a western perspective. Because the Avey we discover at the beginning of the novel has completely repressed the African diasporic part of her culture and identity in favor of a western, white materialist culture, she cannot at first make sense of what is happening to her. After her dream at the beginning of the story and through most of the novel, Avey repeatedly notes that she is not feeling herself, an impression her friends confirm when they catch her packing in the middle of the night to sneak off the ship. In her account of ceremonial spirit possession in Africa and America, Sheila Walker identifies as the most obvious sign of possession the fact that, to the observer, "the possessed person exhibits motor behavior very different from that which is characteristic for him." Significantly, the way in which the reason for such behavior is interpreted largely depends on the cultural and theoretical position of the observer: "In Western psychological terms the individual may be considered to be suffering from some form of psychopathology, whereas in folk terms, a god, spirit or demon has assumed control of his faculties" (10). If Thomasina rather logically concludes from Avey's apparently irrational behavior that "she's done gone and lost her mind" (24), it is significant that Avey also describes herself as "crazy," and predicts everyone will consider her so. Reading the novel through possession not only explains—if that is indeed necessary—Avey's apparently irrational behavior, but explains it in a way that throws into relief the two cultural systems the novel holds in tension. Besides, it does so using a theoretical and philosophical frame that precisely emerges from the African diaspora cosmology the novel relies on.

Avey's association of her own behavior with madness also highlights the fact that she views her condition as debilitating. Yet, if possession alters consciousness, it does so in a way that is actually enhancing and empowering. Over the course of the novel, Avey experiences most of the effects Sheila Walker identifies as characteristic of this state of altered consciousness: alteration in thinking (notably disturbed memory), disturbed time sense, loss of conscious control (which may actually lead to greater control or truth), change in emotional expression, change in body image (notably depersonalization, body-mind split, and dissolution of boundaries between self and others), perceptual distortions (such as hallucinations), change in the meaning or significance attached to subjective experiences in such states (feelings of profound truth, insight, illumination), sense of ineffable (difficulty to communicate the experience to those who have not experienced it, or even to remember it), feelings of rejuvenation or renewed hope, and hypersuggestibility (in the sense of an increased propensity to accept and/or automatically respond to specific statements or commands) (13). Because most of these effects are profoundly disturbing at best, and physically and psychically painful at worst, Avey first considers them as a burden, and her initial reaction is to flee the environment in which they emerged in order to free her mind, as well as body, from them. However, she simultaneously finds herself being drawn toward more occasions for altered states. After leaving the *Bianca Pride* and later her hotel room in Grenada, where the first two spirits—her great-aunt and her husband, respectively—visited her, she finds herself accepting to postpone her return to the safety of her home in the New York suburbs to go on an excursion to the nearby island of Carriacou. Although she is unable to account for her own decision, repeatedly questions it, and soon comes to regret it, her behavior can be read as her unconsciously registering the enhancing effects of her altered state. If she never explicitly identifies these effects positively, no more than she recognizes her experience as spirit possession, by the end of the novel she will feel enhanced in her consciousness.

On a general level, the effect she experiences can be described as double vision, or second sight.[5] A lexical field related to vision runs through the novel, as the narrator describes the disturbing things Avey sees as hallucinations or tricks of the eye and comments on her seeing the world or the past with more or less clarity; Avey spends as much time gazing at or watching other people as they do looking back at her; and mirrors, masks, and veils are recurring symbols in the novel. Described through Avey's perception, double vision often takes the form of superimposition or, significantly, a ghosting effect, an effect through which a secondary, spectral image appears on an object. The ghost image that appears is at times negative, a vision of horror that casts a shadow on the object Avey is actually looking at, and at other times positive, like "subliminal memories" (245) that bring to her mind, or bring her mind to, a joyful and sustaining moment in her past. Double vision can thus be described as the ability to make connections between objects, people, places, or events whose meaning and significance are highlighted by their superimposition, by "holding" them all "into focus at the same time" (DeLamotte 169 n. 7).[6] Avey's visions quite literally open her eyes not only on the world but also on herself, her life, and her choices. Double vision, which amounts to a form of re vision, allows her to see through the veneer of her complacent life and to see it for what it really is: a form of spiritual dispossession that is akin to enslavement.

In the novel, this double vision is often referred to as "*li gain connaissance*." Also spelled *konesans*, the term comes from Haitian vodou, in which it is defined as "an insight into the invisible causes and ends of things," a form of "second sight which allows [the devotees] to understand the hidden meanings of human and divine actions" (Murphy 19). This "special quality of mind . . . , which might be seen as both ritual knowledge and spiritual insight" (17), is the foundation on which the vodou community is organized, as the position of each member in the liturgical hierarchy is determined by his or her level of *konesans*.[7] The novel identifies several characters who have *konesans* and who serve as guides or models for Avey. Although the spiritual and cultural elements Marshall uses come from various traditions, *Praisesong for the Widow* can be read as following the vodou ceremonial "path into *konesans*," in which the devotees are initiated "so that their eyes may be opened" (Murphy 19).

The Call

In his account of possession, Joseph M. Murphy points out that "an initiate does not choose to join a vodou community, but responds to a call from the lwa" (19), or spirit. In this initial phase, the "called one" experiences the manifestation of the spirit in his or her body as a "wild" call that must be "civilized" (18) under the guidance of trained initiates. The call may take the form of a powerful dream, an illness, or "a series of ordinary misfortunes," which the leader (*houngan* or *mambo*) will help interpret as spiritual "interference" (20) aimed to "awaken human beings to the limitations of their perspectives" (191). What happens to Avey aboard the *Bianca Pride* at the beginning of the novel, prompting her to interrupt the cruise, closely corresponds to this initial phase of possession. One night, she has a dream in which she finds herself back in Tatem, a Sea Island in South Carolina where she used to spend her summers as a child with her great-aunt Cuney. At least twice a week during her visits, Cuney would ritually take Avey to Ibo Landing to tell her the story of the Ibos, these Africans who, when they were disembarked from the slave ships, looked around them, saw what future awaited them in America, and walked back home across the Atlantic.[8] In the dream, Avey is standing on the mud path to the landing and sees the old woman waving and "silently calling" her, "*Come, won't you come?*" (42). Avey's mild curiosity soon turns to irritation when she realizes that Cuney means to take her to the landing across the mud field, against her will if need be. Her resistance leads to a "silent tug-of-war," which itself quickly turns into a fight when her great-aunt's hand closes on Avey's wrist like a "manacle" (43), and the two women start hitting each other.

The dream conflates different times and spaces, bringing the places of Avey's past and her present together. The sound of her fight with Cuney starts "ranging over Tatem and up and down her quiet streets at home" in North White Plains (45). The two time-spaces collapse here, as her home in the New York suburbs is not only geographically removed from Tatem but also corresponds to a much later period in Avey's life than her childhood visits to the Sea Islands. This superimposition reveals the distance that separates Avey from her younger self. While the child loved the trips to Ibo Landing, and was always ready to follow her great-aunt before she even called her to go, Avey now ignores and then resists her call. The young Avey dressed in imitation of her elder, wearing a similar hat and even an imaginary second belt because Cuney wore two, one on her waist and one on her hips for "extra strength" (32). In the dream, Avey's clothes reflect her material success and respectability and her assimilation into the white middle-class model of womanhood. It is because of these clothes that she will not go to the landing: after all, she is dressed for a luncheon given in honor of her husband, not for an "obstacle course of scrub, rock and rough grass" (40).

Avey's refusal to go with Cuney to a site of memory, as well as her overall feeling of coercion in the dream, conveys her negative view of memory and her reluctance to let it take hold of her. But her stubborn resistance and her subsequent reaction to the dream also suggest her inability to make sense of, and submit herself to, the "wild" call of her great-aunt's spirit. That the dream was in fact a manifestation of possession is confirmed by the lasting physical effects it has on Avey, who wakes up sore and tired, as if she had actually been in a fight. Her body shows the effects of Cuney's "riding" it, which initiates a slow and quite literally painful process of re-membering. Following the dream/possession, Avey experiences another kind of physical discomfort that can be assimilated to a form of illness, another sign of spiritual call. The "mysterious clogged and swollen feeling" (52) begins one night at dinner, when she is faced with a dessert she finds herself unable to eat. The lush parfait that so impresses her friends makes Avey sick. This feeling of bloatedness, like a lump of undigested food in her stomach, regularly returns to plague her long after that night.

The effects of possession continue in the form of what Avey perceives as a series of incidents. Looking absently around her in the dining room, she catches a reflection of a table with three older women in a mirror;

identifying two as her friends, she fails to recognize the third as herself. Similar incidents happened before when she saw her reflection in store windows but did not register it as such. Depersonalization is a characteristic effect of possession. Avey's subsequent realization that she failed to recognize herself may also be one of the first manifestations of her double vision: it again registers the distance between the person she used to be and the life that this woman in "beige crepe de Chine and pearls" (48) sitting in the Versailles Room of a cruise liner named *Bianca Pride* incarnates. But this incident is only one aspect of the overall disorientation that Avey suddenly feels on the cruise ship, which suddenly seems to turn into a slave ship. Like the African captives during the Middle Passage, she finds her sense of time and space disturbed, and everything around her becomes a source of distress. The "troubled heave and roll" of the liner, which only she seems to feel, makes her uncomfortable and anxious and sends her wandering "in a dazed, shaken state" for a quiet spot (54, 57). The inescapable proximity of the other passengers becomes so unbearable that their mere presence is an aggression. Hoping to shut them out by closing her eyes, plunging herself in a dark that evokes the slave ship's hold, she is continually assaulted by "their voices crashing into the dusky orange silence behind her lids" and "their faces looming abnormally large and white for a second as her eyes opened" (54). The voyage throws her, like her captive ancestors, into physical and psychological agony.

This overwhelming sense of violence and victimization is only reinforced by what she takes for hallucinations, double images that seem to superimpose themselves on the once-familiar and carefree life aboard the ship. The view of a game in progress on a lower deck turns into a "brawl" and becomes a scene from her past in which she witnessed a black man being beaten up in the street by policemen. The "thud" of the quoits hitting the deck becomes "the sound of some blunt instrument repeatedly striking human flesh and bone" (56). Turning away only to see other passengers shooting clay pigeons, she fancies the targets are "something human and alive" (57), cruelly thrown overboard with undue violence. In her desperate flight from the scenes of horror that assail her, she brushes against an old man who appears to her as a "skeleton" (58). Like the runaway slave of Robert Hayden's poem that serves as the epigraph to this first section of the novel, Avey feels "hounded" by a "mob"—a term that indeed "inevitably call[s] up its modifier 'lynch'" (DeLamotte 94)—of white passengers, while the cue sticks, golf clubs, and sporting guns of the nearby crowd on the sports deck become real sticks, clubs, and guns.

By associating the *Bianca Pride* with the Middle Passage and racial violence, Marshall does not imply that white consumerist culture is in itself a modern form of slavery. As a number of critics have argued, the novel does not present, let alone condemn, Avey's pursuit of material security and middle-class comfort as "a sin" (DeLamotte 82) or "some unpardonable moral transgression" (Sandiford 382), but instead depicts it as an understandable and necessary act of self-preservation that nevertheless came at a high price. However, the novel does suggest Avey's unwitting complicity in a consumerist culture and an unequal society that was built on the exploitation of slaves and the symbolic, social, economic, and political oppression of black and colonized people. The Versailles Room, in which Thomasina insisted they should dine in order not to "[let] these white folks keep the best to themselves" (46), evokes not only the luxury of old France but also, as Avey's politically conscious daughter points out to her, the treaty that divided the Caribbean and put the islands—including Carriacou, which Avey will soon visit—under European control. The sugary parfait that makes Avey sick is another symbol of Europe's exploitation of its colonies and dominions, and the *Bianca Pride*, as its name itself indicates, is "huge, sleek, imperial, a glacial presence in the warm waters of the Caribbean" (16).[9] As another mindless consumer of the exotic, Avey participates in this act of cultural cannibalism and economic exploitation. Her initial impression of the cruise ship is reminiscent of that of the child narrator in "To Da-Duh," who stands in awe of the tall buildings and machines of her native New York and tries to make the beauties of her grandmother's Caribbean island seem slight in comparison. Although Avey readily admits to her own slightly childish admiration for the ship's "dazzling white steel," its turbines, console, and computer, she at first appears unwilling to question it, self-indulgently exclaiming that there is simply "no resisting it" (15).

What overthrows her initial enthusiasm and triggers her re-vision of her surroundings is the visitation of her dead great-aunt. The fact that she finds it impossible to eat the parfait that the other passengers relish and that she feels compelled to leave the ship suggests her confused sense that something is amiss and that, as Thomasina correctly though misguidedly suspects, "Somethin's behind this mess. Somethin' deep" (23). But if Avey feels "in the grip of a powerful hallucinogen—something that had dramatically expanded her vision," what this nascent double vision allows her to see at this point remains "beyond her comprehension" (59). Not really knowing what she is fleeing from, she thinks she is fleeing to the comfort of her suburban home in North White Plains, a place whose name echoes that of the *Bianca Pride*, and to her "familiar objects there, the sterling silver tea and coffee service on the buffet, her special crystal and china in the breakfront, the chandelier above the great oval table"—objects that depict a room not very different from the Versailles, with its "Louis XIV decor and wealth of silver and crystal on the damask-covered tables" (83, 46).

Remember the Good Times

Avey's escape does not go as planned, however. Having missed the only flight of the day leaving Grenada—another one in a series of misfortunes—Avey is forced to stay in a hotel in which the staff, furniture, and view are uncannily similar to those of the *Bianca Pride*. Like the ship, the hotel evokes a glacier, with its "towering structure of stark white concrete and glass done in a 'ski slope' design" that makes it look like "some transplanted Matterhorn" (80). Feeling the undigested lump of food again, she is "like someone in a bad dream who discovers that the street along which they are fleeing is not straight as they had believed, but circular, and that it had been leading them all the while back to the place they were seeking to escape" (82–83). She is quite right, of course; but she has yet to realize that the nightmare is not her recent crisis aboard the *Bianca Pride* but the last thirty years of her life. Now alone in her hotel room, she notes that "whatever rebel spirit" (83) compelled her to leave the cruise ship has now left her with only her doubts. This "rebel spirit" is both the part of her own psyche that somehow felt something was wrong with the cruise, and the ghost of Cuney, as the two forces were conflated through possession. If Cuney has indeed left her for now, Avey is soon visited by another spirit: her late husband.

Appearing to her on the balcony on which she took refuge from the overloaded emptiness of the room, the ghost startles her by asking, "What the devil's gotten into you, woman?" (87). Critics—including the few who read this apparition as a ghost—unanimously interpret these words as a rebuke for Avey's decision to leave the ship, thereby wasting a considerable amount of the precious money her husband worked himself to death to earn. This is indeed what Avey herself understands. However, it is significant that the ghost hardly speaks at all, and that it is Avey, through her focalization, who glosses his words for us. When he tells her, "You must want to wind up back where we started," she explains he means Halsey Street, the place where they lived as a young couple and family, and more generally a time of their lives that so traumatized Jay he would never name it but refer to it as "back where we started" or "back you know where" (88). However, Halsey Street is not only a cramped, cold apartment where they struggled to make ends meet through Avey's three pregnancies and Jay's regular and odd jobs; it is also a place where they shared love and complicity, sustained by a vibrant culture that tied them to a symbolic and actual community. Despite their difficulties and the decisions these compelled them to make to keep their family safe, it was a time when they lived in touch with their spirituality, when they felt what Amiri Baraka, in a poem that provides another of the book's epigraphs, calls "the strong nigger feeling" (8): a sense of cultural and spiritual wholeness and connection.

Whatever Jay's ghost actually means to tell her, his words and presence, like Cuney's call, have strong effects on Avey, sending her into another swirl of memories. The chaotic structure of this section of the novel mirrors the workings of Avey's memory, as she thinks back to both the hard and the good times. She—and the reader with her—loses track of time, "the years telescoping" as her mind goes "leapfrogging back" (143) over the last three decades, and more. Reality, dream, and memory blend to the point that it is no longer clear what is Avey's present reactions, what corresponds to the feelings she experienced in the past, and what is a figment of her imagination. The title of the section, "Sleeper's Wake," as well as the fact that the next section begins with Avey waking up as if from a dream, suggests that these thoughts take place in a trancelike state induced by possession. Like in her dream of Cuney and the sensations it triggered, Marshall continues using the technique of superimposition to contrast Avey's present life with what it used to be when she and Jay were younger, living in Halsey Street. She thinks back with nostalgia to their nightly ritual, when Jay would play blues records to recover from the fatigue of his two or three jobs. The sustaining power of the blues and the attentive reverence with which they listened to it starkly contrast with the lame, soulless "Begin the Beguine" that played in the dining room of the *Bianca Pride* as a background to the sound of silver spoons on crystal. While Avey felt ashamed when Thomasina joined a local dance during a previous cruise, there was a time when the "ridiculous dances" she and Jay staged in their living room were part of those "frivolous" (123) things that were nevertheless "of the utmost importance" (137). In her dream with Cuney she worried about ruining her shoes by walking across the mud field to Ibo Landing; in Halsey Street she would kick off her shoes as soon as she set foot on the "earth brown" floor of the apartment, "a rich nurturing ground" that reverberated music and "restored [her body] to its proper axis" (12). But even more important were "the times when it was just the two of them" (126), when she and Jay would tell each other, in ritualistic fashion, how the sight, touch, and taste of each other's bodies "felt like," when their bodies would speak "another kind of poetry" (127).

The effects of these "small rituals and private pleasures" (136) are expressed in the idiom of possession. The blues worked on Jay as a kind of "magic," a "special mojo" that allowed him to shed his tired skin so that "his body . . . would look as if it belonged to him again" (94). The black voices that emerged from the radio on Sundays were "like spirits ascending" (124). Even Sis, their first daughter, would sit "enthralled" (126), holding her breath, when Jay recited fragments of poems by Langston Hughes, Paul Laurence Dunbar, or James Weldon Johnson. Sex connected them not only to each other but to a whole "pantheon" (127) of African diaspora deities, including Erzulie, Yemoja, and Oya, who took residence in Avey's body. The sacred character of their sexuality and the description of Avey's orgasms as a "private miracle" during which she "gave the slip to her ordinary everyday self" (128) further associate these moments with a form of possession. Indeed, possession induces "a sense of security" and an increased capacity to "live one's desires and fantasies," as "the possessed individuals are actualizing themselves on a plane of reality more powerful, sacred, and meaningful than the everyday" (S. Walker 84). Possessed by these African deities and by the spirits of the great musicians and poets of the diaspora, Avey and Jay could re-possess themselves, and each other.

Indeed, possession not only effects individual fulfillment, but is also an essentially collective process. It requires that the devotees feel "a part of the all" (S. Walker 97), that is, understand their place and role in the community and their interdependence with the other members that compose it. Possession both requires and affects community, in that it is at once "built upon group solidarity" and "a promoter of this social solidarity" (98). It is therefore no coincidence that during the years they perform rituals that make them feel in touch with themselves and with each other, Avey and Jay are also well integrated in their community. Avey's engagement as a union organizer indicates her social and political consciousness. Their reverence for the great blues singers and writers of the diaspora inscribes them in what Equiano called "a nation of dancers, musicians, and poets" (34). They often go dance in Harlem, and they regularly see their friends, even after they have left their old neighborhood for Brooklyn. Their yearly trips to Tatem and Ibo Landing also keep them connected to Avey's family history and give Jay, who does not have such family connections of his own, a sense of belonging.

The various levels on which these activities sustain Avey and Jay also suggest they function as redressive practices. Although Hartman does not mention possession as a form of redress, the similarities between the two ritualistic forms are evident. Just as slave dances and other forms of performance "aimed at relieving the pained body through alternative configurations of the self and the redemption of the body as human flesh, not beast of burden," Jay and Avey find in their own rituals a way to ease the pain of a day's work and reconstitute the sense of self and agency violated and dislocated by debilitating living conditions.[10] Through music, dance, poetry, and sex, they reconfigure their bodies "into a site of pleasure, a vessel of communication, and a bridge between the living and the dead" (Hartman, *Scenes of Subjection* 77). In calling on a long tradition of music and poetry, reenacting the dances of the past—the Tatem Ring Shout that Avey saw her great-aunt perform, itself a reenactment of the Ibos' shuffle—and invoking the gods of Africa, their rituals also counter a much broader and older experience of dislocation by re-membering the diasporic body. However, as I suggested in my analysis of similar redressive moments in *Feeding the Ghosts*, redress is defined as much by its necessity as by its inevitable failure, as those breaches can be re-membered but cannot be undone. For Hartman, this incompleteness precisely explains the repetitive character of redressive practices. While Avey and Jay persistently reenact their rituals every night to temporarily restore their physical, social, and cultural integrity, these rituals cannot in themselves change the actual conditions that break their bodies and their community.

As soon as they leave the protected space of their bedroom or living room, their vibrant, playful personalities give way to the very different public selves they must show to the white world. Jay particularly feels compelled to put on a mask to make his life easier in a tough, racist world, playing the good black worker who makes no trouble, does the job of two people, and does not complain about his incompetent boss getting all the credit and money. "[L]et them only see us, while / We wear the mask," wrote Paul Laurence Dunbar, a poet who is part of Jay's repertoire and who Marshall acknowledges as one of her earliest and primary influences ("From the Poets" 632). More than a protection for Jay, Avey also sees his mask as a veil behind which his true, passionate self—which only she is entitled to see—remains safely out of view, notably from the salesgirls that she thinks covet him. This aspect of the mask can be read in relation to the collective function it serves in African cultures, in which "the mask is a vehicle for the primary evocation of a complete hermetic universe, one of force or being, an autonomous world, marked both by a demonstrably interior cohesion and by a complete neutrality to exterior mores and norms." In other words, by creating a boundary between the inside and the outside, the mask serves a cohesive function as it "effects the 'spiritual consolidation' of the race" (Gates, *Figures in Black* 168). In that sense, the mask Jay wears at work seems not only to cover his and Avey's private life but also to "re-cover, in an almost mystical sense, [the] self-contained, virtually autonomous world" (169) of their cultural, spiritual, and intimate existence.

At first, under the soothing effect of the blues, Jay drops the mask as soon as he gets home. But eventually, after years of his exhausting and unsuccessful attempts to better his family's situation, the mask turns out to be all that anyone, including Avey, is given to see. The "clenched and dogged look" Jay had to adopt in his job seeking and professional training "marathon" (115) slowly becomes his sole expression. Before, in Avey's view, her husband's face "mirrored everything she felt" (90); now, not only has he come to constantly wear the mask, but his face has become the mask. Avey notices that his face has become that of a "pallid" stranger "superimposed" on his face "as in a double exposure" (131). This ghost image, this mask of death—which he will indeed keep after his death—clearly evokes the extreme to which Jay's efforts to improve his family's condition lead him: what he commits is nothing short of spiritual suicide. More precisely, by being compelled to work three jobs that never even allow him to advance himself, and by progressively abandoning all the social, cultural, and spiritual nourishment that used to give his life meaning, Jay is slowly turned into a mere commodity. That he becomes one even in Avey's eyes is confirmed by her description of everything he worked himself to death to possess—the house, insurance policies and annuities, and all the money that became hers after his actual death—as "the whole of his transubstantiated body and blood" (88). His forced self-subjection to a capitalist system that does not reward black people equally is so complete that it turns him into a zombi.

Jay's transformation is indeed an extreme example of the fragmentation of the self enforced by zombification. His mind has been so severed from his body that it seems to have dissolved and disappeared, leaving only an empty shell. But his body itself also appears to have broken apart, so that the elements that compose it are animated individually. His face, more particularly, has taken a life of its own—if life can be used to qualify this existence. In a rather gothic evocation of his corpse as she perceives it at his funeral, Avey thinks she can hear, "in the midst of his immutable silence, the sound of *its* mirthless, triumphant laughter . . . through the high nave of the church" (133, my emphasis). Not only can Avey hear this laughter emerge from Jay's dead body, but the impersonal pronoun, which refers to his face, indicates that the sound does not come from Jay but from this now independent and alienated part of his body. This face that she cannot bring herself to look at is not even his face but the mask she has often seen him wear, a mask that remains very much "alive" (133) even though Jay himself is dead.

The mask that has become Jay's face does not only signify his spiritual death or zombification. The symbol of the mask also clearly brings to mind Fanon's *Black Skin, White Masks* and what this book diagnoses as the pathological effects of racist and colonialist ideology. Marshall's description of Jay's fractured condition in both life and death indeed echoes Fanon's account of the dislocating effects of the white gaze on his own black body: "My body was given back to me sprawled out, distorted, recolored, clad in mourning in that white winter day" (113), Fanon writes; "completely dislocated" by the white man's gaze, "I took myself far off from my own presence, far indeed, and made myself as an object" (112). While Fanon puts much emphasis on the singular event that marked his first confrontation with "the fact of blackness," his account—which is really an account of trauma—insists in fact on the day-to-day debilitating effects of racism and colonialism on the black psyche. Similarly, if *Praisesong for the Widow* gives examples of single traumatic events, such as Avey and Jay's witnessing policemen beating up a black man, what the novel foregrounds is rather the more quotidian, insidious traumatic effects of a racist society that will not give black people the same opportunities.

Fanon is also helpful for articulating the relationship between the psychological and the material that is at the heart of Avey and Jay's transformation. If his analysis is a psychological one, Fanon insists that the psychological effects he describes are primarily the result of an economic reality; only subsequently do they result from the colonized subjects' internalization of their alleged inferiority. Avey and Jay's transformation—their putting on white masks—is not, at least not originally, motivated by a desire to be white. Even when he is constantly turned down by employers despite his "neat, personable, well-spoken" (113) demeanor and his qualifications, Jay does not seem to doubt his own worth or start internalizing the racial prejudice that underlies his failure to get a better job. However, these constant rejections and the economic insecurity in which they lock the family compel the Johnsons to progressively take their distance from the community and culture in which they used to find support. In Avey's retrospective view, the decisive moment in their transformation is when Jay, coming home late one night to be assaulted by his lonely and suspicious wife's questions and rebukes, compares her to the woman living down the block who trails her husband to the local bar to publicly accuse him of spending all their money on alcohol and women. The very embodiment of the destructive effects of poverty, overwork, and despair, the woman has come to represent for Avey and Jay an image of what they refuse to become, an image that they ward off by joking about it—until that one night when it all becomes too familiar to laugh. Tempted, for a brief moment, to leave Avey and save himself, Jay chooses to stay and takes it upon himself to get his family away from these people they have become too dangerously similar to.

They first move away symbolically and socially, by rejecting their former values and interests and ceasing to engage in their habitual activities; and later, when money finally permits, they move away geographically by buying a house in North White Plains. Not only do they stop going to Harlem and engaging in the fantasies that turned their small living room into a dance hall, but Jay even begins to view such leisurely activities and places as disreputable and distracting and to identify them as a part of the reason for black people's position on the social scale. He who so painfully learned that hard work, competence, and education do not necessarily mean success for a black man becomes ruthlessly critical of those who do not seem willing to sacrifice what he had to sacrifice for material security. Refusing to "blam[e] the white man for everything," he starts taking "his anger out on himself" and "out on his own" instead (135, 134), finally yielding to what Fanon describes as the "mutilations" (*Wretched of the Earth* 155) of an alienating society. His internalization of, or assimilation into, the "unsparing, puritanical tone" of the dominant white, racist discourse has become so complete that even his voice sounds to Avey like that of another man, as if "someone . . . had slipped in when he wasn't looking and taken up residence behind his dark skin" (132, 131). Thus ventriloquized, Jay now speaks of these "proverbial niggers" as if they were "a race apart" (45, 140). Such talk dramatically contrasts with the "Vaudeville-like jokes which they sprinkled like juju powders" to protect themselves from the fate embodied by the woman down the block: "Oh-oh, here come your folks again, Jay," Avey would tease him, watching the woman and her no-good husband in their usual squabble; to which he would reply "*My folks?* Who told you I was colored, woman? I'm just passing to see what it feels like" (107). While Jay is not passing in the usual sense of the term, he has now fully endorsed the white mask "of customs and values, of norms and languages, of aesthetic standards and religious ideologies" (Gubar 38).

As Jay and Avey take their distance from the community, their relationship as a couple is also affected. They no longer engage in the activities and playful exchanges that nourished their bond. Sex also loses its fulfilling power, as it becomes marred with a constant concern over more undesired pregnancies that would only worsen an already precarious economic situation. Avey on some level registers her estrangement from her husband, as she notices that she no longer thinks of him as the lively, playful Jay, but as Jerome, his bitter, sinister alter ego. She even starts imagining that her husband really did leave that fateful night after all, and that what remained is only this shadow of the man Jay used to be. Paradoxically, despite their estrangement they somehow grow more and more alike, as their friends start pointing out. Avey realizes that she has also started to think of herself as "Avey Johnson" in "the same formal way" (141). Over time she also got a mask of her own, as she started holding in the bottom lip she used to let appear to show her displeasure. This "held-in lip" has "become a permanent part of her expression over the years" (28)—until it suddenly reappears when she decides to leave the *Bianca Pride*. When earlier she would have vehemently protested, she has "developed a special silence" she uses with anyone, including her daughter and her friends, who says something "unpleasant" (14) to her.

This refusal to speak or engage in conflicts may seem like indifference, but it is the result of a defensive reaction to racial violence. Confronted everyday with stories and pictures of black victimization, Avey begins to act—or precisely to *not* act—as if violence and racism "did not pertain to her"; she even resents her daughter's political engagement because it makes "denying her [own] rage" (140) more difficult. Only able to see her community as victims, she thinks the best way to escape victimization is to leave that community by putting on a mask of respectability and white values, and then moving to the suburbs. The story of the Ibos, the foundational story of resistance to white violence and domination she used to know by heart, becomes "some far-fetched story of people walking on water which she in her childish faith had believed till the age of ten," and a story she now feels she has to "rid herself of" (42). Her private summer trips to Tatem with Jay stop, and are replaced by a company outing to the Laurentians, where Jerome can network with his white colleagues. Whereas Ibo Landing was a site of memory celebrating the ancestors, the Laurentians, which call to Avey's mind the practice among Eskimos of banishing their elders on the ice to die alone, signify the severing of family and more largely community connections. Thus, while she is troubled by the pale-faced man her husband has become, Avey's transformation has been just as profound and dramatic, as she suddenly comes to realize when confronted with her husband's ghost. And the pale face she starts punching on the hotel balcony in an outburst of rage is only a mirror image of her own.

In her discussion of *Praisesong for the Widow*, DeLamotte wonders at the "warmth with which some white readers have greeted a novel that may appear quite safely focused on a criticism of African Americans for aspiring to too much material prosperity" (97). Indeed, when Avey, in her trancelike state, repeatedly screams "*Too much!*" at the end of the book's second section, her outcry may be taken to signify her belated revolt at her own burial under what the minister of her childhood's church—who will appear to her in a later vision—calls "the shameful stone of false values, of gimme gimme gimme and more more more" (201). However, what she rejects is not this quest for material security, or even the values it compelled her and Jay to endorse, so much as the price they had to pay for it: the "death and burial," as Fanon calls it, of their "cultural originality" (*Black Skin* 18); the loss of their self-worth and of their empathy for their own people; their estrangement from each other and from themselves. The title of the novel's second section, "Sleeper's Wake," therefore carries a double meaning, pointing both to Avey's awakening after years of spiritual stupor and to her long-delayed wake for her late husband, and for their former life. Although he has been dead for several years, Avey has been unable to properly mourn her husband because all she could remember of him was the man with a "pale and shadowy" face superimposed on his, lying in a "cream-colored satin" coffin (132), in "the white lambskin apron and the white gloves" (87) that identified him as a Master Mason. The man she finally starts mourning after this second visitation is not Jerome, but Jay: Jay died long before Jerome, but she could not honor his memory because she thought such nostalgia would be "a betrayal. A sin against the long, twelve-year struggle" (122) to take them out of Halsey Street, a struggle in which Jay almost literally killed himself, and spiritually did.

However, by dissociating Jay from Jerome, by finally mourning Jay and further banishing Jerome to the limbo of forgetting, Avey also consigns their disastrous choices to the past, so that she can only grieve over what they "could have done" (139). Her violent outburst against the ghost of Jerome, which she starts punching—as she did with Cuney—as the incarnation of their demise, shows that her anger and frustration are still misdirected and that she is not yet ready to incorporate her visions into her present, let alone her future. The stunned state in which she falls asleep and wakes up the next morning confirms her inability or unwillingness to come to terms with the possession and the emotions it aroused. The fact that she leaves the hotel forgetting her watch, pocketbook, and hat seems to suggest she is on her way to stripping herself of the trappings of white materialist culture; yet the beginning of the novel's third section continually emphasizes her lack of awareness and conscious choice in these moves. As she walks farther and farther away from the hotel on the beach, she feels "the caul over her mind lifting" and starts "looking around her" (154). This reference to the caul associates her state with that of a newborn, an association that permeates the first pages of this section of the novel; but it also introduces a significant element in African diaspora culture, in which people born with a caul are traditionally thought to be gifted with second sight and the ability to see ghosts. The fact that she feels the caul "lifting" thus implies that she is actually losing what enabled her visions the night before. Still in the initial, "wild" phase of possession, she will need the guidance of an initiate to make sense of her visions and fully and consciously embrace her cultural re-possession.

Enter Papa Legba

She finds this guide in the person of Lebert Joseph, an old man she meets on the beach while she is desperately looking for a refuge from the heat. Lebert not only helps Avey interpret her dream of her great-aunt and understand why spirits have been tormenting her, but also persuades her to go on an excursion that will allow her to complete her initiation. As Lebert answers Avey's questions about the excursion to Carriacou, for which she saw many out-islanders leaving and for which he is preparing to go himself, he actually offers an explanation for all the discomfort and disturbing events she has been experiencing. The main reason for which he and the other Carriacouans return to their island once a year is, he tells her,

> "The Long-time People. Each year this time they does look for us to come and give them their remembrance.
>
> "I tell you, you best remember them! . . . If not they'll get vex and cause you nothing but trouble. They can turn your life around in a minute, you know. All of a sudden everything start gon' wrong and you don' know the reason. You can't figger it out all you try. Is the Old Parents, oui. They's vex with you over something. Oh, they can be disagreeable, you see them there.

> Is their age, oui, and the lot of suffering they had to put up with in their day. We has to understand and try our best to please them . . ." (165)

Lebert's account of what happens when people do not give the dead "their remembrance" strikingly corresponds to what has recently been happening to Avey. In her own admission, until two nights earlier she had not thought about her great-aunt for a very long time. Her life has indeed been "turned around in a minute," as a result of the dream in which a particularly "vex" and "disagreeable" Cuney caused "trouble" for a reason Avey is still trying to figure out.

However, Avey does not make sense of most of what the man says at this point, and fails to see any connection with the recent events. Her first reaction to his "bizarre" talk is to wish for the return of the "saving numbness" (166) to which she awoke that morning. She dismisses his description of the ritual of remembrance as "voodoo," an association that is ironically quite right, although her disparaging notion of voodoo has little to do with the vodou rituals the novel describes.[11] Significantly, her conclusion that the old man must be mad mirrors the judgment she has been expecting people to have of herself since the beginning of her troubles. She is even more confused when Lebert includes *her* in the cultural traditions he describes: after explaining the nation dance that is part of the Big Drum and identifying himself as a Chamba, the old man asks her, "And what you is?" He then explicates his question to a dumbfounded Avey with another question that she finds just as incomprehensible: "What's your nation?" (166). The list of suggestions—Arada, Cromanti, Yarraba, Moko, Temne, and the rest—makes no more sense to her. As she did when confronted with the out-islanders that seemed to mistake her for one of them when she landed on Grenada, she reasserts her essential difference by defensively answering that she is "a visitor, a tourist, just someone here for the day" (167).

Yet she is not completely insensitive to the old man's ramblings, and is even forced to acknowledge a certain familiarity with some of the cultural elements he mentions. She vaguely recognizes the sound of the nation names as "hav[ing] something to do with Africa" (167), and thinks she has heard or read about the juba dance; she is moved when he sings the tragic song of the Bongo man, the slave sold away from his wife and children, and empathizes with his own grief at losing his grandchildren, who moved to the United States and who, like Avey, do not know their nation. Most importantly, she is strangely compelled to open herself to him, and is surprised to suddenly hear herself telling him much of what has been happening to her. As he sits silently listening to her, she realizes that he knows it all already, that he has the power to see through her, that he has "*Li gain connaissance*" (172). This ability the narrator recognizes in Lebert clearly associates him not only with the other Carriacouans Avey saw on the wharf, whose eyes also seemed to see through the trappings of white materialist culture that she wore and recognize her as one of their own, but also with the Ibos, who had the similar ability to "see in more ways than one" (37).

This association with African ancestors is reinforced by the description of Lebert's wrinkled face as bearing "the scarification marks of a thousand tribes," and his tempered body as having "the essentials to go on forever" (161). The impression of immortality the man gives Avey, as well as the way he looks extremely old and lame at times, and young and swift at other times, further identifies him as an ancestral figure. Like Cuney, he embodies both the ancient wisdom and the resilience of the ancestor. His affiliation with Avey's great-aunt is also heightened in the way he interacts with Avey, the mix of gentleness and firmness with which he reaches out to her and his repeated injunctions that she "must come" with him to Carriacou. When Avey finally agrees to go with him, she feels "as exhausted as if she and the old man had been fighting—actually, physically fighting" (184), as she did after her dream with Cuney. Though not a spirit himself, Lebert clearly has a close connection with the spiritual world. His gift of second sight, the energy he deploys despite his old age, and his apparently incoherent ramblings suggest he is possessed. But his is a state of perpetual possession: no longer needing a spirit to possess him, he possesses himself. Empathizing with Avey for her lack of cultural connection, he is eager to share his condition with her by serving as her *houngan*.

Lebert is not only an initiate who can guide Avey through the ritual of possession: many details also clearly associate him with the African diaspora spirit Legba. Also variously called Elegba, Esu, or Esu-Elegbara, Legba is a prominent figure that appears across cultures in West Africa, South America, the Caribbean, and the United States. A trickster figure, Lebert/Legba seems to constantly shift shape, putting on an "endless array of personas," appearing at times like a "crippled dwarf of a thousand years" (243) walking with a stick and at other times taller and endowed with the vigor and grace of a young man. He even at times appears as a woman, such as when he sings the song of the Bongo with the voice of a "grief-stricken mother" or performs the juba dance with "a noticeably feminine tone" and gestures, holding and snapping his imaginary skirt (177, 179).[12] It is no coincidence, then, that once on Carriacou, Avey herself feels that Lebert "tricked her into coming on the excursion" (230). Also known as the guardian of crossroads, Legba is "the point where doors open or close, where persons have to make decisions that may forever after affect their lives" (Thompson 19). Lebert meets Avey at a symbolic crossroads, where she can either fly home to the safety and familiarity of North White Plains, or take a detour through Carriacou to her cultural heritage; and later when she meets him on Carriacou on the night of the Big Drum, he will be waiting for her at an actual crossroads.

In *The Signifying Monkey*, Henry Louis Gates Jr. views Legba as a prominent example of the myths and metaphysical systems that the Africans who survived the Middle Passage carried within them to the New World (4–6). As the spirit of the crossing, he is in fact directly linked to the Middle Passage and its limbo space, and to the spider-god Anancy, whose moves the limbo dance evokes.[13] Legba is also the keeper of the door between the world of the living and that of the spirits, having a foot in each. Lebert's description as an old man with one leg shorter than the other is thus also clearly reminiscent of this intermediary position between the two realms. As the "gatekeeper between the worlds of Ginen [Guinée, Africa] and Haiti" (Murphy 39), Legba is the master of ceremonies in vodou rites, and the first spirit to be invoked. Lebert is thus the "Papa Legba" of the epigraph to the third section of the novel, who "opens the gates" for Avey. The title of that section, "Lavé tête," refers to the stage in Haitian vodou ceremonies during which the devotee's head is "'washed' to remove impurities and resistance" (Mitchell 112) as a preparation for becoming the receptacle of a possessing spirit. Lebert, as both *houngan* and Legba, instructs Avey on the path to *konesans* by helping her let go of her resistance against the changes she feels taking place in her. Significantly, after speaking to him, Avey feels the caul "clos[ing] over her mind again" (172): after the numbness she felt when she woke up that morning, which prevented her from consciously engaging with what she had been experiencing over the last couple of days, she is now getting ready to *see*.

The Middle Passage

And indeed, during the short boat trip to Carriacou, Avey is able—though still not quite consciously—to see beyond the immediate reality and make connections with other phenomena and memories from her personal and cultural past. Even before she boards the schooner, the wharf filled with its busy and colorful crowd offers a view that is somehow familiar to her.

It first reminds her of pictures of a ceremony in Ghana she saw in a film her daughter Marion made during one of her trips to Africa, a ceremony in which the rulers and people honor their ancestors and revive their unity as a community. Significantly, Avey registers this without the mild irritation and bewilderment that generally characterize her thoughts about her daughter's interest in African cultures. In contrast to her previous exasperation at being mistaken for a local, she even makes a connection between the scene before her eyes and a scene from her own past. Conjuring a memory from her childhood, she recalls how her family would go on the Hudson River to the park of Bear Mountain on an annual trip organized by the Harlem neighborhood social club. The superimposition of the Hudson trip on the crossing to Carriacou throws into relief something Avey only unconsciously feels at that moment: she remembers how, as a child, she spied her parents dancing on the deck of the boat, and realized that she and her siblings were both literally and metaphorically born of such intimate and loving moments. On that scene is superimposed a third one, the Ring Shout she witnessed as a girl in Tatem and correctly interpreted as another important moment of communion. From those events she remembers the connection she felt with all the people around her, even the "disreputable" ones who would always cause a fight—those "proverbial niggers" Jerome would much later despise and complain about. She imagines this organic bond as "threads streaming out from her" (190) and entering the people around her. This umbilical cord of sorts and the broader metaphor of the web symbolize her early, but later on repressed, consciousness of a not only familial but more largely communal affiliation. Feeling part of a "confraternity" (191)—in contrast, perhaps, to the historically white male Freemason fraternity of which Jerome was a member—the young Avey thinks they are all going together on a voyage much more significant than a boat trip to Bear Mountain, something "momentous and global" (192) whose meaning nevertheless eludes her.

While the adult Avey is aware, as she boards the *Emanuel C* with Lebert, that the out-islanders who have already taken their place on the schooner are similarly engaged in something both "festive" and "solemn" (187), she does not consciously include herself in that experience as anything but an outsider, a guest, a witness. Even when, with "a shock of recognition," she sees in three elderly women the "presiding mothers" of her childhood church, she does not linger on the obvious similarities between the rituals of her childhood and the cultural phenomenon in which she is now taking part. Similarly, although she acknowledges that her mind somehow made a "connection" (196) between the patois she heard when the *Bianca Pride* called in Martinique, the patois she now hears on the *Emanuel C*, and the patois she used to hear in Tatem, she still does not link the excursion with her own cultural heritage. Watching and listening to the out-islanders, the only conscious connection she allows herself to make between them and her is their shared excitement as the schooner leaves the harbor and sets sail for Carriacou.

As if to force her to make these connections, a new vision seizes her while aboard the schooner. Triggered by the superimposition of the presiding mothers on the Carriacouan women, the vision takes the form of a dream-memory that so intensely possesses Avey that dream and reality, past and present, fuse. As the two time-spaces of the schooner and of the church of her childhood conflate, it becomes impossible to say whether it is the rocking of the boat on the treacherous channel that conjures the nausea the young Avey fights in the church, or whether the memory of the intense sermon and the chocolate egg she ate before Sunday class causes her body to react in the present. Proving to a dramatically ironic extent Murphy's point that "discomfort [is] a necessary ingredient in the instruction" of the *lavé tête* (22), Avey experiences the bodily effects of possession as she uncontrollably empties her stomach and bowels. Like on the *Bianca Pride*, what was at first only a cause for curiosity or vague concern becomes, in her physical agony, unbearable: the foreign but obviously kind words of the women become an indistinct whisper in her ear; the pleasantly unfamiliar character of the boat on the sea turns into a bewildering and threatening experience; and the "small multitude" (193) that crowds the deck becomes an unbearably close and overwhelming presence from which she cannot get away. Disoriented, surrounded by a mass of people who speak in tongues both familiar and incomprehensible on a vessel on which she feels trapped and anxious, Avey is once more connected with the captives of the Middle Passage, her shipmates. But it is only when she is taken inside the deckhouse and has another vision that she makes this connection herself. Although she is alone, "she had the impression as her mind flickered on briefly of other bodies lying crowded in with her in the hot, airless dark. A multitude it felt like lay packed around her in the filth and stench of themselves, just as she was. Their moans, rising and falling with each rise and plunge of the schooner—the depth of it, the weight of it in the cramped space—made hers of no consequence" (209). Concluding the third section of the novel, this passage conveys Avey's "dimming consciousness" (207) of not only her connection with a collective past, but also of her duty toward those who came, and suffered, before her. Directly following this episode, the title of the next section, "The Beg Pardon," announces her eventual engagement in giving these and other dead their remembrance.

It takes Avey some time to fully integrate the embodied memories that the schooner episode triggered, partly because they leave her in a daze that lasts a few hours after she is disembarked in Carriacou and put to bed like an infant. It will require the expert hands of Rosalie, Lebert's daughter, to put her "back together again" (229). Rosalie not only shares her father's "special powers of seeing and knowing" (218), which identify her as an initiate and therefore another guide for Avey on the path to *konesans*; like Lebert, she is also a shape-shifter who seems to become, in Avey's confused perception, "any number of different people over the course of the night" (217), including Avey's mother and her great-aunt, as well as the nurse who looked after her when she gave birth to her three daughters. These three important nurturing female figures in her child and adult life are superimposed on Rosalie, whose firm but gentle treatment of Avey's body transports her through time and space. Significantly, the woman closes Avey's eyes before she starts bathing her, as if to allow her to see in other ways. The smell of soap and the soft sound of water in the galvanized tub brings her back to when she was a child in Tatem bathing in her great-aunt's tub; the way Rosalie stretches her limbs reminds her of the way she nursed her own daughters, creating a continuity through generations. When the woman finally turns her attention to the flesh of her thighs, grown "sluggish" from being girdled and untouched, Avey experiences an awakening that turns into orgasm, a "sense of a chord being struck" (224) and reverberating throughout her body, just as when she was with Jay.

In many ways this scene brings to mind Baby Suggs's bathing of Sethe after her escape from Sweet Home, tending to a body broken much more by the violation of slavery and the price she paid for running away—the chokecherry tree on her back, her "unrecognizable feet" (*Beloved* 93)—than by the delivery of Denver. Like Rosalie, Baby Suggs bathes Sethe "in sections," thereby putting her back together. When Paul D returns to 124 after his violent rejection of her, a broken Sethe wonders if he will know how to bathe her in this way, and if "the parts [will] hold" (272). Rosalie's massage thus functions as a moment of redress, as it reconnects Avey not only to her body, by rekindling physical sensations she had long forgotten, but also to the social body, by reactivating her spiritual connections with significant people in her life. This social body here remains limited in her consciousness to her close family—her mother, her great-aunt, her husband, and her children—but the novel again gestures toward a broader, older community she is still unaware of. Taking place right after her own Middle Passage, and after her vision of a slave ship's hold in the deckhouse of the *Emanuel C*, Avey's bathing is reminiscent of the way the African captives were washed and oiled before landfall in America. But while the captives were tended to in order to mask or attenuate the toll the voyage had taken on their bodies and make them more attractive for the slave market, Marshall here reconfigures this moment as one of pleasure.[14]

Joining the Circle

For her initiation to be complete, Avey has yet to reconnect with this larger community, by participating in a collective ritual. This happens progressively, as what she originally saw as an unbridgeable distance between herself and the behavior, practices, and identities of the Carriacouans continues to shrink. Seeing for herself the ritual feeding of the Old Parents in Rosalie's house, Avey realizes that what seemed unquestionably foreign and exotic in the description made by a "senile" (167) old man is in fact not very different from the familiar wake rituals of her childhood in Tatem. The textual and actual juxtaposition of the plate of food that lies on the buffet as an offering to the Old Parents and the plate of food that is placed on the table in front of Avey further confirms the non-supernatural character of this tradition by marking the proximity of the dead and the living. According to Mbiti, in African cultures "libation and the giving of food to the departed are tokens of fellowship, hospitality and respect; the drink and food so given are symbols of family continuity and contact" (9). This continuity is suggested in the term "living-dead," which Mbiti prefers to "ancestors" or "ancestral spirits," in order to convey the fact that the departed are very much "'alive' in the memories of their surviving families, and are thought to be still interested in the affairs of the family to which they once belonged in their physical life" (104). After Avey's experience of the visitation of her great-aunt and husband as an invasion, the cultural practices that are still so much a part of the everyday life of the Carriacouans now remind her not only that her conception of the relationship between the living and the dead is only one among others, but also that other conceptions might indeed be more sustaining. The dead plagued her because she failed to remember them, as Lebert obliquely informed her; rather than refusing and quite literally fighting—with her mind and body—the presence of the dead in her life, she would gain by welcoming them and opening herself to what they have to tell and show her about herself. Only by acknowledging and taking her place in that circle will she heal the emptiness she has recently identified at the center of her life.

The Big Drum marks the climax of Avey's initiation. This collective ritual confirms the fundamentally communal nature of possession: with Lebert/Legba as master of ceremony and Rosalie's maid, Milda, as initiate-interpreter, Avey finds herself responding to the ritual and naturally drawn into it. Keeping to the edge of the circle at first, watching attentively and listening to Milda's explanations, she begins to make conscious connections between the social, cultural, and spiritual significance the Big Drum holds for the participants and her own memory, history, and identity. The first dimension she identifies, as well as personally experiences, is the link the ritual creates between the living and the dead. Derived, like the Ring Shout, from the circle rituals that were an integral part of West African religions and cultures, the circular movement of the dance and the continuous track left by the performers' shuffle symbolize the unbroken connection with their ancestors (Stuckey 11). Not only do the dancers and drummers, Lebert the first among them, call to the spirits by honoring them, but the spirits actually join the dance. These spirits include the Old Parents, the dancers' kin, but also more distant ancestors that the ceremony "draws up . . . from their homes in Africa" (Murphy 28). In Murphy's description, the function of such ceremonies thus goes well beyond the proximate temporal and spatial borders of the community: they bring the past into the present and the distant into the immediate circle by actualizing and opening access to Africa in the here and now, so that "in the construction of the space of ceremony and in the limited time bounded by the ceremony's opening and closing, the people may enter an African space and time." The ceremonial space—whether it is a church, an open field outside a church, or Lebert's backyard—"can be recognized to be Africa," whereas the time that extends from the rhythms and music "becomes the time of the ancestors who are contemporary in the bodies and minds of the people" (186) involved in the ceremony. While watching the Beg Pardon, Avey feels the presence of her great-aunt in Milda, who is standing next to her. When she finally joins the dance and naturally falls into the shuffle that reproduces the Ring Shout of her childhood, she finds herself once again "standing beside her great-aunt on the dark road across from the church" in Tatem (248).

If the dance brings Avey back to Tatem, or Tatem back to Avey, it also actualizes a more distant past beyond her own memory. As she glides forward "as if the ground under her was really water," her shuffle mirrors and honors the walk of the Ibos back to Africa. When Lebert proudly exclaims he knew "she wasn't the kind to let a little rough water get the better of her" (248), he refers of course to the painful crossing to Carriacou, which she experienced as her own Middle Passage, but also situates her in the lineage of these African ancestors. Avey has "finally after all these decades made it across" (248): she has at last joined the Tatem Ring Shout that was forbidden to her because of her great-aunt's (self-) exclusion; she has crossed the line that separated her from the circle of the initiates; but, more fundamentally, she has made it across the waters, like the Ibos, and returned "home" to her African diasporic culture. In vodou ceremonies and diasporic traditions more generally, the ability to see Africa ("Ginen") in the here and now, and to "'see' simultaneously the spiritual and human worlds" (Murphy 192), are signs that the initiate has attained a higher level of *konesans*. Avey's sight has changed so dramatically that she now not only sees the connection between the Big Drum and other ceremonies like the Ring Shout and her own Halsey Street dance rituals with Jay, but also sees Africa, the ancestors, and herself as part of one temporal and spatial circle. By placing herself literally and symbolically in the circle with her ancestors, both the direct and the more distant ones, she finally takes her place in a cultural community.[15]

The participants in the Big Drum, like the greater crowd of out-islanders on the wharf in Grenada, looked all along at Avey with "eyes which refused to see any differences" (235) between her and them. But it is only at the end of her initiation that she finally and fully acknowledges her familiarity with them. The "tangible feeling of togetherness" that anthropologists have largely attested as one important function of the Big Drum (McNeil 192) is notably based on the way the bodies and minds of the participants dancing to the rhythm of the drums are "attuned, so that they may share the same *konesans*" (Murphy 42). This connection through *konesans* is symbolized in the novel through the recurrence of the metaphor of the threads: this time, however, the threads do not stream out only from the people's navels and hearts, but also from their eyes. Conflating the physical bond she felt as a child with her newly acquired *konesans*, this image also marks the climax of the experience of possession in the dissolution of boundaries between self and other, as all the participants are organically connected. This communion is confirmed when the other Carriacouans, Lebert and Rosalie leading the way, respectfully bow to a bewildered Avey.

The novel's title therefore means, as DeLamotte notes, "both a praisesong for the widow to sing—a fellowship of voice in which to merge her isolated self—and also a song of praise *for herself*" (111). An African traditional heroic poem, the praisesong is usually sung in the context of rites of passage to "mark social transition . . . from one group to the next" (Busia 198). This transition is signaled by Avey's self-identification at the end of the ceremony as "Avey, short for Avatara" (251), a name that is suggestive of all the dimensions of her transformation. Renaming is an important part of spirit possession, as "the old meanings," associated with the "master," are "questioned, replayed, kicked around, and, finally, dismissed" (Dayan 72). In the process, "the self is also liberated from normal conventions and societal and economic constraints" (68). In dropping the formal and distancing "Johnson," Avey signifies her reclamation of the vibrant personality that characterized her before she became "Avey Johnson" even to herself. In a key moment of the ceremony, Avey rejects Jerome's ventriloquized voice—*"If it was left to me I'd close down every dancehall in Harlem and burn every drum!"*—and follows instead Jay's self-possessed and loving appraisal of her ability to "out-jangle Bojangles and out-snake Snake Hips" (247, 123). In joining the dance, she does not only recover, by setting it into motion, the body that Rosalie contributed to re-enliven: she also reclaims the "stylishness and sass" (249) that used to characterize her.

By appending to her familiar name the reference to the first Avatara, who saw the Ibos come and leave, Avey not only acknowledges her genealogy but also symbolically accepts the mission with which her ancestor entrusted her by visiting Cuney in a dream and predicting Avey's birth: she will become a culture bearer, too. As an initiate "incorporat[ed] back into ordinary life with a new identity and vision" (Murphy 191), Avey is now ready to act as a guide for non-initiates. Acquiring double vision has allowed her not only to re-vision the past to integrate it in the present, but also to look to the future with confidence. Comparing herself to the Ancient Mariner, upon returning from her journey she plans to tell her tale to those who are still "unaware, unprotected, lacking memory and a necessary distance of the mind," in order to help them change their ways. Like a spirit, she will "haunt the entranceways of the skyscrapers," the "glacier buildings" (255) where cultural memory is left alone to die. She will take children to Tatem to show them Ibo Landing and continually and ritually tell them the story of the Ibos, like her great-aunt before her. This project, she thinks, will also help her reconnect with Marion, the child she had so desperately "tried to root from her body" (255), the daughter who has ironically always shown the greatest interest in, and respect for, her roots. Having mended both her ascending and descending lines, she will no longer be a genealogical isolate but will be anchored in a community of memory.

The Long Journey Home: Praisesong for the Widow *and Diasporic Identity*

This idealistic ending has given rise to criticism. Angelita Reyes views it as the culmination of an overly "romantic approach to history, myth, and social-political issues." Comparing *Praisesong for the Widow* with Morrison's *Tar Baby*—a novel that also addresses the issue of cultural continuity and spiritual reconnection and includes ghostly figures—Reyes praises the latter for its more sociopolitically realistic treatment of "the precarious relationship of myth and history" (193) and its author's uncompromising awareness that "historical reconnections are elusive for some" (194). Without denying the obviously hopeful conclusion of *Praisesong for the Widow*, which indeed contrasts with the more ambiguous and ambivalent ending of *Tar Baby*, I want to argue against a simplistic reading of Avey's journey. First, some elements in the last few pages of the novel, which relate the plans that form in Avey's mind as she leaves Carriacou, betray a certain degree of naïveté on her part. When read against earlier similar episodes in the novel, the validity of her projection and the flawless, everything-going-according-to-plan character of her new, enlightened life are cast in doubt. After all, her visualization of her escape from the *Bianca Pride*—finding a taxi as soon as she lands on Grenada, jumping on a plane to New York and comfortably sitting in her living room before the end of the day—could not have been more wrong. Her desire to tell her story to "those young, bright, fiercely articulate token few . . . rush[ing] blindly" (255) through New York streets might be similarly frustrated by their unwillingness to heed her, just as she was at first annoyed at Lebert's ramblings. And her decision to instruct her own grandchildren about the Ibos does not guarantee that they will listen to her with the same awe as she did her great-aunt, or that they will hold on to the story through their adult lives, since she did not.

Even if her initiation over the past three days may seem to ensure that her vision is now indeed better, other details suggest that the level of *konesans* she has reached is not ultimate or definitive. Possession is a dynamic and disturbing process that always somehow exceeds the comprehension of the possessed. After all, even those like Lebert who serve as models of *konesans* must reaffirm their connection to both the living and the dead and beg pardon for their failures every year. What my reading of the novel through possession suggested, but my linear analysis of the novel downplayed, is the rather chaotic movement of Avey's progression on the path to *konesans*: one step in the right direction is often followed by two steps backward, as what seem like profound realizations on her part turn into doubts or willful forgetting the next moment. Rather than marking "a journey's end, a mission accomplished" (Eko 143), the reaching of "the desired destination" (Pettis 1), or a full and simple "closing of the circle" (Collier)—formulations that all suggest *telos* and closure, two problematic notions, as I have argued—the end of the novel suggests the liminal or intermediary nature of Avey's condition and identity.[16] Her journey is therefore a (reversed) Middle Passage in the sense I defined in chapter 1: just as the effects of the Middle Passage persist long after the captives' landing in America, Avey's journey is far from over, and the life she has planned for her return to the United States might turn out to be more difficult than she thinks.

That Avey seems unaware of the long way that still lies ahead indeed casts a doubt on the success of her project. Her confidence in her new vision is contradicted by how quickly her individualist, unmindful ways actually return. She indulgently dismisses Lebert's proposition that her nation might well be Arada as one of those "things about her which could only be of his imagining" (253). Though largely justified by her understandable reluctance to endure another crossing by boat, the fact that she takes a plane back to Grenada sets her apart from the people she felt so close to the night before, few of whom could probably afford that mode of transportation. Money, as Carissa Turner Smith rightly points out, is strangely invisible throughout her journey (728 n. 4); financial considerations similarly do not seem to enter her plans to have not only her grandsons but also Marion's schoolchildren sent over to Tatem. Even more puzzling is her last view of Carriacou from the plane as "fleeting and ephemeral," an island that is "more a mirage rather than an actual place. Something conjured up perhaps to satisfy a longing and need" (254). Suddenly oblivious of the reality of the place and the people she met and whose hospitality, care, and sympathy she freely received, and in a way that disturbingly "echo[es] the superficiality of the tourist's experience" (Felix 91), Avey relegates them to backdrop and token roles in her own personal story.

Contradictory as it may seem, Avey's perception of Carriacou as somewhat ghostly, an elusive and transient presence that was conjured from some other realm, can also be read as actually pertaining to Marshall's conception of the process of cultural recovery. According to Brogan, who also points out the degree to which Avey's "startling observation" contrasts with the description of her "apotheosis" in the preceding chapter, this ghostly character is to be linked to the "imaginative faculty" (151) that is deployed in the process of cultural recovery and, more broadly, to the role of the "interplay of memory and imagination" at work in what she calls "ethnogenesis" (28). Brogan's discussion of the construction of ethnicity through the trope of haunting briefly refers to Hall's work on ethnicity, identity, and cultural memory. In what remains of this chapter I want to give Hall's insights a more central place, as they are helpful not only for analyzing Marshall's ambivalent approach to diasporic identity, but also for explaining the aptness of the ghost trope with respect to that particular aspect of the novel.

What's Your Nation?

Praisesong for the Widow oscillates between the two conceptions of cultural identity Hall offers in his essay "Cultural Identity and Diaspora." The first defines it

> in terms of one, shared culture, a sort of collective "one true self," hiding inside the many other, more superficial or artificially imposed "selves," which people with a shared history and ancestry hold in common. Within the terms of this definition, our cultural identities reflect the common historical experiences and shared cultural codes which provide us, as "one people," with stable, unchanging and continuous frames of reference and meaning, beneath the shifting divisions and vicissitudes of our actual history. This "oneness," underlying all the other, more superficial differences, is the truth, the essence, . . . of the black experience. It is this identity which a . . . black diaspora must discover, excavate, bring to light and express through [artistic] representation. (223)

Avey's repeated efforts to assert her difference from the people she encounters are constantly contradicted by these people's recognition of her as part of their community, however vague its contours may be; and they are finally overcome by Avey's own acknowledgment of her place in that community. The emphasis the novel puts on African diasporic people's common history, such as the references to the Middle Passage, and on shared cultural practices, like the Ring Shout and the various forms of circle rituals, unites these diverse people beyond their "other, more superficial differences" by tracing them to a single common point of origin, Africa. Recurring references to blood, family, and lineage throughout the novel suggest that cultural transmission functions in biological terms. Avey and Jay's rituals are imbued with qualities that she cannot fully account for but that she knows "sp[eak] from the blood." A part of "an ethos they h[o]ld in common," these qualities "join them to the vast unknown lineage that had made their being possible" (137) and that is somehow related to the color of their skin. Lebert, the narrator tells us, remembers Africa "from memories that had come down to him in the blood," and the sounds and rhythms of the Big Drum trigger in Avey a comparable "host of subliminal memories" (178, 245). This essential, biological link to Africa and to all its children scattered around the Atlantic may be obscured or forgotten, but it can, the end of the novel seems to suggest, always be reclaimed.

To read the end of the novel as univocally celebratory of this restorative possibility is, however, to overlook the profoundly ambivalent undertone of the Big Drum. While the ceremony is a "fete," a happy gathering and a celebration of past, present, and future communities, it is also underwritten by a "theme of separation and loss" (244). Lebert's drumming is not only joyous: it also "sound[s] like the distillation of a thousand sorrow songs." Conveying an "unacknowledged longing," it is a "lamentation" emerging from "the bruised still-bleeding innermost chamber of the collective heart" (245). It reminds the participants that the ritual they are engaged in is not only a celebration of the ancestors and of cultural, "national" unity: it is also a mourning, a respectful but painful tribute to an origin that was lost and can never really be recovered.[17] The Big Drum is an expression of what I described in chapter 1 as the dual significance of the Middle Passage as a moment of rupture and creation. Avey's perception of the ceremony as "the bare bones of a fete" (240) suggests this ambivalence: her disappointment at the crude simplicity of what she expected to be a grand ceremony reveals the distance that irremediably separates the Big Drum from its African origin; but her initial disappointment quickly turns into curiosity and respect for the ritual and the people engaged in it, as she understands that what she is witnessing is "the essence of something rather than the thing itself" (240). The "bare bones" are not the poor, sad remnants of a distant culture these people desperately try to hold on to, but a skeleton that they creatively flesh out with their own cultural needs and capacities (Rogers 92). Like Candle Walk in *Mama Day*, the Big Drum is both reenactment and creation. Memorializing a foundational act whose original content and meaning cannot be fully recovered, Candle Walk has evolved through generations to adapt to the needs and creativity of its participants, for whom it has nevertheless retained its "essence" as a moment of exchange and solidarity. Similarly, the Big Drum, like all diasporic cultural traditions, both depends for its meaning on its African antecedents and defines itself independently from, or even against, these antecedents (Murphy 178).

Ethnogenesis, Brogan argues, takes place largely through storytelling, through what she calls tales of cultural haunting. "The focus on storytelling," she notes, "shifts emphasis away from biological to adoptive models of cultural transmission" (18). Candle Walk and the Big Drum are not only rituals; they are also narratives. As such, they play a fundamental role in identity formation: by telling the story of Sapphira, albeit in a provisional, nonauthoritative way, Candle Walk participates in the construction of the collective identity of the people of Willow Springs; the Big Drum, with its successive episodes (the Beg Pardon, the nation dances, and the creole dances) even tells several stories in one, but as a whole tells the story of diaspora, from its rupture with Africa to its re-creation in myriad variations in the New World. Narratives of this kind are part of the way in which ethnicity is constructed (Hall, "Ethnicity" 348). The nation dance, like Candle Walk, is not only a performance; it is also performative. Despite Marshall's claim that the names of the nations have "been carefully passed down through the generations" (*Triangular Road* 144), the dances do not really evoke the authentic, original African nations from which the dancers are descended, but they rather *produce* these nations in their present forms.

The concept of nation so central to *Praisesong for the Widow* is therefore much more complex than it seems: when Marshall asks, through Lebert's insistent question, what Avey's nation is, she may be asking not so much who her African ancestors were—a question that cannot possibly be answered—but rather what the very notion of a distinguishable, coherent African ancestry might mean. Cultural practices like the Big Drum and Candle Walk do not "represent" a cultural identity, no more than that identity should be seen as "an already accomplished fact" (Hall, "Cultural Identity" 222). This second and, according to Hall, "much less familiar, and more unsettling" (226) understanding of cultural identity defines it as "a 'production,' which is never complete, always in process, and always constituted within, not outside, representation." African diasporic identity, or indeed identity in general, is thus the always unfinished result of a "continuous 'play'" between similarity and difference, continuity and rupture, with respect to origins, to other people, and to what one has been and will be. Rather than essential, transcending, and fixed, identities are a "matter of 'becoming' as well as of 'being'"; not only do they "have histories," but they also "undergo constant transformation" (225).

Phantom Africa

While Marshall has often insisted that "a spiritual return to Africa is absolutely necessary" for black people to "feel a sense of unity" and counteract the fragmentation that characterizes diasporic experience (J. Williams 53), the Africa evoked in *Praisesong for the Widow* is not that continent on the other side of the Atlantic but, in Glissant's words, "a source and a mirage" (*Poetics of Relation* 58). A presence that pervades diasporic consciousness and constantly returns when repressed, this phantom Africa is a spiritual, cultural, and political signifier, but a signifier whose meaning is, as Hall puts it, always "necessarily 'deferred.'"[18] This definition contrasts not only with the traditional western view that "normalizes and appropriates Africa by freezing it into some timeless zone of the primitive, unchanging past" ("Cultural Identity" 231), but also with the definition of cultural identity supported by movements like Négritude and Pan-Africanism, which, in response to the disfigurations and distortions of colonialist representations, sought to transcend diaspora's actual diversity and disunity through a mythical unitary origin (223–24).

This dynamic and unstable view of Africa is largely supported by the way *Praisesong for the Widow* troubles the notions of "home" and "roots," by never quite mapping one onto the other and never locating either in a single place. Significantly, it is not in Africa that Avey reclaims her African ancestry, but in the Caribbean. When, at the end of the novel, she resolves to share the experience of her journey through memory, it is not about Carriacou but about Halsey Street that she means to tell people. Having felt somehow at home in the Caribbean, she nevertheless returns to the United States, not to settle definitively in one place but to navigate between New York and Tatem. Rather than a source of confusion or schizophrenia, this lack of unity and fixity can be read as productive and sustaining. As Glissant suggests, an identity based on the unitary notion of roots is a source of suffering for the emigrant who feels split between a point of origin and a new point of anchor, two points that can never be reconciled (*Poetics of Relation* 143). Drawing on Gilles Deleuze and Félix Guattari, Glissant proposes the non-unitary image of the rhizome, or "submarine roots . . . floating free, not fixed in one position in some primordial spot, but extending in all directions in our world through its network of branches" (*Caribbean Discourse* 67). Avey's redefined identity at the end of the novel is a rhizomatic one, as is, in fact, Marshall's own identity.[19] Her work, as Lisa D. McGill points out, "does not displace an African American self for a Caribbean one; instead, it evokes and establishes the African American and Caribbean communities' relationship to each other" (73), a gesture that is also central to her activism. As a second-generation immigrant, Marshall resisted the pressures to choose between the Barbadian and the African American communities. Raised in Brooklyn, which she considered as home, she also grew up with her family and her community's evocations of that other home in Barbados, and it is this sense of doubleness that compelled her to explore these questions in her novels ("From the Poets" 629).

Marshall's visit to Barbados as a child, as I suggested at the beginning of this chapter, was crucial to her sense of identity, as was her much later visit to Africa (J. Williams 52). The importance of traveling is clear in *Praisesong for the Widow*, which, to the static and essentializing notion of roots, prefers the metaphor of the journey to highlight the unstable quality of identity, both individual and collective. Marshall's emphasis on a dynamic relation to an origin that is encountered and reenacted in diaspora through journeying thus also aligns her with Gilroy, for whom identity is not a matter of "roots" so much as "routes" (*Black Atlantic* 19). But if journey is a central metaphor in *Praisesong for the Widow*, the novel does not in fact suggest that physical mobility is itself necessary to, or indeed guarantees the success of, the reclamation of cultural identity. Before the cruise she decides to interrupt at the beginning of the novel, Avey had already been on several similar journeys and returned to North White Plains unchanged. In contrast, the closed space of their apartment in Halsey Street allowed Avey and Jay to "Take the A-Train" with Duke Ellington and see the rivers of the black world with Langston Hughes, or to go dance at the Savoy, the Rockland Palace, or the Renny without even leaving their living room. Significantly, while Avey makes connections throughout the novel between various kinds of grounds on which she somehow felt "centered and sustained" (254)—the wooden floor in Halsey Street, the mud field in Tatem, the dirt floor of Lebert's rum shop and that of his backyard on Carriacou—these fixed places are also characterized by the movement—the dances of all kinds—that they support.

This play between stability and movement suggests a tension, rather than an opposition, between roots and routes.[20] In *Praisesong for the Widow*, Marshall "revises an earlier definition of diaspora structured by a teleology of origin, scattering, and return" (Hayes 74); yet she does not do away with the notion of roots altogether—no more than do Hall, Gilroy, and other cultural theorists and writers from the 1980s on. Rather, her ambivalent treatment of roots can be identified as an act of "queering," in Jarrod Hayes's use of the term: while *Praisesong for the Widow* reads like a return narrative, it is a return narrative that "queer[s] the relation between diasporic identity and its roots by acknowledging [its] own fictionality" and "propos[ing] alternative, multiple roots that ground an identity based on . . . diversity." Produced as an effect of the narrative rather than existing prior to it, queer roots are, as Hayes puts it, "origins that are not original" (73). I introduce the notion of queer roots here as a step toward the next chapter, which focuses on Cliff's work. Indeed, if Marshall can be said to queer roots and diaspora in *Praisesong for the Widow*, she does so only in what Hayes would call "a rather abstract way": if she "bring[s] the narrative paradox out of the closet" (81), by showing that narratives of return construct the origin they claim to merely discover, she does not out the sexual paradox, insofar as she does not address the sexual normativity that underpins the concept of diaspora itself. The term "diaspora," as Stefan Helmreich has remarked, is etymologically and symbolically linked to paternity, as it "summons up the image of scattered seeds," a metaphor for "the male 'substance' that is traced in genealogical histories." In this respect, diaspora "refers us to a system of kinship reckoned through men and suggests the questions of legitimacy in paternity that patriarchy generates" (245). While Marshall does not in my view—except in rare and, to me, inexplicable occasions[21]—relate diasporic identity to a patriarchal or more generally male lineage, her evocation of diaspora as kinship or enlarged family nevertheless bears the mark of an unquestioned heterosexuality through "its dependence on a genealogical, implicitly heteronormative reproductive logic" (Gopinath 10). Cliff's work, in contrast, constantly interrogates this logic and denounces its exclusionary and normative power in both white colonialist discourse and diasporic postcolonial narratives.

Cliff's exploration of cultural identity also takes issue with the racial premise that underwrites the nationalist conception of diaspora in analogy to family, whether conceived in purely biological terms or in the more flexible and unstable terms of culture. According to Gilroy, "the growing centrality of the family trope within black political and academic discourse points to the emergence of a distinctive and emphatically post-national variety of racial essentialism."[22] In my reading, Marshall's *Praisesong for the Widow* is in line with this neo-nationalist position: it oscillates in its representation of identity between essentialism and constructivism, taking the form of what Gilroy calls a "flexible essentialism" (*Black Atlantic* 99); yet it clearly positions itself as part of a black cultural nationalist project. Although few critics have analyzed Marshall's work in light of her activism, her novels can be seen as the "creative sphere" through which she explored and defined her position toward black cultural nationalism and her relationship with the civil rights and black power movements and with (white) American left-wing politics (McGill 75).

In that sense, *Praisesong for the Widow* marks "a significant step" in Marshall's literary and political development, for it reflects her growing suspicion about the "efficacies of white and black political alliances." Abandoning the leftist class struggle in favor of a race-based struggle, the novel "embrac[es] a black nationalist ideology that denies that whites can play a role in the creation of an independent black cultural sphere" (McGill 99). Whites are indeed strikingly invisible in *Praisesong for the Widow*, appearing only as a structuring, oppressive absent presence. What could be seen as—at least partly—a class-related problem is presented in the novel solely as a racial issue: only black people appear as the victims of poverty, insecurity, and the spiritual degeneration that results from the maddening struggle against these conditions; the other American poor remain invisible, outside the frame of the novel. Race, in this conception, seems an unproblematic notion, defined either negatively through its association with disenfranchisement, poverty, exploitation, and slavery, or positively as a vibrant culture surviving despite—or because of—racism across the diaspora. If interracial alliances are absent or implicitly rejected, intraracial bonds are presented not only as crucial and necessary but also as natural and freely available, as long as those who have unduly forsaken them want to reclaim them.

The question Marshall's novel does not address, indeed does not even allow itself to pose, then, is what happens to those who, despite their genuine desire to be a part of the diasporic family, race, or community—whatever name we wish to give it—are considered as strangers by that very community, outside the family, or as belonging to another race. This, as I show in the next chapter, is a question that Cliff's work incessantly poses. Avey identifies herself as a stranger for most of the novel, yet she is always welcome by the members of the diaspora and is integrated as a "native daughter" as soon as she opens her eyes, mind, and heart to her diasporic identity.[23] Cliff's characters, in contrast, constantly have to struggle—and often in vain—to be accepted in the community they long to be a part of. While my reading of *Praisesong for the Widow* has partly contested Reyes's critique of the novel as too romantic and idealistic in its portrayal of historical reconnections, her point that "pariahs exist in order to constantly be a reminder that everyone will not come into a heroic awakening—or even desire it" (194) is indeed crucial: Cliff's characters also embark on many journeys, more or less willingly, but their success does not depend simply on their willingness or ability to acknowledge historical and cultural connections that would just be there for the taking. Without denying the difficulties that Marshall sows on her protagonist's path, the success of Avey's journey of recovery requires only that she give the dead their remembrance and reclaim what she has forsaken; when she does, her great-aunt's house in Tatem will be waiting for her to "fix it up" and move there (256). Things are not so easy for Cliff's protagonists, and endings not as happy. The spiritually damaging repression of African diasporic culture is not (only) of their own doing, as it is first repressed by their parents, their teachers, and colonial society; their ancestors do not call to them through possession, but have to be called by them, the gaps left by their absence turned into a source of questioning and a quest for sources. For Marshall, the central concern is the "psychological and spiritual return back over history" black people must undertake in order to "mold . . . a more truthful identity" ("Shaping the World" 107); for Cliff, the question is how to "claim an identity" when one is denied the right to.

[4]

"A GHOST-LIFE": QUEERING THE LIMITS OF IDENTITY

The terms that we use to name ourselves . . . carry their strings of echoes and inscriptions. Each represents an original misnaming and the simultaneous constant striving of the dispossessed for full representation. Each therefore must be used provisionally; each must be subject to new analyses, new questions and new understandings if we are to unlock some of the narrow terms of the discourses in which we are inscribed. In other words, at each arrival at a definition, we begin a new analysis, a new departure, a new interrogation of meaning, new contradictions.
—Carole Boyce Davies, *Black Women, Writing and Identity*

AS A JAMAICAN WHO lived most of her life in the United States, a light-skinned woman who identified herself as Afro-Caribbean, a nonheterosexual writer whose work was long surprisingly seldom analyzed from a queer perspective, Cliff does not fall easily into any one category. She is one of several Caribbean women writers who, as Carole Boyce Davies points out in *Black Women, Writing and Identity*, "tend . . . to exist marginally in all the literary traditions to which they belong: namely, African-American literature, Caribbean literature, Caribbean women's writing, African-American women's writing, women's writing, Black writing" (116). This was presumably not a problem for Cliff. As her literary works, interviews, and essays generally make clear, she was not comfortable with clear-cut categories, especially when they were imposed on her. The title of her first poetry collection, *Claiming an Identity They Taught Me to Despise* (1980), clearly stated her project, one that is both literary and political. Throughout her writing she claimed "my right to name myself" (*Claiming an Identity* 8), to be "who I am" rather than "what you allow me to be. Whatever you decide me to be" (*Land of Look Behind* 70).[1]

Who she was, however, is not in any way a simple question. "The question of my identity is partly a question of color" (8), the persona of *Claiming an Identity* explains. The other part, one that remains furtive and elusive in Cliff's early works but becomes more prominent in her later texts, is a question of sexuality. Her works explore what Valerie Rohy has referred to as "a crucial nexus: a site of the relation between notions of racial and sexual identity whose intersection becomes a productive space in which to interrogate identity itself" (219). This nexus, however, has not been sufficiently explored in discussions of Cliff's early work, which have generally focused on one issue or the other — with the vast majority focusing on race.[2] Moreover, while her first two novels have received considerable critical attention, her poetry, and to an even greater extent her collections of short stories, have been largely ignored. There is, therefore, both a necessity to address her treatment of race, gender, and sexuality intersectionally and a real interest in reading her various texts together. Because many recurring images, motifs, and themes run throughout her work, each text throws light on the others. The ghost is one among several tropes that appear frequently, albeit in shifting forms, but whose significance may easily go unnoticed when considering each text for itself.

As in its other manifestations examined in the previous chapters, the ghost enables Cliff to re-vision traditional narratives and discourses. More specifically, it serves to address, question, and destabilize fixed definitions of identity. It appears as the repressed that haunts racist, heterosexist discourse and society. In relation to race, it conveys the condition, experience, and paradox of passing, which is simultaneously presented as a protection and the promise of a privileged life through invisibility, and suffered as the painful absence of connections to community and culture. In relation to sexuality, the trope conveys the abjection and invisibilization of the queer subject by patriarchal, heteronormative society. Yet because the repressed is also that which keeps returning, the ghost not only signifies what, or who, has been effaced and silenced, but also exposes the workings of this effacement and silencing. A deconstructive trope that breaks down the hierarchizing and normalizing binaries that underpin the dominant discourses on race and sexuality, the ghost allows Cliff to contest these dominant discourses by debunking their essentialism and denouncing their inherent paradoxes. In relation to passing, the ghost thus both suggests the invisibilization and repression of blackness and demystifies the very boundary between whiteness and blackness — which the passing subject purportedly crosses—as a fiction. Similarly, by showing how heteronormativity is "haunted" by the sexual identities it excludes, the trope foregrounds how heterosexuality is actually constructed on and legitimized by this very process of exclusion. The foundational categories of race and sexuality are defined by a hegemonic discourse "predicated on binary structures that appear as the language of universal rationality" (Butler, *Gender Trouble* 12). As a trope of liminality, elusiveness, and ambivalence, the ghost creates a breach in this traditional binary configuration and functions as a "critical resource in the struggle to rearticulate the very terms of symbolic legitimacy and intelligibility" (Butler, *Bodies That Matter* 3) on which racist and heterosexist discourses are based. In doing so, it gestures toward a less limited and limiting definition of identity.

Cliff's double use of the ghost trope also allows her to question not only the boundaries that traditionally operate within master categories but also those that delimit and constitute these categories as distinct and independent. Analyzing the ghosts throughout her work thus enables me to avoid the myopia that long characterized much of black and postcolonial studies on the one hand, and queer theory on the other, and to explore "the crack between discourses [in which] the black *and* queer subject resides" (Holland 104, my emphasis).[3] Generally focused on the particular workings of the master category they seek to interrogate, postcolonial, black, and queer studies have too often failed to address the ways in which race and sexuality do not work independently, but intersect. Many women, lesbians, and queers of color have denounced the limited perspective of black heterosexual male theorists and writers on issues of race power relations, in which gender and sexuality are often subordinated or simply erased. Just as heteronormative discourse constructs heterosexuality through the repression and disavowal of homosexuality, E. Patrick Johnson has described homosexuality as "a repressed site of study within the field [of black studies]" ("Introduction" 4). On the other hand, a number of black and postcolonial scholars have also been critical of the similar inattention to racial issues in queer theory.

More particularly, many black and postcolonial writers and scholars have criticized queer theory for being inattentive to cultural and sociohistorical specificities and for positing a universalist and imperialist conception of nonnormative sexuality. Rejecting the term "queer" for its embeddedness in dominant western, white notions of sexual difference and identity, they have called for alternative terminologies and frameworks that better account for the particularities of their lived realities, experiences, and subjectivities. Critics from the Caribbean—a region in which same-sex relations are prohibited or invisibilized in specific ways—have notably mobilized vernacular vocabulary or reappropriated and redeployed historically derogatory concepts to theorize and politicize nonnormative sexual practices and subjectivities in their own terms.[4] Similarly skeptical of imported terms and configurations, Caribbean literature has rather been characterized, Alison Donnell argues, by an "un-naming" of same-sex desire (184). Ronald Cummings, on the other hand, notes that Caribbean writers have addressed the need for cultural specificity through the use of "imaginative, new and intriguing tropes and metaphors to the narration of queer sexualities" (327). The ghost is of course not a trope specific to Caribbean literature, nor is it a new trope for addressing queer sexuality. But I will argue that Cliff's use of the ghost pertains both to this attempt at narrating nonnormative sexualities outside imported linguistic and conceptual frameworks and to this process of un-naming. I thus read the presence of the ghost and the absence of terms that identify sexual categories in Cliff's works in a double way: on the one hand, it conveys the discursive (self-)invisibilization of queer sexuality and queer subjects, a symbolic violence that mirrors and reinforces the physical violence done to them; on the other hand, it also strategically un-names these identities in order to eschew normative and prescriptive categories, in a way that is—at least potentially—empowering and emancipatory. Queer is, in fact, the ghost in these texts, the absent presence that makes itself known but never speaks its name.

One may thus take issue with the use of the term "queer" when discussing Cliff and her work. Despite its limitations and connotations, however, it remains the term that most successfully signifies the fluidity I understand as characteristic of Cliff's evocation of sexuality and sexual identities, and is therefore the term I will use in this chapter—except when I refer to particular critics and theorists and use their own terms. Similarly, if my analysis largely draws on white American queer theorists, it is because in spite of their overly general or specific focus, their insights into the processes of invisibilization, exclusion, and abjection of homosexuality are helpful for explaining Cliff's use of the ghost trope. My analysis of race is in fact also informed by the questions and propositions raised by these queer theorists. As the title of this chapter suggests, I understand and use "queer" as a term and a critical project that has potential well beyond the registers of gender and sexuality and can be productively mobilized and used as "leverage . . . to do a new kind of justice to the fractal intricacies" of "identity-constituting, identity-fracturing discourses" (Sedgwick, *Tendencies* 9). In its broadly destabilizing function, the ghost is in fact the queering figure *par excellence*.[5] In this respect, my choice to discuss race and sexuality in succession rather than in parallel may seem at odds with my argument that Cliff's ghosts draw attention to the intersection of these two master discourses, and to the necessity to undo both at the same time. But this two-part structure is first necessary for disentangling the many levels at which the ghost trope functions and the shifting significations it performs in the various texts. Rather than constituting separate discussions, however, the two parts of my analysis are intimately related, as the section on the queer ghost builds on the section on passing as ghost-life. This structure also better demonstrates an important aspect of my argument, namely the fact that queer manifests as a ghostly subtext in much of Cliff's work. In the second part, I thus occasionally return to my first reading of particular scenes or figures and re-vision them to analyze their queer dimension.

Another useful resource for my analysis is the gothic, which actually has strong affinities with queer theory. According to Nicholas Royle, "The emergence of 'queer' as a cultural, philosophical, social and political phenomenon, at the end of the twentieth century, figures as a formidable example of the contemporary 'place' and significance of the uncanny" (*Uncanny* 42–43), a central concept in gothic studies. In Royle's formulation, "The uncanny *is* queer. And the queer is uncanny" (43). The fact that prominent queer scholars like Eve K. Sedgwick and Judith/Jack Halberstam also happen to be influential theorists of the gothic further confirms the proximity of the two fields.[6] Their common preoccupation with "boundaries and their collapse" (Halberstam, *Skin Shows* 23), surface and depth, self and other is, of course, also central to the issue of racial identity, and to passing in particular. As critics like Howard Malchow and Justin Edwards (*Gothic Passages*) have shown, gothic discourse and racial discourse are historically intimately linked, and the gothic has often been a privileged mode for addressing the anxieties related to passing and the way it troubles racial categories and disrupts certainties about identity. Although I would not qualify Cliff's texts as gothic, critical readings of the genre's emphasis on anxiety, terror, and horror are useful for grasping her complex use of the ghost. An even more ambivalent trope than in the other texts I have examined, the ghost highlights in Cliff's work the contradictory and unpredictable effects that queering the limits of identity can lead to—effects that are not, as some of her protagonists learn to their cost, necessarily empowering.

Disclaiming an Identity

In their introduction to *Her True-True Name: An Anthology of Women's Writing from the Caribbean*, Pamela Mordecai and Betty Wilson note the general neglect Caribbean writers, and Caribbean women writers more particularly, suffered in literary studies up to the 1980s. Hoping to contribute to "the long overdue task of making the writing of Caribbean women easily accessible to a wider audience," they open this 1989 anthology by confessing the "immense difficulty" they had putting it together because of the selective choices they were forced to make in order to arrive at this "final, tiny, sample" of Caribbean women's writing (ix). As the book's title suggests, what brings these writers together is not only that they are Caribbean women but also that they share a concern with precisely what being a Caribbean woman may mean. Noting the impressive volume of writing that anglophone Caribbean women, more particularly, produced in the 1980s, the editors assess this literature as generally "optimistic" compared to the "sickened vision" of the earlier generation of writers (xvii, xvi). Yet they single out Cliff as "the only one of the recently published Caribbean writers who does not affirm at least aspects of being in the Caribbean place" (xvii). What they exactly mean by this is not clear, but can perhaps be inferred from an earlier, comparatively positive comment on other Caribbean women writers who "articulate in their work a powerful sense of the island place and are able to affirm island culture and living" (xi). Cliff, in contrast, because of her "personal history," betrays a "compromised authenticity" as a Caribbean writer and should be situated "more in the alienated tradition of a 'francophone' than an anglophone consciousness" (xvii). This alienation is illustrated through Clare Savage, the protagonist of Cliff's first two novels, *Abeng* (1984) and *No Telephone to Heaven* (1987), who, unlike the other characters that appear in the anthologized texts, does not find her "true-true name" (xviii).

Mordecai and Wilson's critical comment on Cliff's work, and indeed on Cliff herself, would perhaps not deserve more attention if it was only two critics' isolated "crack"—as Cliff glossed it (Schwartz 607)—about one writer. It is significant, however, for two reasons. First, the charge of inauthenticity against Cliff is neither new nor unique: it has been made against other "white creole" writers, such as the Dominican Jean Rhys.[7] Nor is it the concern of a particular but foregone time: the question of who can claim to be an authentic Caribbean was still very much current at the time of the 1997 elections in Jamaica, during which the People's National Party questioned the legitimacy of a white leader—in opposition to its own black candidate—for representing the people of Jamaica (Robinson-Walcott 93–94). Second, the issue of authenticity also comes up in discussions that make a very different, in fact opposed, assessment of Cliff's work, by critics who celebrate it as an attempt at "establishing authenticity for her female and mixed-race characters (and potentially herself as a light-skinned Jamaican living in the United States)" (Stitt 53–54). If this chapter aims to contribute to this debate, it is not to support one or the other proposition—namely, Cliff as an authentic or an inauthentic Caribbean writer—but on the contrary to show why, in Cliff's own view and in her work, such a question is not only misguided but ultimately pointless. Not that the question of authenticity does not surface in Cliff's poetry, novels, and essays, works that are all largely concerned with identity; but rather than assessing the legitimacy or success of Cliff's supposed literary and political project, I will argue that her work deconstructs and ultimately rejects the notion of authenticity as a criterion for defining "Caribbean identity" or, for that matter, any kind of identity. In many ways, her work poses the question not of "who belongs," but of "the possibility and desirability of clear criteria of belonging" (Gamson 402).

In that respect, my discussion will show that it is not only Cliff's work, but indeed Cliff herself, through the ways she has been defined and has defined herself, that can serve "as a catalyst for working through of some of the most politically sensitive conflicts in Caribbean criticism" (Hoving 32). Indeed, a closer look at the reasons for and ways in which the editors of *Her True-True Name* qualify Cliff as an inauthentic Caribbean writer is very useful for initiating a discussion not only of what I think is Cliff's perspective on identity, but of identity more generally. Mordecai and Wilson's introduction offers a good example of the prescriptive and exclusive view of identity that Cliff resists, as a person whom such a view precisely relegates outside, or at least to the margins of, Caribbeanness. Although the editors readily acknowledge the linguistic, social, cultural, and historical diversity that composes the Caribbean literary landscape that their anthology can but attempt to map out, their comment presupposes the notion, already suggested in the title of the anthology, that there is such a thing as a true Caribbean woman's identity, an identity that not everyone can have a claim to. If they do not directly and explicitly define this identity, throughout their introduction they provide various elements that draw an image of it in both negative and positive and throw into relief the intersection of race and sexuality, among other categories, in their construction of Caribbean identity.

Place, Class, and Race

First, it is noteworthy that Cliff's "alienated" place in Caribbean literature does not seem to result, as one might have expected, from her early and definitive exile from Jamaica. Although the editors note this as an obviously significant fact in their presentation of Cliff, many of the other writers in the anthology similarly left their native island to settle more or less permanently abroad, generally in Britain, Canada, or the United States. However, Mordecai and Wilson explain, "Even those like Rosa Guy and Paule Marshall who have lived the greater part of their lives outside the Caribbean manage in almost every case to retain and articulate in their work a powerful sense of the island place and are able to affirm island culture and living" (xi). While one may wonder whom the phrase "in almost every case" alludes to, the fact is that living away from the Caribbean does apparently not in itself preclude a truthful rendering of Caribbean life.[8]

If authenticity—or the lack thereof—is not a matter of the writers' location in the world, it may be conditioned by their location on the social ladder. Noting that most anglophone Caribbean literature up to the 1980s has been "a literature of middle-class values and bourgeois preoccupations," mainly reflecting the concerns of male writers, Mordecai and Wilson celebrate the new literature by women for its focus on "grass roots concerns and ordinary people" (xiii). In this literary history, the middle-class Cliff, and her middle-class Clare, would appear as less interesting and significant, addressing concerns that are properly outdated for the 1980s and reflecting the life and dilemmas of an elite that does not speak to the larger population of Jamaica. This is of course a very narrow reading of Cliff's work, a reading that can partly be explained by a tendency Kathleen M. Balutansky has identified among critics of Caribbean literature—and, I would add, of nonwhite literatures more generally—to "read . . . novels as social documents" (267). If such readings may have "provided valuable insights into the significance of female protagonists in Caribbean fiction in general," Balutansky acknowledges, they were also "fundamentally reductive" because they offered a portrait that "neglected the complexity and flexibility of folk culture in the region" and "reproduced a binary paradigm that polarized the folk, on the one hand, and the middle class, on the other, rather than explore their complex historical development" (268). This tendency is evident in *Her True-True Name*, in which the editors judge it "important to underline the fact that recent writing by anglophone Caribbean women is rigorously honest in its rendering of the societies." Cliff's "compromised authenticity," in contrast, appears notably "in some aspects of her rendering of the creole" (xvii). Arguably, the editors may be referring here merely to how Cliff—unsuccessfully, in their view—uses language in her work, mixing "the King's English" and Jamaican patois. But even read in this limited way, their comment contends that Cliff is incapable of rendering the language of "the Jamaican people" in a truthful way, because her middle-class, British colonial education sets her apart from the folk.

In Mordecai and Wilson's comments, class and race also coalesce to justify the distrust toward the middle-class, light-skinned Cliff.[9] The two categories are indeed difficult to disentangle in the context of Jamaica, a society that, as Cliff's own work clearly illustrates, is based on "a class system notable for its rigidity and absolute color stratification" (*LLB* 14). Mordecai and Wilson's assessment of Cliff insists more directly on her skin color in a formulation that is particularly interesting: after making clear in the general introduction to the anthology that "Cliff is 'white'—or as light-skinned as makes, to the larger world, difference" (xvii), they explain in the brief introduction to the excerpt from *No Telephone to Heaven* that Cliff "*considers* her identity as mixed-blood Jamaican" (48, my emphasis). This apparent discrepancy between what Cliff *is* and what she *considers herself to be* suggests that Cliff is not what she claims to be, and claims to be what she is not—in other words that she is trying to pass as a nonwhite, or at least a mixed-race, writer.

This is confirmed by Belinda Edmondson's comment that many Caribbean women critics and writers "feel" that Cliff's "discovery of a black identity is a foreign fashion that she has appropriated." Their distrust of Cliff, according to Edmondson, is based on their interpretation of her work as "emanat[ing] from an American feminist sensibility" (182). This statement sheds light on Mordecai and Wilson's somewhat obscure comment that another mark of inauthenticity in Caribbean women's writing is the "ritual pursuing of pseudo-feminist agendas" (xvii). The editors do not say what these agendas exactly consist of, but Edmondson's allusion to American feminism may provide an answer. In her analysis, race converges with nationality, as this "American feminist sensibility" is presumably understood as white and in opposition to a black ("Afrocentric") Caribbean feminist sensibility.[10] But race also converges with gender in a "conflation of geo-political and gender categories that is highly suspect" and that associates American, or "First World," sensibilities with a "colonizing culture" identified as "male," whereas Caribbean, or "Third World," sensibilities are associated with a "colonized nature" identified as "female" (Edmondson 182). In this perspective, Cliff's works "are not truly part of an Afrocentric Caribbean discourse" (181–82), because she is aligned with America, whites, and men.

Invisible Sexuality

Cliff herself may provide another explanation for Mordecai and Wilson's marginalization of her. In an essay titled "Caliban's Daughter: The Tempest and the Teapot," she notes that in Caribbean literature "the proposition of one woman loving another woman has too often been used as a heavy-handed emblem of western decadence, the seduction of the tropics by Europe, the colonization of the dark woman by the white one" (48). Other Caribbean writers and scholars confirm this association of queer sexuality and cultural inauthenticity. Rosamond S. King notes that to identify as a Caribbean lesbian is to be "dismissed" and to lose one's claim on Caribbean identity, to be considered as having not "been raised with 'Caribbean values,'" having not "spent enough time in the region," or having "been 'contaminated' by the U.S.A." ("More Notes" 191). Similarly, Makeda Silvera denounces the general belief held in Jamaica that lesbianism is "'a white people ting,' or 'a ting only people with mixed blood was involved in'" (346). She argues that heteronormativity in the Caribbean is linked to the demand for reproductive sexuality that slavery enforced in order to increase and domesticate the labor force. Slaves also followed this norm, albeit for different reasons: insofar as sexuality was one aspect of their lives through which they could assert their humanity against the dehumanizing conditions of slavery, they conformed to the gender roles that prescribed men as procreators and women as fecund (351–52).

This patriarchal and heterosexist ideology persisted well beyond Emancipation, as it also pervaded anticolonial nationalist discourses as well as postcolonial Caribbean states' definitions of citizenship. M. Jacqui Alexander debunks the promises of equality of the new decolonized nations, which have "revised the very terms of citizenship to exclude [nonheterosexual people]" (5): "Not just (any) *body* can be a citizen any more, for *some* bodies have been marked by the state as non-procreative, in pursuit of sex only for pleasure, a sex that is non-productive of babies and of no economic gain" (6). By policing nonheterosexual, nonreproductive bodies, the postcolonial nation has naturalized heterosexuality and reproduction and posited them as necessary to its survival and development. More recent studies also continue to find that heterosexuality is still often perceived in the Caribbean as "a common signifier of maturity," as it is attached to fertility and the notion of becoming a "real" Caribbean woman (Kempadoo 10). This correlates with the notion that lesbianism is a foreign import or contamination, as heterosexuality thus becomes the sign of a mature and successful decolonization.

It is significant that Mordecai and Wilson's introductory remarks on Cliff make no mention of her sexuality. If, as Cliff conjectured, they included her in their anthology of Caribbean women writers simply because "they could not exclude [her]" (Schwartz 607), then the fact that her sexuality is invisibilized can be viewed as a confirmation of King's provocative statement that "Caribbean lesbians do not exist" ("More Notes" 191). Mordecai and Wilson's treatment of Cliff may seem profoundly at odds with the stated purpose of their anthology, which is to give Caribbean women writers a visibility they have long been denied. However, it can also be seen as supporting and reinforcing this project, insofar as the notion of authenticity that they mobilize is intimately connected to authority, the authority they claim for the writers they present. Identity is largely constructed on the exclusion of an Other whose difference reinforces the coherence of the subject, whether individual or collective. If "the whole *notion* of authenticity . . . is one that comes to us constructed by hegemonic voices" (Spivak and Gunew 195), what is interesting in the present case is that the hegemonic voices are those of Caribbean women who have themselves traditionally been marginalized. This reversal of power relations ironically puts Cliff, who is presented as privileged in *Her True-True Name*, in the subaltern position of the excluded Other whose voice is not as worthy of attention. In a way, Mordecai and Wilson conjure the ghost of Cliff in order to better affirm the coherence and authority of the community of Caribbean women writers their anthology constitutes. This is, as my discussion of race and sexuality will show, a typical identity-building gesture of hegemonic culture. But it is precisely Cliff's ghostly status that gives her power to destabilize fixed and prescriptive definitions of Caribbean identity.

The Passing Ghost and the Fictions of Race

Much of Cliff's poetry, and her first two novels, portray a light-skinned protagonist who struggles to come to terms with her mixed-race heritage in a world where racial categories are clear-cut and fixed. Because she was born "fair" (11), the persona of *Claiming an Identity* (hereafter cited as *CI*), is raised as the daughter of her father, while her "dark" sister is "the daughter of the mother" (25). Similarly, Clare Savage, the protagonist of *Abeng* (hereafter cited as *A*) and *No Telephone to Heaven* (*NTH*), constantly feels divided between the white, Eurocentric, colonial education and values distilled by her light-skinned father Boy and the folk, African diasporic culture of her darker mother Kitty. *Abeng* tells the story of Clare's childhood in Jamaica, a story interrupted and underwritten by details about the history of her family and of her country under colonial rule. *No Telephone to Heaven* relates her life after her family left Jamaica to settle in the United States, her subsequent "life-alone" (109) as a graduate student in England, and her final return to Jamaica to join the revolutionary cause against neocolonialism. Like her poetry, Cliff's two novels explore and denounce the contradictions of racial ideology as it is deployed by various characters, black, white, or otherwise, and in different historical, cultural, and national contexts.

If white or light skin is valorized in both environments, race functions in significantly different ways in Jamaica and in the United States. In Jamaica, racial categories operate in a broad spectrum from "white" to "black" through "brown" and "red." Colorism is supported and reinforced by classism: Clare's and Boy's light skins, associated with their British colonial education, place them on a higher level of the social ladder. In the United States, in contrast, the one-drop rule allows for only two categories: white and nonwhite, or white and black. The Savages are confronted with this new racial ideology as soon as they arrive in the country, as they drive from Miami to New York through the segregated South. When they stop at a motel in Georgia, Boy finds himself under the scrutiny of the innkeeper, who seems troubled by the "apricot color" of his skin and the "unfamiliar cadence of his voice" and is not convinced by the explanation that he is Jamaican. As Boy wonders about how to respond to, and allay, the man's suspicion that he might be "colored," he cannot help thinking about the categories he learned and recited as a schoolboy in Jamaica; mulatto, sambo, quadroon, mestee, mestefeena, and the 120-odd other categories would make no sense to this American who thinks only in the binary terms of white vs. "nigger" (*NTH* 55). Understanding that his light skin, middle-class status, and British education will not mean a thing if he is identified as having one drop of black blood, Boy presents himself as the descendant of a plantation owner—which is true, but only half the story.

This scene—which I will further unpack in a moment—illustrates the cultural contingency of racial boundaries. It also shows how, especially in the United States, these boundaries rely on a visual epistemology. In *American Anatomies*, Robyn Wiegman explains how "the visible has a long, contested, and highly contradictory role as the primary vehicle for making race 'real' in the United States" (21). "While not the only means for the articulation of racial essence," she argues, the "visual economy of race" has determined and configured the identification of human differences since the sixteenth century and remains to this day "the most taken-for-granted assumption of Western racial discourse" (180). In this visual economy, skin color, conceived as the essential marker of difference, is read through a black/white binary that organizes not only the definition of race but also the hierarchy that goes with it. Cliff's early works explore and unravel the limitations and contradictions of this definition of race. One significant way in which they do so is through the theme of passing, which both supports and contradicts the visual epistemology of race.

As Elaine K. Ginsberg reminds us, racial passing finds its origins in "the sexual exploitation of black slave women by white men" (5), despite the legal and moral ban on miscegenation. This exploitation and its repercussions through generations is a fact Cliff's work also repeatedly emphasizes, by exploring the imbrication and mutually constitutive power of race, gender, and sexuality in both the colonial and the postcolonial contexts, in white Eurocentric as well as black folk discourses. As I show in the second part of this chapter, the protagonists' struggle to come to terms with their divided selves thus has to do not only with race, but also with gender and sexuality: compulsory heterosexuality and mothering and antiblack racism notably cohere in the injunction to perpetuate the "lightening up" (*NTH* 169) of the family that is pressed on Clare and the persona in *Claiming an Identity*, an injunction they will resist not only by associating with darker-skinned mates but also by forestalling the reproduction of whiteness by exploring forms of nonreproductive sexuality and seeking alternative affiliations outside the heteropatriarchal family. Queer thus appears as a mode of resistance against the racist, patriarchal, and heteronormative economy inherited from slavery and colonialism. In order to successfully resist, the young protagonists must learn to deconstruct the categories they have been locked in, re-vision their identity in nonbinary terms, and reclaim the parts of their identity that have been invisibilized—ghosted—by normative discourses. While the contradictions of race are visible on other people's bodies and revealed through the paradox of passing, making this re-visionary work both more pressing and more accessible, the complete erasure of nonheteronormative sexuality leaves queer in the shadows.

Invisibilizing Race

In *No Telephone to Heaven*, passing is first evoked as a means of protection against, and survival in, the racist white world. Confronted with discrimination and potential violence as soon as he arrives in the United States with his family, Boy quickly realizes that in order to maintain his privilege and escape racism, the best option is to pass. He therefore teaches his light-skinned daughter Clare about "invisibility and secrets.

Self-effacement. Blending in. The uses of camouflage" (100). In *Claiming an Identity*, and in the poem "Passing" in particular, passing is similarly presented as a way for the persona and her family to "blend in" through "camouflage." This camouflage is glossed as a "pattern of skin" that, like the skin of the diamondback lizard in the persona's schoolyard, "makes a being invisible against its habitat" (3). An act of self-invisibilization, passing is presented as a "ghost-life" (5). For the passing subject, to be ghostlike means not only to look white, to make oneself inconspicuous in a white world, but also to make oneself un-raced in a world in which "black" skin has come to be identified as the marker of race and "whiteness has been normalized and privileged to the point of profound invisibility" (Shugart 118).[11]

What is invisibilized in the act of passing, however, is not only the racial origins of the passer in the sense of phenotypic traits—what Fanon called the "epidermal schema" of race (*Black Skin* 92). The ghost-life that is passing also requires "An ignorance of connections" (*CI* 5), that is, the voluntary or forced suppression of vertical relationships with previous generations whose skin color as well as cultural heritage and history would threaten the passer's invisibility. "Ignorance" here means both deliberate omission and unawareness: "I hid from my real sources," Cliff's persona says, "But my real sources were also hidden from me" (*LLB* 71). The verb "hide" operates on several levels here, as it evokes skin and reminds of Fanon's epidermal schema and links it, through the word "sources," to both genealogy and history. To be a ghost, in that sense, is close to Fanon's own metaphor of the angel in *The Wretched of the Earth*, which he uses to describe the condition of the colonized (intellectual) who has undergone the "mutilations" imposed by the supremacy of white culture: "individuals without an anchorage, without borders, stateless, rootless, a body of angels" (155). It also echoes the ghostly paleness that characterizes Jerome Johnson in *Praisesong for the Widow*, in which it connotes the repression of African diaspora culture and the assimilation into white values. The insubstantial character of Cliff's ghost, like Fanon's angel and Marshall's spectral white mask, conveys the sense of disconnection and forgetfulness that passing requires.

In *Abeng* and *No Telephone to Heaven*, Clare's repressed black heritage is embodied in the ghost of Nanny, the Maroon warrior. A leader of the rebel runaway slaves and a powerful obeah woman, Nanny is remembered today as one of Jamaica's national heroes. While her exploits are recorded in both the oral tradition and colonial documents about the Maroon wars, Nanny was long considered more as a mythical figure than a historical one (J. Sharpe 1). Despite the extensive work produced by historians and cultural critics in the postindependence era, Nanny remains located in what one of these historians has called a "twilight zone" between reality and myth, history and folk memory (Mair 53). In *Abeng*, Cliff confirms and laments Nanny's absence from the official, colonial history of Jamaica that Clare learns at school. In this history that is told only "as it pertained to England" and in which the slave past of the island "is slight compared to the history of Empire" (84, 30), Nanny's presence and significance are "negated because she threatens Jamaica's foundational narrative, which would prefer to trace its sources to Europe rather than Africa" (Gikandi 245). For the same reason, she is just as absent from the education Clare receives at home: Boy's "carefully contrived mythology" about the Savages' identity cannot accommodate nonwhite protagonists, and Kitty has decided, for the sake of her light-skinned daughter, not to "give her any false notion of alliance which she would not be able to honor" (*A* 29, 129). The ghost of Nanny does not clearly appear in the story, but her presence as a "duppy"—a spirit in Jamaican culture—is mentioned on several occasions, often in relation to birds, which, "the old people say," are "ghosts; the spirits of Maroons" (*NTH* 193).[12] But Nanny not only literally haunts the Jamaican landscape: she also metaphorically haunts Clare's historical consciousness, and formally haunts her coming-of-age story. In *Abeng*, Nanny's (hi)story appears in vignettes detailing her deeds and her powers that fragment the main narrative. Clare's and Nanny's stories are thus juxtaposed but never meet. The blanks and section dividers suggest structurally as well as graphically the impassable break that separates them and reflect both Clare's ignorance of this subtext to her own story and her sense of identity as fragmented because of this ignorance.

Clare grows more and more unsatisfied with her father and her teachers' easy or evasive answers about the black part of her cultural heritage and starts investigating for herself. But by the end of *Abeng*, the twelve-year-old girl is not yet ready to fully grasp her developing oppositional consciousness. When her family leaves Jamaica for the United States in *No Telephone to Heaven*, she seems even further removed from that part of her identity. But her questions and critical mind find a new object in the acts of violence and racism she witnesses in her new environment. She is particularly shocked by the news of the Birmingham church bombing, which killed four girls nearly her own age, and by the utter lack of interest these deaths seem to elicit among her classmates. In *Praisesong for the Widow*, this event marked Avey's dissociation from black people, prompting her to "[avoid] the headlines and pictures on the front pages of the newspapers and the nightly television newscasts" (140) in an attempt at repressing her rage and dismay; in contrast, Clare cuts out a picture of one of the girls from a newspaper and keeps it in her wallet, as a haunting memento of her desire to remember the victims and maintain her capacity to be shocked by such events. When Boy discovers the picture, he takes it away, arguing that to "ponder these things" (*NTH* 102) will only prevent Clare's proper assimilation as an American.[13]

The "ignorance of connections" that passing demands therefore concerns not only the vertical, genealogical ties with (darker) ancestors like Nanny, but also the horizontal relations with people whose proximity might raise suspicion, including within the family itself. Only just arrived in the United States, Boy must make sure that "his slightly darker wife and mango and guava daughters" remain "out of sight" (*NTH* 55) if the family is to be allowed to stay at the motel in segregated Georgia. Once settled in New York, the Savages break off all contact with Kitty's darker relatives who put them up when they arrived in the city, following their own advice that they should try to pass. Thus, if passing makes the passers ghosts in (white) society because of the invisibility and distance it demands, it also makes them ghosts to their own family, and their family ghosts to them. When Kitty understands that she will never feel "at home with pretense," whereas Boy is "making himself at home" with his new "white" self (75), she takes the daughter that looks more like her, Clare's younger and darker sister Jennie, and returns to Jamaica, leaving Clare and Boy to look after themselves.

Racial Anxiety and the Uncanny

The phrase "ghost-life" takes a new meaning here, as it comes to suggest a sort of nonexistence, a life marked by absence. It also captures the persona's ambivalence toward this situation, an ambivalence that is also suggested in the oxymoronic quality of the line "Passing *demands a desire* to become invisible" (*CI* 5, my emphasis). While Boy is proud of his own ability to pass—an ability that, like the diamondback lizard's "mottled skin" (*CI* 3), is a sign of evolutionary adaptation to a hostile environment—Clare and the persona of *Claiming an Identity* have difficulties adapting to this life that, after all, has been imposed on them. Later on in *No Telephone to Heaven*, the adult Clare tries to explain to her lover Bobby the consequences that "blending into the majority with ease" (152) has had on the way she relates to other people: the price she has had to pay for growing up as an "invisible neger" is to feel "like a shadow . . . like a ghost . . . like I could float through my days without touching . . . anyone" (154, ellipses in original). She thinks that Bobby, as an African American whose visually self-evident and coherent racial identity she envies, does not "trust her in her skin" or understand that "there are people who look one way and think another, feel another" (152). She cannot blame him, however, for she does not trust herself either, knowing only too well that "This kind of splitting breeds insanity" (*CI* 11).

The ghost is thus also an apt trope for capturing the anxiety that accompanies the experience of passing for the passing subject. For Clare as much as for the persona, being a ghost—that is, being there and not there at the same time, both visible and invisible—is profoundly unsettling. It creates a cognitive dissonance, a crisis in their self-perception and self-identification. This dissonance is interestingly played out at the beginning of "Passing," when the persona compares passing with camouflage:

> Camouflage: ground lizards in the schoolyard rustle
> under a pile of leaves—some are deep-green, others
> shiny blue: all blend in. I fear they might be there—
> even when there is no sound.
>
> To this day camouflage terrorizes me.
>
> The pattern of skin which makes a being invisible
> against its habitat.
>
> And—yes—this camouflage exists for its protection.
> I am not what I seem to be. (*CI* 3)

Sliding from the lizards to the persona through the metaphor of camouflage, an ability they share, the text blurs the boundary between who is looking and who is hiding and shifts the source of the persona's anxiety from what she sees, or does not see, to what she is, and, precisely, is not. The last line, "I am not what I seem to be," does not sound like a provocation, such as Boy thinks to himself after fooling the innkeeper; rather, it conveys a profound uneasiness, a sense of defamiliarization that shatters the very meaning of the words "I am."

This defamiliarization associates the experience of passing with the uncanny. The uncanny is difficult to define; in fact, as Andrew Bennett and Nicholas Royle observe, "To try to define the uncanny is immediately to encounter one of its decisive paradoxes, namely that 'the uncanny' has to do with a *troubling* of definitions, with a fundamental disturbance of what we think and feel" (36). For Freud, the uncanny can be described as the effect experienced when a sense of unfamiliarity appears at the heart of the familiar, or when the unfamiliar suddenly seems strangely familiar, when the homely (*heimlich*) becomes unhomely (*unheimlich*) and vice versa. It is also related to the visible and the invisible, as it has to do with appearances, with the sense that things are not what they seem. But the uncanny is also "that which 'ought to have remained . . . secret and hidden but has come to light'" (F. W. J. Schelling, qtd. in Bennett and Royle 40), a definition that relates it in a direct way to the anxieties that arise from the experience of passing. These anxieties, however, do not emerge only in the passer. Just as it creates a cognitive dissonance in the passer's self-perception, passing produces a crisis in the witness's ability to trust appearances: if the passing ghost is troubled by its own absent presence, for the witness of passing the presence of a ghost or, more precisely, the feeling of being in the presence of a ghost even as it cannot be seen, is just as disturbing. This is particularly well illustrated in the scene where Boy checks in at the motel. When the innkeeper looks at Boy, he is confused by what he sees, and wonders about what he cannot see. As his "trained eye" closely examines his visitor, the man registers, but is at a loss to identify, Boy's physical characteristics: "Thin lips—but dark curly hair. Large nose—but no tinge to the voice. Colored skin—but a manner that was quite white." The innkeeper is confused by Boy's foreign accent and sophisticated manner, which he cannot quite reconcile with the kind of people he imagined could originate from Jamaica, a place where he thinks "only spics and niggers" live (*NTH* 56). But even Boy's physical features—his lips, hair, nose, and skin—in which he looks for clues, seem contradictory, familiar and unfamiliar at the same time.

This scene also confirms that, as an act of transgression of the color line, passing is "about the individual and cultural anxieties induced by boundary crossing" (Ginsberg 2).[14] For the "dupe," that is, for the purportedly rightful member of the dominant—generally white—group into which it occurs, passing is experienced and defined as deception. "You could not relax for a moment," the innkeeper muses while looking at Boy. "Someone might slide by. Sometimes it felt to him like the *Invasion of the Body Snatchers*" (*NTH* 56). The innkeeper's comparison of blacks passing for white with monstrous aliens invading the world and replacing "normal" people is suggestive of the many levels on which the anxieties and fantasies about passing work: they are not based merely on the risk of unwittingly accepting, or even welcoming, a deceiver—a "body snatcher"—into one's group: passing also poses a threat to the security of this group's own identity. By conveying a fear about the loss, through "invasion," of normal (white) identity, passing invokes the threat of rampant miscegenation—the "lightening up" that Boy in fact proudly claims and casually calls for. "Vigilance," the innkeeper concludes, "secure[s] the safety of the people" (56) by allowing the race to remain pure.

More than the fear of transgression, passing thus induces fears about the dissolution of the boundaries it is considered to transgress. If to pass is to be invisible in the white world, then the very possibility of this invisibility breaks down the logic of the visual epistemology of race and reveals its inherent paradox. Passing is based on the presumption that "one cannot pass for anything one *is not* unless there is some other, pre-passing, identity that one *is*" (Ginsberg 4). The *OED*'s definition of the verb "to pass" suggests as much: "To be accepted as or believed to be, or to represent oneself successfully as, a member of an ethnic or religious group other than one's own, esp. one having higher social status." In this definition, what corresponds to the groups out of and into which passing occurs seems unproblematic and self-evident. This is even clearer in the more general definition of "to pass for/as": "to be taken for or to serve as (usually *with the implication of being something else*); to be accepted or received as equivalent to" (my emphasis).[15] Yet the irresolvable paradox at the heart of passing is that its practice is made possible precisely by the fact that the groups out of and into which one passes are not as clearly delimited as they claim—and are generally considered—to be. Through the act of passing, both the categories of white and black are revealed as arbitrary and fictitious, and their respective signifiers are called into question. As Ginsberg puts it, "If 'white' can be 'black,' what is white?" (8). But also, I would add, if "black" can be "white," what is black in the first place? This redefines passing not as the betrayal of a true identity, a definition it long had and in many contexts continues to have, but rather as the betrayal of the very notion of "true identity" (Rohy 226). In this sense, passing shifts the question of (racial) identity from the realm of ontology to the realm of epistemology: it tells us not about "true" identity but about how identity is constructed and perceived in racialist terms.

The scene between Boy and the innkeeper is particularly revealing of the way that, rather than *describing* "apparently observable . . . markers of difference," the visual economy of race actually *constructs* these markers by "actively 'visibiliz[ing]'" them (Wald 6). The concept of the uncanny is useful here not only for the implicit link it draws between (in)visibility, appearances, and the ghost, but also in the way it helps articulate the contradiction inherent in the visual epistemology of race and thereby show that race is, in this visual definition, a fiction. According to Bennett and Royle, the uncanny is not an essential quality that a thing possesses but rather an effect produced by the *reading* of that thing: the uncanny "is not so much *in* the text," or, I would add, in the body, that "we are reading," but in "the experience of *the reader*" (43). The reading of the body as a racialized text can therefore be, as in the scene at the motel, an uncanny experience. This relocates the identification of race not in the body itself—in identifiable markers—but in the *reading* of that body, a reading that is based on what Judith Butler would call the "naturalized knowledge" of race. This knowledge is "based on a series of cultural inferences" (*Gender Trouble* xxiii) that support our visual assessment of a person's (racial, gendered, sexual) identity. In other words, "what can be seen, what qualifies as a visible marking" is not in the body under inspection itself but in the viewer's ability "to read a marked body in relation to unmarked bodies, where unmarked bodies constitute the currency of normative whiteness" (Butler, *Bodies That Matter* 170–71). Boy's race thus paradoxically depends on the innkeeper's ability to *see* the specific markers he looks for—"Tell-tale hair, thick noses and heavy mouths" (*LLB* 41). The man's inability to do so in any definitive way leaves Boy un-raced, as it were, a ghost that can move back and forth between identifications.

Living (and Dying) as a Ghost

To lead a "ghost-life" is thus not only to escape and subvert the binarism of traditional racial categories by sliding through them and thereby making them inconsistent; it is also to fundamentally contest the essence of identity itself by making it utterly unstable. While this instability can be experienced as disturbing and damaging for the subject's sense of identity, it is also—at least theoretically—productive. The trope of the ghost indeed gestures toward a way out of the dilemma that torments Clare and the persona in much of Cliff's poetry. Throughout *Abeng* and *No Telephone to Heaven*, Clare feels "split into two parts—white and not white, town and country, scholarship and privilege, Boy and Kitty" (*A* 119). Reluctant to make the choice that she thinks will "be expected of her" (37), she longs to be allowed to embrace all the parts of herself, to find both a way out of her father's tautological precepts—she is a Savage because she is white, and she is white because she is a Savage—and a place for, and a connection with, the mother she feels so physically, emotionally, and culturally estranged from.

A description of Clare near the end of the story—but, in the nonlinear structure of *No Telephone to Heaven*, situated in fact in the middle of the novel—suggests she has reached something akin to this more inclusive self: "She is white. Black. Female. Lover. Beloved. Daughter. Traveler. Friend. Scholar. Terrorist. Farmer" (*NTH* 91). The list, it seems, could go on and on. Clare's self is "composed of fragments" that sometimes pull in opposite directions but that somehow still hold together, like the group of guerrilla fighters among which she has, both literally and symbolically, "taken her place" (87, 5). The heterogeneity of the band, which is made up of people of diverse races, genders, nationalities, and backgrounds, is largely what makes its power, as each member brings something to the group—weapons, knowledge of the land and its ancestral language, experience of armed revolution, or, in Clare's case, an estate on which to grow sustenance, hide away, and prepare for the fight to come. At this precise moment and for the particular action they are engaged in, these people have chosen to identify as freedom fighters, as is suggested by their uniforms, "signifying some agreement, some purpose." But they can also be identified—and distinguished—by "the shades of their skin, places traveled to and from, events experienced, things understood, food taken into their bodies, acts of violence committed, books read, music heard, languages recognized, ones they loved, living family" (4)—and the list, again, could go on and on. All the features that compose the members of the group are not fixed but dynamic, the result of processes, actions, choices, confirming Hall's point that identities "come from somewhere, have histories" and "undergo constant transformation" ("Cultural Identity" 225).[16]

Yet Cliff does not allow her protagonist—or the guerrillas—to live through this fragmentary and incoherent but ultimately more fulfilling self. Like Nanny of the Maroons, in whose name they fight neocolonialism, the band is betrayed by a "quashee," and Clare is killed in action. Instead of "offer[ing] a utopian conclusion" to the protagonist's story, as Judith Raiskin puts it, the end of *No Telephone to Heaven* "dramatize[s] the way individual choices occur within historical paradigms" ("Inverts and Hybrids" 168) that they are often unable to surpass. Clare's death under the bullets of an invisible army shows the "arbitrariness and anonymity" (J. Smith 157) of the forces that support and preserve the system that her non-unitary identity contests; it confirms Anne McClintock's statement that "the colonials . . . all too often succe[ed] in settling matters of indecision with a violent excess of militarized masculinity" (qtd. in J. Smith 158). In the last scene of the novel, as the sounds of gunshots and helicopters dissolve into the morning song of birds, Clare's and Nanny's spirits seem to be finally united. Turning her protagonist into an actual ghost, rather than allowing her to live as a metaphorical one, Cliff ultimately seems to confirm that this world—as Clare's patronizing American school principal warned her—has "no place for in-betweens" (*NTH* 99). Refusing to naïvely celebrate ambiguity, instability, and elusiveness as essentially productive and empowering for personal and political affirmation, Cliff recognizes the cost and the anxieties that an unconventional positioning outside master categories entails. Despite its subversive and liberating potential, for Cliff's protagonists, to live a ghost-life is confusing at the least, more often painful, and sometimes simply no life at all.

This is not the end of the story, however. Not only does *No Telephone to Heaven* close with the beginning of a new day, but, as Cliff herself pointed out, we do not know what happened to the other guerrillas, in particular to Harriet. I will return to the question of Clare's death; for now, as a conclusion to my discussion on race and passing, I wish to reflect on the possibility of Harriet's surviving. Cliff described Harry/Harriet as "the real revolutionary in the book," a term that clearly applies in several ways. Harry/Harriet is instrumental in Clare's reclaiming her cultural and political heritage, in convincing her to return to Jamaica after her American and European exile, sharing his/her knowledge of the land and its history with her, and eventually introducing her to the guerrillas.[17] Moreover, he/she is also, in Cliff's own view, "the most complete character in *No Telephone to Heaven*" (Schwartz 602) and can be read as a model in Clare's own quest for coming to terms with her fragmented identity. Clare feels "drawn" to and "at home" with Harry/Harriet because they are both "neither one thing nor the other" (*NTH* 131). As a mixed-race character with an ambiguous gender and sexuality, Harry/Harriet queers all binaries and fixed categories and offers a powerful—and often playful—illustration of the performative character of identity. That his/her gender and sexuality remain unstable and indeterminate is confirmed by the different ways in which critics have described him/her: as "a homosexual cross-dresser" (F. R. Barnes 23), a bisexual, biracial "non-operative transgendered transvestite" (Elia 352), "a gay 'mixed race' hermaphrodite" (Raiskin, "Inverts and Hybrids" 164), a "mixed-race, gender-complex, male lesbian," and "a male woman" (Tinsley, *Thiefing Sugar* 5, 172). This confusion is only reinforced by Cliff's own ambiguous and often contradictory descriptions of the character in interviews—which she at times calls "Harry" and designates as a "he"—as a "homosexual" who is not "a transvestite" (Raiskin, "Art of History" 69), "a gay hero/heroine," "the novel's lesbian," and "a man who wants to be a woman and . . . loves women" (Schwartz 601). As I will demonstrate in the next part of this chapter, however, un-naming is a powerful political strategy Cliff uses, and it is therefore significant that the novel itself never labels Harry/Harriet in any such way. While he/she predicted both he/she and Clare would have to make a choice, the fact that she does not have a sex change after he/she decides to let "Harriet live and Harry be no more"—not just for economic reasons but also because to her "castration ain't de main t'ing" (*NTH* 168)—shows that to live in-between is not necessarily to "live split" (131). Yet she also knows the danger her life as an in-between puts her in, and that to live safely as only Harriet requires passing as a cis-gender woman, ghosting her "male organ . . . under her bleached and starched skirt" (171). As a liminal character who becomes a passing figure, (Harry/)Harriet provides an apt transition toward my analysis of Cliff's queer ghosts.

The Queer Ghost and the Return of the Repressed

While my discussion of sexuality in the second part of this chapter will take other routes than those I have followed in my discussion of race, and reach a different destination, it starts from a similar theoretical ground. As I pointed out in my reading of passing, whiteness is constructed by essentializing certain bodily features associated with blackness; whiteness is thus defined through the delimitation and inferiorization of blackness. Cliff shows this process of identification at work in racial encounters in *No Telephone to Heaven*. The innkeeper who confronts Boy asserts his whiteness implicitly but powerfully through his rejection of blackness, a symbolic exclusion that is buttressed by the legal exclusion of blacks from his motel in the segregated South. In turn, Boy identifies himself as white through his exclusion of blackness, not only by hiding his darker-skinned wife and daughters and whitewashing his family history, but also by deploying a racist attitude toward black culture throughout the novel. The heteronormative definition of sexuality rests on a similar process of exclusion based on a binary system of identification that is culturally and historically constructed, yet naturalized. The binary definition of sexuality as hetero/homo is effected by the narrowing down of sexuality to the matter of an object-choice based on a particular sex—male or female (Sedgwick, *Epistemology of the Closet* 35). Like all binary oppositions, it is hierarchically structuring, as one term is implicitly valorized and accepted as the norm. The category "heterosexual" thus "depends for its meaning on the simultaneous subsumption and exclusion" of the category "homosexual" (10).

This process of exclusion becomes in Butler's terms one of "abjection." Borrowing Julia Kristeva's concept of the abject as "that which has been expelled from the body, discharged as excrement, literally rendered 'Other'" (*Gender Trouble* 181), Butler theorizes the way normative heterosexuality constructs itself through the foreclosure or disavowal of unlivable identifications. In the "exclusionary matrix" of heteronormativity, these identifications produce and provide a "constitutive outside to the subject," "'unlivable' and 'uninhabitable' zones of social life" whose borders "constitute the defining limit of the subject's domain." In other words, the constitution of the subject takes place not only through the identification with a "normative phantasm" of heterosexuality, but also through the repudiation of "abject"—that is, nonheterosexual—identifications. In a cultural matrix in which gender (masculine/feminine), sex (male/female), and desire for the opposite gender and sex must be aligned, nonheterosexual identities are "unviable" identities, identities that "cannot 'exist'" but inhabit a zone outside the domain of the subject (*Bodies That Matter* 3).

I have quoted Butler's words at length here because her choice of terms and metaphors is significant for my argument about the ghost of queer. Indeed, her evocation of the "abject"—a term commonly used in gothic studies—of borders and limits, and of "unlivable" identifications, resonates interestingly with the ghost trope. *Bodies That Matter* is in fact a good example of the way the trope has been "used as a conceptual metaphor . . . to expose and address the way certain subjectivities have been marginalized and disavowed in order to establish and uphold a particular norm" (Blanco and Peeren, "Spectral Subjectivities" 309–10).[18] This is indeed a rather widespread use of the ghost trope. Writing more broadly about marginalized subjects in the context of the United States, Holland argues that the American nation has built and maintained itself through the exclusion of certain groups—blacks, Native Americans, queers—and their containment in a "space of death." Among those "dead" subjects—or, precisely, nonsubjects—black queers suffer a double "death-in-life" (4), insofar as they are disavowed by both the American nation and the black community. Partly informed by Patterson's definition of slavery as social death, and more directly influenced by anthropologist Michael Taussig's identification of this imaginary space as a politicizing fiction of "societies where the culture of terror flourishes" (qtd. in Holland 4), Holland's notion of a "space of death" confirms the ghost trope's aptness for theorizing those (non)subjects that are in effect alive but symbolically and socially dead, inhabiting the domain of the unlivable.

The trope not only appears in queer scholars' theorizations of the construction of heterosexuality and heteronormative society through the disavowal of homosexuality; it also appears in critical examinations of the representation—or, as a matter of fact, the nonrepresentation—of queer subjects and subjectivities in modern culture and society. As Blanco and Peeren note, queer subjects have a "propensity . . . to be culturally configured as ghosts" ("Spectral Subjectivities" 312). This propensity does not rest solely on the ghost's usefulness for conceptualizing a form of death-in-life, but also has to do with the trope's suggestive play on the visible and the invisible, presence and absence. Thus, it is the master trope in Castle's *The Apparitional Lesbian*, which opens with the observation that "the lesbian remains a kind of 'ghost effect'" in modern culture, "elusive, vaporous, difficult to spot—even when she is there, in plain view" (2). The lesbian "has been 'ghosted'—or made to seem invisible" (4) in culture and society because of the threat she poses to patriarchy. She is invisible in the historical record, in the law—in which, unlike male homosexuality, lesbianism has traditionally been ignored—and, most prominently, in literature. Castle describes western literature as "a kind of derealization machine: insert the lesbian and watch her disappear" (6). Her work explores how, in their constant efforts to disembody the lesbian and decarnalize lesbian desire and love, writers have made much use of spectral metaphors.

Queer subjects thus have clear affinities with ghosts in heteronormative and homophobic discourse, whether as the repressed abject and the unlivable, the socially dead, or the absent and invisible. However, the negative power of the trope must be re-visioned to take into consideration its dual quality. Just as in the case of race, the ghost of queer contains in itself its own subversive double: "The ghost," Castle notes, "is a paradox. Though non-existent, it nonetheless *appears*" (46). "To become an apparition" is therefore "also to be endlessly capable of 'appearing'" (63). As a trope, the ghost not only hides and erases, but also highlights and visibilizes what it signifies. This explains why, after serving to "vaporize" the lesbian in the literature of the eighteenth, nineteenth, and twentieth centuries, the trope was then imaginatively "repossessed" by lesbian writers in order to re-visibilize their repressed sexuality, re-embody their decarnalized desires, reclaim their suppressed subjectivity and identity (31, 47).

The trope's defining paradoxical quality also explains its conceptual power for deconstructing the heteronormative construction of sexual identity. In Butler's work, the trope serves to explain not only the process of repression of the homosexual abject, but also the constant return of the repressed and its disruptive effect on the heteronormative definition of sexual identity. The trope indeed appears repeatedly in *Bodies That Matter* to explore the way normative heterosexuality is "haunted" by the "spectre" of the other sexual identities it excludes and abjects, which it must constantly "repress" in order to sustain the borders of its own identity. The "troubling return" of these repressed identifications threatens the boundaries of the heterosexual subject as "the persistent possibility of their disruption and rearticulation" (23, 8). Writing almost at the same time as Butler, Diana Fuss also notes that heterosexuality is "haunted" by "its terrifying (homo)sexual other." In her introduction to *Inside/Out: Lesbian Theories, Gay Theories*, she identifies in the collected essays "a fascination with the specter of abjection, a certain preoccupation with the figure of the homosexual as specter and phantom, as spirit and revenant, as abject and undead" (3). As a response to heterosexuality's abjection of the homosexual, she argues, gay and lesbian theoretical production "emerges . . . as a kind of ghost-writing, a writing which is at once a recognition and a refusal of the cultural representation of 'the homosexual' as phantom Other" (4).

Holland also demonstrates the critical and political power of forms of resistance that appropriate, rather than reject, the very terms and modes of marginalization. According to her, letting the dead "speak from the space that is familiar to them," that is, from the very space of death-in-life, has more "revolutionary" potential than invalidating the condition of social death and bringing the socially dead back into the realm of the living. "Embracing the subjectivity of death" (4) thus means recognizing that "any move to speak to the center implies a *use* of its vocabulary" (152). "Raising the dead," as Holland terms this process, disturbs the boundaries that delimit the social and symbolic spaces of life and death, troubles the dichotomies of center and margin, oppressor and oppressed, language and silence. Similarly, the ambivalent, dual quality of the ghost shows that the alternative, or response, to invisibility and absence is not necessarily visibility and presence. As Peeren argues in her discussion of marginalized groups—migrants, domestic workers, mediums, and missing persons—in the contemporary British and American cultural imagination,

> subjects designated as ghostly in the dispossessing sense of being considered invisible and expendable are not restricted to the option of rejecting

> the associations outright by insisting on their full visible materiality and social significance. They may also work *with* the metaphor, reshaping it to activate other, more empowering associations of the ghost in order to go from being overlooked to demanding attention by coming to haunt. . . . Living ghosts might be able to manipulate the way they are metaphored, turning the figure to their advantage. (7–8)

Particularly in contexts and situations in which becoming visible and asserting one's presence might make one subject to violence and, in the extreme, literal erasure and actual death, embracing and appropriating ghostliness may be a safer and ultimately more productive option. Exploiting the ghost trope in this dual way "acknowledges both the strength of the spectral metaphor and the difficulty of escaping the designations through which one is socially (un)recognized" (183). As I demonstrate in the rest of this chapter, Cliff uses the ghost in this double way. On the one hand, the trope signifies the abjected, invisibilized—and, sometimes, self-invisibilized—queer subject in heteronormative discourse and society. On the other hand, the ghost's (absent) presence and constant return have destabilizing effects on the forces that seek to repress and erase it. In Cliff's texts, the ghost trope is, to use Peeren's terms, "strategized and, in the process, re-oriented" (184) to critical and subversive ends.

Unlivable Identities

The different forms the trope takes in the texts I examine depend in part on the historical and geopolitical context in which the stories are set. Homosexuality is repressed as much in the late twentieth-century United States as it is in World War II Europe and in colonial and postcolonial Jamaica. But while in the American-set stories the ghosting of the queer subject largely takes the form of invisibilization, it takes more radical forms in the context of fascist Italy and of Jamaica, in which the notion of homosexuality as an unlivable identity translates dramatically literally. If the systematic persecution of homosexuals belongs in Italy's past, "the abominable crime of buggery" is still prohibited in Jamaica (L. Williams 385), while same-sex relations between women, though absent from the legal framework, suffer from wide social intolerance.[19] This largely explains the extent to which queer sexuality long remained invisible in Caribbean literature, though critics and writers disagree on just how long. Although some have noted that queer representations are "not at all a new textual concern" in Caribbean literature, since they can be traced as far back as the 1930s (Cummings 324), others have identified the period since the 1980s as one of "coming to light" in which Caribbean writers have finally brought the issue of sexuality, and homosexuality more particularly, "into the open" (King, "Sex and Sexuality" 31, 34). As recently as 2008, Thomas Glave, editor of *Our Caribbean: A Gathering of Lesbian and Gay Writing from the Antilles*, presented this book, the first anthology of its kind, as an attempt to initiate "an ending of silences and invisibilities" (10).

Our Caribbean contains one short story by Cliff, a story that poignantly evokes the abjection of queer and its rejection into the unlivable zone of social life.[20] "Ecce Homo" offers a particularly dramatic account of both the symbolic erasure of queer sexuality and the literal elimination of the queer subject. Set in the context of World War II, and of the fascists' persecution of homosexuals, the story relates the tragic fate of two men, an Italian and a naturalized American from Africa, who meet in Rome and become lovers. Discovered and arrested by the fascists, they are deported to a concentration camp, from which they manage to escape. After hiding for some time in the woods, they are found by an American company of black soldiers. The Italian is made a prisoner of war, whereas the American is sent back to the United States, promising his lover that he will send for him "when this is all over" (70). When the American hears that his lover killed himself shortly after they were separated, he breaks down and is committed to a mental institution. He spends the rest of his life there, with the ghost of his lover by his side.

The ghost trope more specifically appears in a reference to the pink triangle the lovers have to wear in the concentration camp, which identifies them as homosexuals and which, when the Americans find them, is "but a ghost on [their] chest[s]" (69). The two men are ghosted because of their sexuality by being removed from society and sent to a camp to work, and likely die; if the pink triangle actually visibilizes them as homosexuals, it does so only within the unlivable space of the camp, a space they share with all those identities—homosexuals, Jews, ethnic minorities, enemies of the regime—that cannot exist. But when the American soldiers find them in the woods—another zone of unlivability in which they can freely live their love but could not survive for long—they must invisibilize the reason for their persecution from their saviors, join the domain of the livable if they indeed want to live. If their self-ghosting is necessary, the tragic end both men meet, one in death, the other in a psychiatric hospital, shows that they ultimately cannot escape the unlivable domain, that they remain impossible identities.

In *Abeng*, the ghost trope also suggests the unlivable character of queer identities, but it takes a different form, one more directly related to the Jamaican context of the novel. In an episode that is relatively brief but reappears several times in the novel, the narrator relates how Clinton, a man who, the rumor said, "preferred the company of his mama to any other woman," was left to drown in the river to the shouts of "battyman, battyman" (63)—the derogatory term in Jamaica for a homosexual man. Not only did Clinton die, but because the men his mother paid to take care of the proper burial rites ignored her instructions, his duppy rose from the grave to restlessly roam the land. The people's indifference to Clinton's life and to his death, denying him the right to either because of his deviant sexuality, literally condemns him to the limbo of living death, in effect defining his identity as unlivable. In a way similar to D'Aguiar's use of the zombi, Cliff turns the figure of the duppy on its head, showing how this traditionally malevolent and monstrous figure in Jamaican folklore is here actually the victim of far more cruel and dangerous forces. Clinton's duppy figures, both literally and symbolically, as the (dis)embodiment of the violence against queer people in Jamaica.

Clinton's (living) death finds an echo in the novel in the equally tragic fate of Clare's uncle Robert, who "caused some disturbance when he brought a dark man home from Montego Bay and introduced him to his mother as 'my dearest friend'" (125). Forced to discontinue this relationship and keep to the normal, quiet life that would preserve the family's respectability, Robert finally "did what Clare understood many 'funny' 'queer' 'off' people did": just as Clinton drowned in the river, Robert "swam too far out into Kingston Harbor and could not swim back" (126). The memory of Robert, who is actually not Clare's real uncle but "happen[s] to be her godfather" (125), significantly surfaces in the narrative, and in Clare's consciousness, in the midst of her confused feelings and reflections regarding her friend Zoe, after the two girls have been bathing in the river. Robert's story, as Timothy Chin points out, serves "as an implicit warning to Clare against the dangers of transgressing the boundaries of what is culturally sanctioned as acceptable or 'normal' sexual behavior" (137) within the family and the larger community. These are precisely the boundaries that Clare's relationship with Zoe could easily lead her to cross. By loving, like Robert, someone who is not only of the same sex but also darker than herself, Clare would act in double contradiction to her father's exhortation to lighten up the family. She has already transgressed gender boundaries by taking her friend on a wild pig hunt armed with a rifle—clearly a man's job. When a cane cutter happens upon the girls lying naked on the river rocks after they gave up the hunt,

Clare fires the rifle in order to scare the man off and accidentally shoots her grandmother's bull. Banished from Miss Mattie's estate, thus also effectively separated from Zoe forever, Clare is then sent by her parents to live with "a family friend," Mrs. Phillips, an old white widow who will teach her to become a proper "lady" (148, 150)—that is, a woman who knows, and keeps to, her place.

Clare's isolation and confinement at Mrs. Phillips's, where she is forbidden to interact with anyone but her mentor, echo a common motif in queer gothic narratives. As Paulina Palmer notes, lesbian gothic writers have often resorted to the genre's typical depiction of women's persecution by their husbands or parents and their incarceration in locked rooms or mental asylums, motifs in which they find "references to interests and experiences corresponding to [their] own" (*Lesbian Gothic* 11). Clinton was the victim of the community's violence but had the love and support of his mother, however powerless she was; Robert's death and Clare's confinement, on the other hand, show that this violence is often perpetrated within the family itself, confirming Palmer's assertion that the family unit is often a primary site of repression and oppression of nonnormative sexuality. But it is in the short story "Bodies of Water" that Cliff engages most fully with the motifs Palmer identifies with lesbian gothic, in particular the evocation of home and family relationships as "oppressive and claustrophobic" (11) for the queer subject. This story also makes much use of the ghost trope, but in a way that conveys invisibility rather than unlivability. The ghost works here on various levels to suggest both the ghosting of queer by heteronormative society and the queer subject's self-ghosting.

Ghosting and Self-Ghosting

"Bodies of Water" opens with the view of an old woman, later identified as Anne Dillon, fishing on a frozen lake. Through Anne's stream of consciousness we gather that her partner, Bessie, recently died and that the mention of Anne as "sole survivor" (124) in the local newspaper caused a bit of a scandal and prompted her "unimaginative" but nevertheless "dangerous" niece to threaten to "make arrangements" for her (123). Anne resists the idea of being removed to and contained in an institution. Should the threat be carried out, however, her only solution would be another form of disappearance: she would "take off, head West, change her name" (125). Her desperate plan confirms Castle's point that the invisibilization of lesbians is often reinforced by their "self-ghosting, hiding or camouflaging their sexual desires or withdrawing voluntarily from society in order to escape such hostility" (7). Moreover, although she is still free and alive, Anne is not immune to symbolic and rhetorical ghosting. Her love relationship with Bessie is never named for what it is, suggesting that it is impossible: the niece calls Anne's lover her "friend," while the niece's husband, attempting to assuage her fear of scandal, says that people will see them only as "two old maids. That's all" (124). Anne attempts to resist this symbolic erasure, however, not only by naming herself Bessie's "sole survivor" but also by refusing to take Bessie's name off the mailbox where it stands next to hers, perhaps the most affirmative statement of same-sex love in the story.

As she is fishing, Anne is being watched by a younger woman, Jess, who occupies a neighboring house in her brother Bill's absence. Most of the story unfolds through a letter from Bill that Jess is reading, and through the thoughts and memories the letter conjures in her. We learn how, after the parents of the fourteen-year-old Bill found out about his queer sexuality by reading his diary, they subjected their son to symbolic, psychological, and physical violence. As they go see a doctor for advice about his deviant condition, they lock him on the glass porch, a closet of sorts that is simultaneously a part of the family house but not really inside it, suggesting both the parents' control over the boy and their exclusion of him from the "normal"—heteronormative—family space. With the sun "magnified in the glass" (140), the porch becomes a torture chamber, as Bill's skin burns, his throat closes, and he vomits in the unbearable heat and light. Significantly, the only way out he contemplates is through death, imagining he could smash the glass with a lamp and cut his wrists with the shards; helpless as he is, he does not even consider smashing the glass in order to escape the porch, let alone his oppressive home and abusive parents. His reaction recalls Anne's: faced with the threat of being sent to a nursing home, Anne thinks to herself that they will not "take her alive" (125), preferring death to a closet that her niece sells her as "a pleasant place" (124) but that she knows would be really something between "a nursery" and a "padded cell" (123).

While the adult Anne can perhaps resist her niece's project to internalize her, young Bill is utterly powerless when his parents decide to have him treated with electroshock and, when that fails, send him to "some tough place" (122) to toughen him up. Like Anne's ghosting, Bill's invisibilization by being locked away in an institution is paralleled and reinforced by his symbolic and rhetorical ghosting. When his parents go see the doctor, they are dressed in the clothes "they had worn to the great-grandmother's funeral the year before" (142), glossing his condition as a symbolic or social death, or as pertaining to the unlivable. The boy's efforts to defend himself against his parents' violent reaction are "silenced" (141) by his father, who will not even look at him, thus making him in effect invisible to him. Just as Anne and Bessie's love is unnamable, Bill's sexuality is qualified as a "sickness" and referred to as an undefined "it" whose referent is never spoken in the story. This elusion is partly explained by the fact that the events are related through the consciousness of Jess's younger self, who at the time did not understand what was going on, beyond the vague sense that "there is something wrong with her brother" (142). But it is also dramatized by the persistent failure of the adult Jess and Bill to name it. Bill's confession as a child in his diary is strikingly elliptical: "*I think I may be. I think I am*" (143). Similarly, in his letter to Jess he admits to his inability to use the word "lover" to refer to his neighbors Anne and Bessie, just as he shies away from using the verb "die" to refer to Bessie's death, preferring the euphemism "pass away" (132). This is presumably because of the fear that his own oncoming death provokes in him: although it is never stated clearly in the story, it seems that Bill is ill with what one would imagine to be HIV/AIDS.[21]

It is also probably because of his illness that he left his house and retreated somewhere not even his sister knows about. Not only ghosted by his parents and the heteronormative society they stand for, Bill is thus also forced to ghost himself: as a boy, he had to efface his queerness on his return home after his "cure," passing as a "tough" boy who has learned carpentry and takes girls to the prom; as an adult, he feels compelled to erase himself physically by removing himself to a place unknown, and to rhetorically erase himself in his letter. Whereas the third-person narrator repeatedly draws attention to Jess's body by relating her physical desires and sensations—she is warm, she is cold, she drinks coffee and vodka, she smokes, she takes a bath—Bill's own words in the letter suggest that all these simple, bodily pleasures and needs no longer concern him: Jess can eat all his food and dispose of his old clothes, he tells her, implying he will no longer need them. Appearing in the narrative only through his written words, Jess's memories, and the memorabilia in the house he deserted but somehow haunts, Bill is, indeed, a ghost in the story. For all we—and Jess—know, he might already be dead. While the narrative often alludes to the ghosts that are rumored to haunt the lake by which Bill's and Anne's houses stand, the real ghosts in the story are those who are so ghosted that they are not even referred to as such in any direct way.

This motif, the ghosting of the queer subject, also appears in Cliff's poetry, in particular in the last poem of *Claiming an Identity*, "Separations."

The poem evokes an unnamed woman, who is not only qualified as a ghost but indeed appears as a ghostly presence in the text. Already dead at the time of narration, she appears only "in photographs. Occasional flashes. The complicated indications of dreams" (62), as the persona is helping her sister and mother sort through the latter's possessions. Information about this woman is scarce and scattered. We gather that she held an important place in the persona's childhood, caring for her and taking her on trips, and that she died of breast cancer despite her mastectomy. The persona, a very young child at the time, was deeply impressed and affected by the view of the sick, emaciated, flat-chested woman, and mourned her deeply and privately after her death. At the end of the poem, the woman is finally identified as the persona's aunt, her mother's sister.

The way the aunt appears and disappears in the poem, like a fleeting memory that the persona is trying to hold on to but that keeps eluding her, conveys her ghostlike quality. While nothing explicitly identifies her as a lesbian, several details and the general sense of mystery and secrecy that surrounds her code her as a queer figure. First, the aunt, and more particularly her body, are simultaneously visibilized and invisibilized in the poem. In the descriptions of the photographs, attention is given to her clothes, accessories, and hairdo: a girl in a silk dress with a watch, ring, and bracelet and curly hair; a young person in white trousers with a necktie as waistband, her hair wet from a swim in the sea; a thinner woman in "Sunday dress, hat, gloves" after her surgery. Her face, however, always remains "[i]ndistinct," or is described in vague terms, such as "long" and "solemn" (63), terms that tell us little about her features. Despite her descriptions she remains a blur in the mind of the persona, who is trying to conjure her from the images on the photographs and in her memory. If attention is repeatedly drawn to her body, this body is in fact generally marked by absence, notably that of her breasts and of the fleshiness she lost to illness—a ghostly presence in themselves.

The fact that the persona's mother refuses or is unable to talk about her sister suggests there is something unspeakable, secret, beyond or behind the pain caused by her death. Her portrait in one photograph from the thirties, dressed in what at the time would have been considered men's clothes—trousers and a necktie—creates an uncanny effect, one of "radical uncertainty about sexual identity—about whether a person is male or female, or apparently one but actually the other" (Bennett and Royle 38). The way the persona compares her to "a cricketer announcing his affiliation" (*CI* 63), identifying her with a man and imbuing the word "affiliation" with suggestive meanings, confirms this confusion in gender and sexual identity. In these descriptions, the aunt troubles what I referred to earlier, quoting Butler, as the "naturalized knowledge" about these categories. In the striking "final image" of the poem, a photograph captioned "Baby and the ghost," the persona appears as "an infant, seated on the lap of a shrouded figure. A woman covered by a bedspread to look like a chair" (64). Associating again the aunt with the uncanny, this time troubling the boundary between animate and inanimate, person and object, the photograph seems to offer an extreme example of both the invisibilization and the dehumanization of the queer subject: the literal covering up of the queer woman and her identification as a piece of furniture, a nonsubject, an unlivable identity.

Traveling with Ghosts

"Separations" traces the persona's attempts to—quite literally—*see* her aunt, as well as to make her intelligible, to recover her from the domain of the unlivable to which she seems to have been condemned. What the persona reclaims here, however, is not only her aunt but also herself. Palmer's statement that queer subjects living in a heteropatriarchal society often suffer from "a sense of deprivation at being denied a history and the sense of identity which it promotes" (*Lesbian Gothic* 20) is useful for understanding the relationship between the persona and her ghostly aunt. According to Palmer, the oppressive and repressive nature of traditional family relationships for queer subjects makes it necessary for them to create "alternative attachments and groupings" that can offer sites of "self-definition and emotional fulfilment" (18). This search for sustaining bonds outside the biological, heteropatriarchal family is often associated with a search for identity and for origins, both individual and collective. This quest for historical, cultural, and symbolic precursors is also an important theme in queer Caribbean literature, in which it contributes to contesting the notion that homosexuality is a western import (Calixte 132) and challenging the homophobia often deployed in nationalist discourse (Cummings 329).

In "Separations," the aunt plays an important role in the persona's attempt at self-definition and identification with a sense of collective history. Despite her absence, the aunt appears as a nurturing figure throughout the poem, in ways that significantly oppose heteropatriarchal representations. The breastless aunt seems more caring than the persona's mother, who did not breastfeed her. She is also more nurturing in the sense that she is associated with history and memory, while the mother is associated with forgetting and erasure. After she decided to "live without her possessions," the mother is ready to "[t]ear everything up" (59, 60), including the photographs, the persona's diplomas, awards, degrees, and letters. The aunt, on the contrary, is repeatedly associated with the desire to remember, not only because she appears as a trace in photographs and memories, but also because she apparently shared experiences and trips with her niece. "I have had a history with this woman—she is not my mother" (62), the persona says of her aunt, associating her with history while separating, through the dash, her mother from both. Even after her death, as a ghost, the aunt stimulates the persona's connection with the past in a way that the mother consistently refuses to do. "I have traveled with this ghost," the persona remembers; and she continues traveling with her in memories, following her "through the places of [her] past." In one of these places, "a small child waits for [them]—dirty, pale, with open sores," who asks her, "Will you take me with you, this time?" If we read this child as the persona's young queer self, who was abandoned, neglected because of the pressures of compulsive heterosexuality, then the role of the aunt becomes clearer: by choosing to "leave [her mother and sister] to themselves" (64) at the end of "Separations"—the poem that also closes *Claiming an Identity*—and to travel with the ghost of her aunt, the persona rejects the heteronormative structure of her family and embraces a quest for the recovery and rehabilitation of her queer self.

"Separations" thus ends on an affirmative, albeit bitter, note. Whatever the persona will do and allow herself to be with this recovered sense of self and history lies outside *Claiming an Identity*; but her departure, following the ghost of her aunt, certainly holds promises. In this respect, the persona's fate contrasts with those of the queer protagonists in the other stories I have examined, who significantly do not have any alternative, sustaining social structure outside the heteronormative family. In "Ecce Homo," the two lovers have no one but each other, and when one dies the other withdraws into himself and waits for death. In "Bodies of Water," Anne seems to have been completely isolated since Bessie's death. As for Bill, despite his claims that he is with people who "know what to do"—presumably about his illness—and that he "still ha[s] friends in the city" (137), he confesses in his letter that he is "lonely" (132). Even his loving sister is unable to help him, as an adult as much as she was as a child, and is only a powerless witness to his absence. *Abeng* and *No Telephone to Heaven*, on the other hand, include several characters who could serve as guides for Clare. But, as a young girl, she is either ignorant of their existence or unaware of their queer identity.

One of these characters is Bertha, a character Clare does identify with, but only in her attempts to come to terms with her mixed racial and cultural identity. Yet the dialectic opposition of Jane Eyre and Bertha Mason, which also appears in *Claiming an Identity*, not only distinguishes between the British, white Jane that Clare has been brought up to become and the Caribbean, creole Bertha with whom she ultimately chooses to identify: it also differentiates the loving and devoted female heroine who becomes Rochester's wife from the wild creature he once married for money rather than love. As Palmer has noted, Charlotte Brontë's Bertha can be read as an example of threatening female sexuality: the attic in which she is kept locked and hidden "exudes an air of frustrated female passion which on occasion breaks free from constraint to pervade the mansion as a whole" (*Lesbian Gothic* 65). Not only a female gothic figure and a ghost who haunts Thornfield Hall, Bertha is also, according to Cliff herself, an image of the lesbian monster. Brontë's descriptions of her, she notes, emphasize her "virility" and "maleness"; Jane's reference to her predecessor as "the clothed hyena" further identifies Bertha as a queer figure in Cliff's mind, for the hyena is commonly believed to be "a hermaphroditic creature, capable of switching his/her dominant sexuality." In keeping with the gothic motif of the wife incarcerated by her husband and certified as dead, Thornfield Hall's attic is therefore also a closet behind the doors of which the "sexual monstrosity" ("Caliban's Daughter" 48) that Bertha is remains securely locked, a space where her unlivable identity can be confined. Indeed, her queerness is so closely controlled that it does not even appear in Clare's consciousness—or, for that matter, in critical discussions of Cliff's work.[22]

More obvious among Clare's "historical precursors" (Chin 137) is Mma Alli, a much-respected slave on Judge Savage's plantation, whose existence Clare knows nothing about. Significantly described as a one-breasted woman, Mma Alli "had never lain with a man" and "loved only women in that way." She teaches women not only "the magic of passion," but also how to "keep their bodies as their own," and contributes to freeing them from the most violently enforced form of compulsory heterosexuality by helping them terminate rape-produced pregnancies. As a figure of resistance and an obeah woman who knows "the ways of the Maroons" (*A* 35), Mma Alli is directly linked to Nanny. Nanny is herself often represented as a queer figure in literature and criticism. Her descriptions often trouble gender boundaries, as she is portrayed as a mix of ferociousness and caring and is commonly referred to as a "childless mother" in Jamaican folklore and literature. In a poem by Jamaican writer Lorna Goodison, she appears as a warrior with flat breasts whose "womb was sealed / with molten wax" to induce "the state of perpetual siege / the condition of the warrior." This operation, as Jenny Sharpe notes, only seems to have reinforced her mother-like qualities and functions, for "then [her] whole body would quicken / at the birth of everyone of [her] people's children" (qtd. in J. Sharpe 32).

Abeng evokes Nanny's mythical role in the foundation of Jamaican society, stating that Jamaicans are descended either from the rebel who chose to flee slavery or from her sister Sekesu, who remained in servitude (18). That Clare is Nanny's spiritual descendant is quite clear, as I noted in the first part of this chapter; but the nature of their rebellious character entails more than my discussion of racial and cultural identity suggested. "Marronage," as Cummings points out, appears in Cliff's novel and in other queer Caribbean texts as a culturally specific trope for exploring Caribbean queer subjectivities, by "link[ing] contemporary sexual dissidence to a history of rebellion" (329). Nanny is therefore a founding figure not only for an anticolonial or postcolonial tradition of resistance, or even for a "female-centered tradition of resistance," as she has commonly been identified: she also functions as a "historical or 'genealogical' precedent for an 'indigenous' lesbian/gay subjectivity" (Chin 137). More than an elusive and unconscious connection to the African diasporic heritage Clare had to suppress, Nanny's haunting presence in *Abeng* can thus also be read as the repressed but potential link to Clare's queer self. This second, less obvious function of Nanny's ghost remains, however, equally unfulfilled in *Abeng*.

As Clare reclaims Nanny in *No Telephone to Heaven*, she also comes closer to claiming her queer identity. It is no doubt significant that the scene the guerrillas interrupt with their aborted attack on the film set at the close of the novel is precisely one that casts Nanny as a sexy, stunningly dressed woman engaged in a romantic exchange with a strong, athletic Cudjoe on the point of rescuing her from a forest monster. Symbolically, what Cliff's guerrillas disrupt here is not only an act of "cultural cannibalism" (F. Barnes) by which the neocolonial power—here represented by a joint British-American film production—appropriates and perverts Jamaica's history of resistance through a gross misrepresentation of its iconic figures: they also disturb, if only temporarily, a narrative that securely circumscribes Nanny in a heteropatriarchal version of history. That nothing suggests this is part of their purpose in attacking the film set, however, only confirms that Nanny's queerness is an aspect of her history and identity that even the guerrillas who fight in her name have forgotten—or repressed.

As I suggested earlier, the end of *No Telephone to Heaven* brings Clare and Nanny together, not only in death but also as ghosts. Clare's death can be read in various ways, and indeed Cliff herself has offered contradictory views on it. In "Clare Savage as a Crossroads Character," she describes it as a fulfilling ending by which Clare becomes one with her ancestors and her homeland landscape, figured as female. In her later interview with Meryl F. Schwartz, she does not fully repudiate this rather positive reading of Clare's end, but she nuances it: being burned into the Jamaican landscape may be seen as "one way of becoming whole," she concedes, but Clare, in the end, is "still dead." More importantly, she links wholeness to sexuality, explaining that "for Clare to claim her lesbianism in the Caribbean would be to become a complete woman." Had Clare not died, she concludes, "she probably would have gone the whole way" (601). She gets close, notably through her relationship with Harry/Harriet, the only person she feels an "ability to feel for" and a desire to "love" (*NTH* 128, 130). Significantly, Harry/Harriet, especially as Harriet, is portrayed as a descendant of Nanny and Mma Alli, whose tradition of folk healing practices he/she perpetuates and puts in the service of the community by serving as a nurse and as a "medical officer" (7) for the guerrillas. Like the persona's aunt in "Separations," Harriet travels with Clare along the back roads of Jamaica, helping her reconnect with both the black folk culture and the nascent queer sexuality she left behind in her exile to the United States. Indeed, their trips through the country and the moments of intimacy they share by the sea and the river are reminiscent of the times Clare shared with Zoe as a girl, until her territorial and sexual explorations were brought to an abrupt end.[23] With Harry/Harriet she picks up exploring again, and her relationship with him/her is, in Cliff's own words, "a step towards herself" (Schwartz 601).

Queer Writing, Ghost Writing

Why, then, does Cliff not allow her protagonist to reach this wholeness, except in death? According to her, the reason why Clare "can't claim her sexuality" even in *No Telephone to Heaven* is that "she's not in a place where she can," because Jamaica is such a "repellently homophobic society" (Schwartz 601). This no doubt explains why Cliff herself decided to settle in the United States and not return to Jamaica (612). Homophobia seems to have also been particularly strong within her own family. It is noteworthy that the incident that provokes Bill's (self-)ghosting in "Bodies of Water," namely his parents' discovery and reading of his diary, is actually a memory from Cliff's own childhood. Inspired, like Clare, by Anne Frank, young Cliff found in writing a diary "a way of survival," a way to "maintain her identity" and to keep herself "separate from [her] family" in what she described—echoing Palmer—as "a very claustrophobic situation" (Raiskin, "Art of History" 68). Her parents' intrusion into her private world had dramatic effects on her: she said she did not write again until her 1978 piece "Notes on Speechlessness" ("Caliban's Daughter" 38).

What is particularly interesting for my argument here is that while Cliff mentioned this incident in three different interviews, she connected it with sexuality in only one of them—the latest of the three. "It's all very fragmented in my mind right now," she explained in the 1992 interview, "but I'm remembering more and more" (Schwartz 604).[24] The diary incident was thus not only a "silencing event" (603) in Cliff's writing history: it also apparently caused her to repress the memory of both the event itself and the girl she was in love with at the time—who, like Bill, was removed (to a boarding school) by her parents.[25] For this repression, as well as for what she acknowledged as her "self-censorship" on matters related to sexuality in her literary writing, Cliff blamed the "internalized homophobia" (604) that growing up in Jamaica, and in her family more particularly, ingrained in her. This may explain why queer, while it figures prominently in her later fiction—notably her last novel, *Into the Interior* (2010), significantly qualified on its cover as "her most intimate, courageous work of fiction"—appears only as a "subtext" (Schwartz 604) in her early writings.

But this absent presence should not be read as a mere defeat against or submission to the repressive and invisibilizing forces of heteronormative discourse and homophobic society. Rather, it also constitutes an oblique mode of resistance against these forces through the re-signification of the very trope that effected the erasure of queer in the first place. Using the same trope to write *about* and *back to* the processes of abjection or invisibilization of queer subjects and identity is fruitful on a number of levels. First, as Peeren points out, "Staying within the logic of spectrality avoids relying on notions of demystification or exorcism in which the 'real' can be fully freed of what haunts it" (23). For example, while the community's definition of Clinton's queer identity as unlivable literally turned him into a ghost, his wandering duppy also signifies the troubling return of the queer presence that will not let itself be erased completely. The very same people who mock his mother's endless efforts to lay his spirit to rest take every precaution to protect themselves from it, because they know that they are responsible for his death and living death and that "his duppy might seek them out" (*A* 65).

Most of Cliff's queer characters, however, do not have this capacity to haunt. Bill, Anne, and the lovers of "Ecce Homo" cannot resist their ghosting, nor in fact avoid self-ghosting. While Peeren locates "spectral agency"—this haunting force that "challeng[es] the mechanisms that produced them as ghosted" (24)—in the protagonists of the texts she examines, in most of Cliff's works the disruptive power of the trope is not to be found in the ghostly characters themselves but in the way the ghost allows the writer to critically re-vision queer identities. Rather than denying or countering the process of invisibilization by bringing queer—queer subjects, queer desire, and queer itself as a textual concern—into broad light, Cliff opts for an elusive mode that, following Fuss, I would call a form of "ghost writing." As Butler's use of the trope suggests, the constant return of the repressed functions "not only as an *imaginary* contestation that effects a failure in the workings of the inevitable law [of heteronormativity], but as an enabling disruption, the occasion for a radical rearticulation of the symbolic horizon" (*Bodies That Matter* 23) in which sexual identities are fixed. By playing on the conditions of visibility and invisibility, presence and absence, voice and silence, Cliff's use of the ghost destabilizes *from within* the dichotomous positions and, hence, identities that these categories delimit. As a trope that cannot be defined in opposition, but only in relation, to the living and the dead—as it is simultaneously similar to and different from both—the ghost enables a reconfiguration of queer identities in non-oppositional terms to heterosexuality. She thereby eschews a traditional opposition that fatally condemns nonheterosexual identities to remain marginal and secondary to the norm.

The ghost thus has much in common with the term and concept of "queer" itself, which is often described as "always ambiguous" or as characterized by its "fundamental indeterminacy" (Jagose 96). Like the ghost, queer "does not assume for itself any specific materiality or positivity," so that "its resistance to what it differs from is necessarily relational rather than oppositional" (98).[26] For all its fluid and unstable significations, however, queer remains a term used to *name*. The ghost, in contrast, conveys the (absent) presence of queer through the unstable, elusive, and ambiguous power of haunting, surfacing in fragmentary and obscure allusions, remaining suggestive rather than explicit and definite. While young Bill's elliptical "*I think I may be. I think I am*" translates his difficulty to express his sexual identity or his fear of outing it—an act of un-naming that, tragically, does not protect him from repressive measures—Cliff's un-naming of queer identity constitutes a theoretical, political, and poetic strategy that refuses the stabilizing and fixing gesture of normative categories and definitions—a gesture that has often been seen as a colonialist one (Calixte 131).

Significantly, this strategy is a response not only to heteronormative definitions, but also to homonormative ones. It notably works against the dominant Euro-American gay paradigm, a paradigm that largely relies on the promotion of public visibility and oppositional identity politics. Many postcolonial critics have denounced "the teleological, Western-centred developmental narrative of coming out and recognising one's homosexuality" (Pecic 12) as "a form of cultural imperialism that imposes a prescriptive framework of same-sex desire" on non-western cultures (Edwards, *Postcolonial Literature* 114). As Omise'eke Natasha Tinsley puts it, the closet can be read as a defining trope for the space in which not only queers but queer studies themselves have been confined. As she pertinently asks, "Is being 'out'/doors a mark of privilege for cane field workers or washerwomen? And for how many Caribbeans is a closet a standard feature of houses?" (*Thiefing Sugar* 26).[27] Similarly rejecting the imperative of visibility and identity politics in favor of an absent presence and unfixed identity, Cliff's ghost writing qualifies as what Halberstam would describe as a "new grammar," a "different, anarchistic type of struggle" (*Queer Art* 129) closer to the guerrilla mode that uses the colonial and neocolonial oppressors' own weapons against them.

As the guerrillas' demise at the end of *No Telephone to Heaven* shows, however, this strategy is not without risk. The signification of a silence, an absence, a ghost is never obvious, but indeed requires decoding, interpretation, interrogation, lest it be understood by those who make, maintain, or endorse normalizing definitions as a mere sign of their power and legitimacy. As Peeren reminds us, "Haunting, like agency, is not a property one simply has" but "is conditional upon being noticed" (182, 16). Donnell has come to a similar conclusion regarding Caribbean writers' endeavors to reconceptualize sexuality in their own terms: "without critical discourse to bring these issues and debates forward," she fears, "the un-naming of sexual subjectivity that characterises these works may not be recognised as a crucial demand for and imagining of new kinds of rights-bearing discourses" (245). Moreover, the two levels I have sketched above in summarizing the ghost's subversive power, namely the level of the characters and that of the writer, suggest the potential limits of this literary and theoretical re-vision of identity, which, as my discussion of race already concluded, represents a crucial resistance to the symbolic violence of hegemonic discourses but may be of little avail when confronted with a physical violence that locks up, abuses, and even disintegrates bodies. "I am afraid my place is in the hills," Cliff writes in *The Land of Look Behind* (103)—in the hills of Jamaica's Cockpit Country, with the duppies of Nanny and Clare. Unlike her protagonist, Cliff did not return to Jamaica, except on occasional visits. She explained she could imagine a life there only "as somebody who would be dedicated to extreme political change," and she did not "see that degree of change as a possibility in Jamaica" (Schwartz 600). It is this "killing ambivalence" (*LLB* 103) that makes her work so complex and compelling.

Cliff's work addresses the dilemma identity has posed to all those who have tried to claim one in a racist, classist, sexist, and heterosexist world: to maintain what Hall calls the "great social collectivities" of race, class, gender, and sexuality that "stabilize our identities" ("Ethnicity" 342) despite their limiting, prescriptive, and exclusionary nature; or to abandon them and, in the process, lose the sustaining ground and the power of the identity politics they support. Cliff's re-vision of identity offers a middle way that points, I think, toward what Butler envisaged as a "new shape of politics" (*Gender Trouble* xxxii). Cliff confirms that the loss of a stable, reified subject-position should not be lamented as a failure "but, rather, affirmed as the promise of the possibility of complex and generative subject-positions as well as coalitional strategies that neither presuppose nor fix their constitutive subjects in their place" (Butler, "Gender Trouble" 210). Through her use of the ghost, Cliff queers the limits of identity even as she acknowledges the importance of claiming the provisional and always fleeting identities that remain necessary to living and "writ[ing] as a complete Caribbean woman" (*LLB* 14)—whatever that might mean.

A chapter on Cliff is an important contribution to a book concerned with exploring the literary and political construction of diaspora. While D'Aguiar evokes the founding moment of diaspora, and Naylor and Marshall show how even those estranged from the community can reclaim it by re-visioning its history and its memory, Cliff complicates the notion of diaspora itself, not only because of her own vexed position in it, but also in the way her work destabilizes the very notion of community. As the texts I have examined throughout this book demonstrate, diaspora as a community is fashioned through the re-membering of fractured (social) bodies, of silenced histories, and of repressed affiliations. But Hartman also reminds us that "the 'warmly persuasive' and utopian quality that the word 'community' possesses, with its suggestion of a locality defined by common concern, reciprocity, unity, shared beliefs and values, and so on" should not lead us to ignore that—in slavery's time as much as today—community is "characterized as much by antagonisms, distrust, contending interests, values, and beliefs as by mutual cooperation and solidarity" and that betrayal and exclusion are "inevitably a part of the making of community" (*Scenes of Subjection* 59). As suggested by her reaction to what she qualified as the "plain bitchy" remark (Schwartz 607) accompanying her semi-inclusion in *Her True-True Name*, Cliff was painfully aware that the light skin and middle-class position that are generally considered as privileges could also serve as a motive for exclusion, just as can a nonnormative sexuality, even a ghosted one. Her texts explore not only the intersecting and mutually constitutive powers of racist, sexist, and heterosexist discourses, but also the way power, privilege, and solidarities can shift. Many episodes in Cliff's fiction and poetry confirm Hall's point that "a transgressive politics in one domain is constantly sutured and stabilized by reactionary or unexamined politics in another" ("What Is This 'Black'" 473). In *Abeng*, two young girls' bond against sexism dissolves when the lighter and wealthier one picks up a rifle and the King's English to assert her authority. In *The Land of Look Behind*, a Jamaican man falls silent in the face of racism in a London bar only to recover his voice to mock the gay waiters in the next restaurant. As Cliff's various personas repeatedly remind us, "the whole business is very complicated" (*LLB* 68).

AFTERWORD

LEARNING TO LIVE WITH GHOSTS

Haunted places are the only ones people can live in.
—Michel de Certeau, *The Practice of Everyday Life*

WHY DO THE DEAD RETURN? This is a question that any study of ghosts is bound to ask. The answer, from psychoanalysis to popular culture, has generally been this: the dead return "*because they were not properly buried*, i.e., because something went wrong with their obsequies. The return of the dead is the sign of a disturbance in the symbolic rite, in the process of symbolization; the dead return as collectors of some unpaid symbolic debt" (Slavoj Žižek, qtd. in C. Davis 2). This is also the answer that Morrison gave in a conversation she had with Naylor, at the time she was writing *Beloved*. Describing her work as a matter of responsibility, toward her protagonist, Sethe, but also toward all "these unburied, or at least unceremoniously buried, people" in history, she understood the novel as her way of "properly, artistically, burying them" (Naylor, "Conversation" 209). Later in the same conversation, she talked about her obsession with the photograph of a dead girl that was, with the story of Margaret Garner, the inspiration for *Beloved*—but ultimately became the starting point of *Jazz*. All her writing, she explained, had been about "rescuing [the dead girl] from the grave of time and inattention. Her fingernails may be in the first book; face and legs, perhaps, the second time. Little by little bringing her back into living life" (217).

Another comment by Morrison helps illuminate this apparent contradiction of a literary project that simultaneously attempts to bury and dig up the dead. In another conversation, she explained that when she first submitted the manuscript of *Beloved* to her editor, it ended with the reunion scene between Sethe and Paul D, and the hope that these two would finally have "some kind of tomorrow" (*Beloved* 273). She admitted she was not sure, at the time, that what she had written could be a book and that, in any case, it was in her view far from complete (Caldwell 241).

While this comment does not explain how or when the two-page coda that now closes the book—but certainly not the story—came to be added, a third conversation, one year after the publication of *Beloved*, sheds light on its meaning and purpose, which by her own admission she came to realize only later: "I didn't know that before or while I wrote it. I can see now what I was doing on the last page. I was finishing the story, transfiguring and disseminating the haunting with which the book begins" (Morrison, "Bench by the Road" 44–45). What Morrison means here by "transfiguring and disseminating the haunting," and how the other texts I have examined in this book also attempt to do precisely this, is what I wish to address in order to bring this study not to a close, but to new openings. For indeed this, I will ultimately argue, is also a function of the ghost trope, as well as of re-vision.

The last two pages of *Beloved* have been read in various ways. They have also often been overlooked, as if the novel still ended with Sethe's incredulous but wishful response to Paul D's affirmation that she is her own "best thing" (273). But the coda, whose poetic density and opacity raise only more confusion as to the identity, origin, and purpose of the ghost, casts a shadow on this hopeful, albeit bittersweet, ending. In the reading most optimistic for the protagonists, it suggests that Sethe and Paul D might indeed find some peace in forgetting, but that their disremembering causes the dis-membering of Beloved, whose worst nightmare comes true as she "erupts into her separate parts" (274) and is swallowed away. In a more pessimistic and, in my view, more careful reading, their dis(re)membering of Beloved will not protect them from a past they have tried to beat back all their free lives, a past that will return, again, and again. At the end of the novel, the ghost is, as Roach would say, "forgotten but not gone" (31). If her traces—the touch of her hand and the rustle of her skirt, her footprints by the stream and her familiar features in other people's faces—eventually fade, it is not because she has disappeared but because the living are no longer able, no longer willing, to look for or decipher the traces of her presence. Unlike the Day women of Willow Springs, they do not know, they do not want to know, that a sound in the wind is *not* "just weather," but really *is* "the breath of the disremembered and unaccounted for" (*Beloved* 275).

The twice-repeated phrase, "disremembered and unaccounted for," which has echoed throughout this book, clearly refers to more than the ghost Beloved—which already signifies beyond itself. Based on the self-serving notion that "remembering seemed unwise" (274), Sethe and her community's failure to remember and be accountable for Beloved and all she signifies puts them disturbingly close to the supporters of the master narrative of History, who deem some memories unsafe, too. Morrison has commented on black people's "struggle to forget the terrors of slavery." If it was "important in order to survive," she admits, it is damaging and ultimately "fruitless," and the aim of her work is, precisely, "to make it fruitless" (Gilroy, *Small Acts* 179). "This is not a story to pass on," *Beloved*'s coda repeats and insists. The dual meaning of this moral pinpoints what Morrison has described as the "perfect dilemma" posed by Beloved and by the memory of slavery she signifies: "Forgetting is unacceptable. Remembering is unacceptable" (qtd. in Goddu 154). What, then, is to be done?

All the writers I have examined in this book address this dilemma, and their texts explore various ways of dealing with it—various ways, that is, of dealing with ghosts. To simply ignore the ghosts is never really an option: as Avey quickly learns, they have a way of making sure you heed them. In traditional stories where ghosts are a supernatural, intrusive presence come to claim payment of a symbolic debt, exorcism is commonly understood as an appropriate way to deal with them: these ghosts return, as Colin Davis puts it, only to be sent away again (2); once our debt to them has been paid, peace restored, symbolic order reestablished, they are generally happy to leave us alone and disappear to finally enjoy some long-awaited rest. The texts I have examined here, however, refuse such resolution. The reasons for this are poetic as well as ethical and political. Not only do Morrison, D'Aguiar, Naylor, Marshall, and Cliff "work very hard" to write books that "haunt" (Morrison, in McKay 146), but resisting closure is also crucial to what I understand as these writers' purpose in "disseminating the haunting" beyond their texts and beyond the particular stories they tell.

By refusing to lay their ghosts to rest, these writers first remind us that, when dealing with slavery, racism, heterosexism, systematic oppressions of all kinds, there is no peace, no original order to restore. Their narratives contradict the notion of a preexisting whole, unified self or community that can be healed, a notion that also overlooks and obfuscates those experiences in which trauma is a normal—that is, the result of social norms and institutions—everyday presence rather than a single disruptive event. If their texts serve redressive purposes, in exploring scenes of subjection and disruption, in tending to the social and cultural body of diaspora, they acknowledge their own necessary limitations through their tentativeness, their fragmentedness, their open-endedness. Just as the slaves' dances invoked but could never enact a return to "an originary plenitude" (Hartman, *Scenes of Subjection* 74) of the mind, the body, and the self, and had to be repeated again and again to sustain life in a regime of social and physical death, writers of the African diaspora conjure the ghosts of the past, again and again, to gesture toward, but never achieve, a remembered history, memory, and identity.

In disavowing the possibility of exorcism, they also suggest that the debt, hardly symbolic in the first place, can never be paid. As D'Aguiar shows, the ghosts can never be fed because their full story cannot be told once and for all; there can never be a last essay, a last novel, a last historical study about slavery. But feed and entertain the ghosts we must, as Cocoa knows, whose conversation with George continues beyond the open-ended end of *Mama Day*. If, like Cocoa, we must mourn the dead, we must do it in a way that remains, as Gordon puts it, partial to the dead as much as to the living (184). In *Specters of Marx*, Derrida associates mourning with exorcism: both are "incantatory" (64, 59) processes that reaffirm the death of the other and bury the dead for good, putting them "in [their] place. A safe place" (9)—a phrase that uncannily echoes Sethe's justification for killing her baby daughter. Rather than exorcism, Derrida calls for a mourning "by right interminable" (121).[1] Against the teleology of traditional definitions of mourning, he invites us, like the writers I have examined here, to "learn to live *with* ghosts" (xvii–xviii), to find modes of being that keep us partial to the dead without foreclosing life. Haunting is what Parham and Brand call this mode of being, in the sense of a consciousness of the persistence of the past in the present, of death in life. Living "in the wake" is what Christina Sharpe terms it, exploring the multivalence of a term that means "the keeping watch with the dead, the path of a ship, the consequence of something, in the line of flight and/or sight, awakening, and consciousness" (*In the Wake* 17–18). Being in the wake means living with the dead, remaining in the shadow of the slave ship; but, crucially, "the knowledge of this positioning avails us particular ways of re/seeing, re/inhabiting, and re/imagining the world" (22).

Haunting, living with ghosts, being in the wake—whatever its name, this way of dealing with the dead is a re-visionary mode that is necessary for approaching not only the past, but also the present and the future. Indeed, as Derrida points out, insofar as it "is always called upon to come and to come back," the ghost, "contrary to what good sense leads us to believe, signals toward the future" as much as toward the past (245 n. 39). Although they are set in the time of slavery, novels like *Beloved* and *Feeding the Ghosts* are not so much "past-obsessed" as they are "forward-haunting," as Dennis Childs puts it, for the conditions they describe "haunted their way into the present" ("'You Ain't Seen Nothin' Yet'" 274).[2] Indeed—and this is the third reason for which these texts refuse closure—to eventually banish the ghost would be to claim that, like what it signifies, it belongs in other times. It would amount to reestablishing a distinction between past and present that, as I argued, only serves a master narrative of progress. In disseminating the haunting in their stories beyond the boundaries of the texts, Morrison, D'Aguiar, Naylor, Marshall, and Cliff pose the same question Hartman raises in "The Time of Slavery"—a time that is anything but past: "How might we understand mourning, when the event has yet to end? When the injuries not only perdure, but are inflicted anew? Can one mourn what has [not] yet ceased happening?" (758). These questions have grown only more pressing in the few years since I began writing this book. In a time in which it must be affirmed and repeated, shouted on streets, written on protest signs, T-shirts, brick and virtual walls, that Black Lives Matter, because it is not self-evident, because "dead blacks are a part of normal life here," in such a time the very condition of black life has become, in Claudia Rankine's words, one of endless mourning.

These writers' engagement with the ghosts of the past is therefore not about what LaCapra describes as a "fidelity to trauma," a "melancholic sentiment" that perceives working through the past as a form of betrayal (*Writing History* 22). Rather than a pathological and debilitating condition, their engagement is an ethical imperative and a political commitment; rather than an isolated and self-isolating position resistant to social and socializing forms of mourning, these texts are engaged together in a larger collective project. Kaplan's concept of "diasporic melancholia" offers a helpful way of articulating these two aspects, the productive fidelity to trauma and the collective dimension. In her discussion of Julie Dash's film *Daughters of the Dust*—a film that bears many similarities with *Praisesong for the Widow* and that would certainly have fit in my discussion—Kaplan proposes a definition of melancholia that re-visions its traditional, Freudian characterization as individualist, past-absorbed, and pathological, and recasts it as collective, present- and future-oriented, and productive. Paying particular attention to the diasporic religious traditions that the film deploys and relies on, the very same traditions I have evoked throughout this book, she argues that diasporic melancholia emerges as a practice that "transform[s] grief into the articulation of grievances that traverse continents and cross time" ("Souls at the Crossroads" 513). If past, present, and future are inextricably linked, it is not only because the horrors and violence of the past keep returning: if the past holds pain, it also holds strength and nurturance for the present and the future.[3]

Learning to live with ghosts is therefore, as Derrida intimated, not only a politics of memory but also a politics of inheritance, a respect and responsibility for the dead as well as for the not-yet-born (xviii). So is the Janus-faced—or Legba-legged—re-visionary project of the texts I have examined. Not only an act of looking back, re-vision is, as Rich proclaimed, "an act of survival"; not only a way to see, but also to live, "afresh" (18). As these texts amply show, learning to live with ghosts is in no way easy or painless, as it means learning to live with loss and absence, open graves and gaping wounds. But the best we can do, in the encouraging words of a ghostly grandmother to a young woman who feared stepping into the world, is to "know it, and go on" (Morrison, *Beloved* 244).

NOTES

Introduction: Tracing the Ghost

1. For an examination of ghosts in Morrison's work see Anderson and Bennett.

2. Dash's novel is a sequel to her 1991 movie, also titled *Daughters of the Dust*, which is narrated by the ghostly voice of the unborn child of two of the characters.

3. Geraldine Smith-Wright devotes one chapter to ghosts in African American women's literature (looking at Zora Neale Hurston, Ann Petry, Toni Morrison, and Paule Marshall) in the collective volume *Haunting the House of Fiction: Feminist Perspectives on Ghost Stories by American Women.*

4. "If so-called 'so-called poststructuralism' is the product of a single historical moment," Robert J. C. Young argues in *White Mythologies*, "then that moment is probably not May 1968 but rather the Algerian War of Independence." Young points out that many of the most influential poststructuralists (Jacques Derrida, Jean-François Lyotard, Hélène Cixous, Louis Althusser) were either born in Algeria or directly involved in the War of Independence (32). Pal Ahluwalia further examines the colonial roots of poststructuralism in a book that also criticizes the subservient position into which the common view of postcolonialism's theoretical debt to poststructuralism places the former, and poses pertinent questions about the reasons for the general silence about, or even suppression of, poststructuralism's colonial affiliations.

5. Sladja Blazan suggests that the current fascination with ghosts may have more to do with "the agenda-setting of leading literary journals and globally-distributed, established publication houses' programs" than with the supposed return of a figure that was, after all—it is its characteristic—"always present, even in [its] absence" (2).

6. Peeren reiterates this point in *The Spectral Metaphor* about Achille Mbembe's use of the ghost trope in his analysis of sovereignty and terror in the postcolony (48–49).

7. In his study of diasporic religions in the Caribbean and the United States (such as Haitian vodou, Brazilian candomblé, Cuban santería, Revival Zion in Jamaica, and the Black Church in the United States), Joseph Murphy identifies as the distinctive and common feature of these diverse beliefs and practices the promotion of a (ritualized) relationship of reciprocity between the living and "the spirit": while the community makes the spirit present through word, music, or dance, the spirit in turn fills the community and its individual members with its power (6–7). This reciprocal and mutually sustaining relationship is as important for the living as it is for the dead.

8. See for example Winsbro; Chireau; Jessee; Christian; and Sandiford.

9. Mbiti's general account of African religions and philosophy has been criticized for its totalizing and homogenizing view of what are in fact diverse regional or cultural traits, as well as for its use of western concepts and categories—such as that be-

tween the supernatural and the natural, the religious and the secular—that some have viewed as "the quintessence of conceptual colonization" (Wiredu 33). The influence his study has had on both subsequent discussions of African beliefs in diasporic cultures and on readings of *Beloved* and other novels shows, however, that this culturally informed perspective on the novel has been useful for critics' understanding of these aspects, including my own.

10. It is commonly believed that the most famous of all slave revolts, the Haitian Revolution, was inaugurated by a vodou ceremony during which the insurgents called upon the spirits for courage and support. Some scholars have recently questioned the historical veracity of the ceremony, or nuanced its influence on the course of the revolution. David Geggus thus notes that although "there is good reason to emphasise the magico-religious world outlook of the slave masses," the success of the revolt certainly rests more on the insurgents' "cautious guerrilla tactics" (51) than on whatever happened on that one day at Bois Caïman. Indeed, other scholars have analyzed the way exoticizing representations of the ceremony served as a fantasy for colonists as much as French abolitionists and the Haitian elite to assert their difference and present Haitian culture as primitive, superstitious, and therefore in need of western control—a fantasy that has continued to justify western interventions in Haiti to this day.

11. Carpenter and Kolmar note that the trope of the haunted house allows women writers to address the violence lurking within the home and the ideals of domesticity within which women have traditionally been confined (Introduction 14). As I analyze in chapter 4, this is a motif Cliff appropriates, but also complicates by showing how not just patriarchy, but heteropatriarchy, restricts women's and queer men's freedom, and how women, and mothers in particular, are complicit in this structure of physical and symbolic violence.

12. Rich calls more specifically for a rewriting of canonical literature, a re-visionary impulse we also see in some of the texts I will discuss. Cliff rewrites such classics as *Jane Eyre*, *Great Expectations*, and *Ivanhoe* through her protagonist's identification with or sympathy for these texts' racialized—and therefore marginalized—characters (Bertha, Magwitch, Rebecca), while Naylor rewrites *The Tempest* by making Miranda the magician and title character and rather emphasizing the powerlessness and inadequacies of the male protagonist.

13. For a more detailed analysis of this association between spectrality and deconstruction see Royle's "Phantom Review."

14. In his introduction to *Invisible Man*, Ralph Ellison addresses a similar paradox as he surmises that it is black people's "high visibility" that actually makes them "un-visible" to white Americans (xxxiii). His protagonist is invisible not because he is a ghost, but because "people refuse to see [him]," because they have "a peculiar disposition of the eyes" that is really a "matter of the construction of their *inner* eyes, those eyes with which they look through their physical eyes upon reality" (3).

15. According to James Ferguson, this paradigm shift in the conception of history was coeval with the epistemic shift in the anthropological schema of human history from the theological conception of a "Great Chain of Being," in which all the creatures in the world, including the various types of humans, were ranked according to their various but immutable degree of perfection (i.e., their proximity to God), to social

evolutionism, according to which societies were classified on the basis of their development from savagery to civilization. As confirmed by the long-standing depiction of Africa as a continent characterized by both its savagery and un(der)development and its lack of history, historiography has been intricately linked to social evolutionist anthropology. Both take the form of developmental narratives, and both were contested in the latter part of the twentieth century.

16. Caribbean writers and cultural critics, in particular, have written at length about the inadequacy of a linear and progress-driven conception of history for the Caribbean, and explored alternative—or, as Edward Kamau Brathwaite writes, "alter/native" —epistemologies and historiographies to the colonial model. These alter/natives, given the situation of the Caribbean, often draw on the movements and qualities of the sea: its cyclic, continual, and shifting ebb and flow inspired Brathwaite's "tidalectics," a model that opposes the synthesizing and deterministic *telos* of Hegelian dialectic ("New Gods" 45–46); Derek Walcott situates history in the timeless and uncharted sea rather than in the human-centered chronology and geography of colonialism ("The Sea Is History"); and Antonio Benítez-Rojo's theory of the "repeating island" describes the Caribbean as a region that is as much in flux as the waters that encompass it, and Caribbean culture and history as resisting the regularity of clock and calendar times (11).

17. A view in which "time is no longer just a neutral form of history but its force as well" (Paul Ricoeur, qtd. in Stone-Mediatore 112) has also served, as Shari Stone-Mediatore points out, to surreptitiously neutralize the responsibility and agency of the actors of history: if time, rather than people, is the motor of history, then faith and patience, rather than critique and contestation, are the adequate attitudes until injustice and oppression disappear. In such a view, time becomes, as Martin Luther King Jr. famously said, "an ally of the forces of social stagnation" (qtd. in Stone-Mediatore 112).

18. That this issue of representation is a common preoccupation of trauma studies and poststructuralism is no coincidence. James Berger identifies in the poststructuralist rhetoric an emphasis on "decentering, fragmentation, the sublime and apocalyptic" (573) that he tentatively relates to the traumatic historical events of the middle of the twentieth century. Many prominent figures of poststructuralism—notably Derrida, Lyotard, Dominick LaCapra, Geoffrey Hartman, Shoshanna Felman, and Hayden White—turned to writing about the Holocaust in their later works, which seems to confirm that there is an affinity or a continuity between poststructuralism and trauma theory. As Berger analyzes, both are "discourse[s] of the unrepresentable, of the event or object that destabilizes language and demands a vocabulary and syntax in some sense incommensurable with what went before," and discourses that strive to "demystify all sorts of 'narrative fetishes' . . . and ideologies" (573, 574).

19. While reading slavery in this way certainly provides another reason for the place it has come to occupy in African diaspora literature, other writers and scholars have taken issue with this view, which makes slavery and trauma the defining and constitutive features of diasporic culture and identity. For Hortense Spillers, the notion that trauma can be transmitted across generations in the form of a collective or racial unconscious is tantamount to a form of social and historical fatalism, as black people would thus "never be anything but haunted" (Haslett).

20. Because my interest in this book is in this discursive formation rather than in a racially (self-)identified group, I will only use the term "black" when specifically discussing the effects of racial/racist discourses and structures.

21. This explains why I do not include African writers in my discussion, even though ghosts, spirits, and other forms of living dead also feature prominently in contemporary African literature, such as in Ben Okri's *The Famished Road* (1991) or in the work of Amos Tutuola and Ngũgĩ wa Thiong'o. On the latter two see Mbembe and Cheah, respectively.

22. Cliff and D'Aguiar were born or spent their childhood in the Caribbean (Jamaica and Guyana, respectively) but lived most of their lives in England or the United States. Marshall was born and raised in the United States as a second-generation immigrant of Barbadian descent; she identifies her first visit to her parents' native island as a crucial moment in her life and an important influence on her writing. Naylor was born in New York but had strong roots in the South through her parents; in setting *Mama Day* in the Sea Islands, a region occupied by communities known for having preserved much of their African linguistic and cultural heritage, Naylor clearly engages with a diasporic tradition and draws connections with *Praisesong for the Widow* and other texts, such as Dash's *Daughters of the Dust*.

23. Bernard W. Bell coined the term "neoslave narrative" in 1987, the year *Beloved* appeared. Ashraf Rushdy contributed an entry on the genre in *The Oxford Companion to African American Literature* in 1997, one year before the publication of *Feeding the Ghosts*, and devoted a whole book to it two years later, at the same time as Elizabeth Ann Beaulieu and her *Black Women Writers and the American Neo-Slave Narrative*.

1. "Voyage through death / to life upon these shores": Representing the Middle Passage

1. On the reception of both Turner's painting and Ruskin's description of it see McCoubrey.

2. Binder offers a useful, though now outdated, overview of the major narrative texts evoking the Middle Passage.

3. Analyzing "*Beloved*'s lapse in, and loss of a novelistic storytelling capacity" in this passage, Sabine Broeck argues that by thus figuring the Middle Passage as "the literary space of a telling narrative void," Morrison "rather purposefully created a want" (par. 3).

4. Kaplan makes this argument in the context of her discussion of discourses on the relationship between Thomas Jefferson and Sally Hemings, which also rely on a traditional dichotomy, that of coercion and consent. Although this is not the focus of my argument, I will briefly return in chapter 2 to the limitations of a dichotomous view of their relationship pivoting on the supposedly mutually exclusive notions of coercion and consent, violence and seduction—notions that Hartman's *Scenes of Subjection* also deconstructs at length.

5. That the trope of the living dead is useful for re-visioning an aspect of history that has consistently resisted expression is confirmed by the fact that it also appears in at least three other texts, all produced in the same decade: in Dabydeen's long nar-

rative poem "Turner" (1995), the persona is the half-submerged African forever floating in the foreground of Turner's painting; in Clarence Major's "The Slave Trade: View from the Middle Passage" (1994), the speaker is the spirit of a captive who jumped overboard and uses this mid-Atlantic position to understand the slave trade by contemplating its three angles; and the voice-over narrator in Guy Deslauriers's dialogue-free film *Passage du milieu* (2000) is revealed at the end to be already dead, as he was killed and thrown overboard before the ship reached American shores. For an analysis of *Passage du milieu* and its many similarities with Smallwood's and D'Aguiar's representations of the Middle Passage see my article in *Atlantic Studies*.

6. Equiano's identity as African-born has however been put into question by Carretta, on the basis of new biographical evidence that suggests he may have been a native of South Carolina ("Olaudah Equiano").

7. By subverting western accounts of European-African encounters and reversing the traditional figure of the monstrous Other, Equiano's description offers an ironic re-vision of European discourses on race and alterity and a clever questioning of western rationalism: the Europeans' alien appearance and incomprehensible language relegate them outside the realm of humanity; *they* are the savage cannibals. Moreover, the technology that made them the masters of the oceans and made the supremely rationalized institution of the slave trade itself possible is presented as "magic" (57).

8. For a similar and more detailed reading of this passage see Baucom's *Specters of the Atlantic* (271–72).

9. The design has often been used for covers, notably for Barry Unsworth's Booker Prize–winning novel *Sacred Hunger* (1992) or for Bob Marley and the Wailers' 1979 album *Survival*. It has also been extensively reappropriated by visual artists, who have tried to work against the dehumanizing nature of the original picture. For a discussion of the *Brooks* as icon and an account of some of its reappropriations see also Francis and Bernier.

10. "middle passage, n.," def. 1, *OED online* (Oxford University Press, December 2016).

11. Smallwood's notion of "kinlessness" refers here to the captives' condition outside a sustaining kinship system and its metaphysical consequences on their understanding of death. As Spillers noted in her seminal essay "Mama's Baby, Papa's Maybe: An American Grammar Book," kinlessness should also be understood in more direct terms as the condition of the offspring born into a system that reconfigures kinship and familial status as property relations (74). This condition, Spillers argues, redefines not only the notion of kinship and family, but also of motherhood and womanhood. Smallwood's book does not pay particular attention to gender in that respect, but I will return to Spillers's point in my analysis of *Feeding the Ghosts*, in which the choice of a female protagonist precisely allows D'Aguiar to explore these issues.

12. Spillers argues that the captives also occupied a liminal position in terms of gender: as commodities, the male and the female captives' identities were undifferentiated, as they were only taken into "account" as "quantities" (72). One should further note that the liminal position that "human cargoes" occupied "between personhood and property" was also problematic for their legal definition (Webster 296). According to Tim Armstrong, this is why slavery "occupies a middle position in the progress from

insurance on goods to insurance on persons, providing a way of thinking about the value of a life" (170). This middle position sometimes led to legal conundrums, as in the case of the *Zong*.

13. In preferring this spelling to the more common "zombie," I mean to associate the figure to the original African *zombi* and its Caribbean developments, following the work of, among others, Alfred Métraux and Joan Dayan. In doing so, I also wish to distinguish this figure from the hordes of North American living dead that have invaded movie theaters, TV screens, and comic books since George Romero's popularization of the genre.

14. Rediker identifies this transformation in Equiano's narrative, as he adopts "a stark, polar, racialized way of thinking [of] and understanding" the various actors on the slave ship. His confrontation with the horrible-looking seamen quickly leads him to identify with the African traders who brought him aboard the ship, whom he now designates as "black people." Simultaneously, when referring to the crew he adopts "the monolithic category 'white people,' which [is], in his mind, more or less synonymous with mysterious and oppressive terror" (128). While Rediker's analysis suggests that these formulations and categories were those of young Equiano as he was living these events, it is important to keep in mind the temporal and cognitive distance that separates the author-narrator from his younger self. Although young Equiano's awareness of racial difference certainly emerged from his social interactions on the slave ship, "black" and "white" might be categories he came to define later in his life.

15. This view has been debunked as one aspect of the "myth of the negro past" (Herskovits) and denounced as "a fiction that has served several economic orders and their attendant ideologies" (Gates, *Signifying Monkey* 4).

16. Smallwood describes slave rituals performed in America in which some details clearly originate in the experience of the Middle Passage. She notably evokes the case of an African-born slave who decorated his deceased son's grave with "a miniature canoe about a foot long, and a little paddle, with which he said he would cross the ocean to his own country." As she explains, "this man's ritual mortuary practice would not have held any meaning for his kin and community in Africa. None had been required to travel a distance so great and so perilous to reach the realm of the ancestors, and none had required the assistance of a canoe and paddle to achieve the soul's departure for another realm. It was a gesture that could be understood only by those who shared the memory of the slave ship" (189–90).

17. As such, the limbo imagination is also an alter/native to linear, teleological History, as it "dislocates (and therefore begins to free itself from) a uniform chain of miles across the Atlantic" (Harris, "History" 159)—just as the dancer's spider-like movements thwart the line of the pole. For a discussion of African diaspora writers' reconceptualizations of history in relation to limbo—as well as to Legba, a figure I address in chapter 3—see Russell.

18. In her recent *Territories of the Soul*, Nadia Ellis theorizes this in-betweenness, this gap between the here and there, as defining of diasporic condition. Articulating "the structural relationship between queerness and diaspora," which both counter "nationalist teleology or conventional reproductive futurity" (99), she reads diaspora as a form of "queered belonging."

19. The underwriters appealed, but historians have found no evidence that a second trial took place.

20. There are many examinations of the *Zong* case, to which the *Journal of Legal History* devoted a special issue, based on a 2006 symposium. The most detailed and complete historical account to date is James Walvin's recent *The* Zong*: A Massacre, the Law and the End of Slavery*. Also of note is Baucom's compelling theoretical and philosophical analysis of the event's economic, cultural, and ethical dimensions and legacies in *Specters of the Atlantic*.

21. D'Aguiar dramatically contrasts the brutal jettisoning of the Africans, dead or alive, with the ritual that accompanies the sea burial of a crewman. While the naked and defenseless bodies of the Africans are thrown straight into the jaws of sharks that follow in the ship's wake, the sailor's corpse is wrapped in his hammock and ballasted with iron so that it will quickly sink. Before the "carapaced body" (108) slides gently off a plank into the sea, the captain opens his Bible and says the name of the dead man, William Pelling. The deaths of the nameless slaves, on the other hand, are recorded as mere strokes in his ledger.

22. The novel also suggests that time does not only resist the Africans' habitual ways of measuring it, but is controlled by the slavers: during the three days at sea that the novel relates, time seems to be regulated by the strokes the captain makes in his ledger to account for the dead, and each day ends when he allows the killing to finally stop for the night.

23. As I further note in chapter 2, the notion that "pleasure" would be at all possible under conditions of unfreedom has been questioned. Spillers also asks whether "'sexuality,' as a term of implied relationship and desire, is . . . appropriate, manageable, or accurate" to describe any situation under the slave system (76). D'Aguiar has spoken enthusiastically about interracial love and described his previous novel, *The Longest Memory*, as a response to the taboo of interracial relations in slavery times (Frías 420). *Feeding the Ghosts* presents Mintah and Simon's relationship as one of love, but it seems possible only because Simon's status is close to Mintah's: he is constantly subjected to verbal and physical abuse by the crew, and the way he embarks on the first departing slave ship when he leaves the courtroom, despite his traumatic experience aboard the *Zong*, suggests he is a slave to the trade in his own way.

24. For a more detailed discussion of D'Aguiar's treatment of gender, kinship, and the maternal see Low.

25. Like Smallwood's example of the boat-carved grave, Mintah's wooden figures can be seen as examples of artifacts born from the Middle Passage itself: originating, through her father, from Mintah's African culture, they prove that this culture did survive the transatlantic crossing; transformed by that experience, however, they would not be understandable by Africans who have not endured it, just as they do not make sense to her visitors in Jamaica.

26. By devoting a whole chapter to the trial, D'Aguiar denounces the whole system that made the dramatic events of the *Zong* not only possible, but justified. His account of the trial makes clear that what happened on the *Zong* was not the deed of a particularly cruel or insane captain, but was inscribed in and justified by the entire legal and moral system that underwrote the slave trade.

27. Deslauriers presumably refers here to the *MC Ruby*, a Bahamian-flagged cargo ship bound for Le Havre, on which eight stowaways from Ghana and Cameroon were murdered and thrown overboard by the Ukrainian crew. One man survived and was able to hide through the rest of the voyage and testify in court. The crew was tried in France in 1995 and found guilty of murder; the captain and second-in-command received life sentences, and the rest of the crew twenty years.

2. *Dusky Sallys: Re-Visioning the Silences of History*

1. In that respect, Hemings is one among a few iconic slave women Jenny Sharpe describes as "singular but not unique" (*Ghosts* xiii), slave women whose historical (and literary) visibility marks as exceptional yet whose lives are also representative of those of many slave women who left no or fewer traces. But unlike Nanny of the Maroons, a figure I will examine in chapter 4, Hemings is known to us only because her name has been associated with Jefferson's and been at the center of a historical—and, as I will suggest, cultural and political—controversy.

2. Many commentators, Morrison included, have noted the irony that the moment when "the white literati" were abolishing the foundations of historical inquiry was also the moment when African diaspora writers, thinkers, and activists were striving to reclaim their history (Gilroy, *Small Acts* 179). For a similar critique see also Deborah McDowell's *"The Changing Same."*

3. Naylor does something similar with the other document that opens the novel, the Days' family tree. There is a striking—and often dramatic—discrepancy between the story the family tree prepares the reader for and what the narrative later reveals. If the tree to some extent helps us understand and remember the relationships within the Day family, it also draws attention to many gaps and absences and raises more questions than it answers. First, it does not provide dates, except for Sapphira, Miranda and her sister Abigail, and Cocoa, whose birth dates are given. This absence is somewhat consistent with the distinctive way the Days, in George's words, "ha[ve] redefined time. No, totally disregarded it" (218), as shown by the fact that they indicate the dead's lifespan with the size of their gravestone rather than dates written on them. But the absence of dates in the tree also silences the premature and tragic end of several members of the family (Jonah, John, Peace, Grace, Hope, and Peace again). Second, the spouses do not appear, thus further silencing other untimely deaths, like the suicide of the first Ophelia, as well as the tragic repetition of "broken hearts" across generations. That generations seem to descend from single parents is particularly significant in the case of Sapphira, who stands by herself at the top of the tree, as if she mothered her seven sons on her own—very much like Hemings.

4. While this difference may seem to be of little significance, the Jefferson-Hemings controversy shows how critical such details can be: establishing the exact dates of the births of Hemings's children—and, hence, the dates of their conception—and confronting them with the dates of Jefferson's presence at Monticello has been crucial to determining whether or not he could have fathered them.

5. Other observers have also pointed out gaps and inconsistencies in the farm book, noting that some entries seem to have been rubbed out, eliminating all trace of the slave's name. This is unusual enough, it has been argued, to suggest that Jefferson

might have wanted to hide incriminating information, such as the existence of illegitimate children. This argument was notably used by Byron W. Woodson, who claimed to be the descendant of Tom Hemings—a claim that was contradicted by the results of the 1998 DNA tests (see note 14 below).

6. Of course, these rules and the methodological principles that support them have changed to some degree since the constitution of the historical discipline, in particular after the "linguistic turn" or "narrative turn" in the last quarter of the twentieth century. However, while most would regard this turn as a paradigm shift in the philosophy of history, commentators disagree on the extent to which it really affected the practice of historiography. In the late 1970s, Lionel Gossman noted that although many historians showed some sign of abandoning the premises and rhetoric of historical realism, the "age of suspicion" seemed not to have affected most of historiography (36). LaCapra reiterated this view in the mid-1980s, claiming that historians "continue to confide in a 'documentary' or 'objectivist' model of knowledge" (*History and Criticism* 17); in fact, he remarks that the repeated assaults launched against this model by philosophers and literary critics had often given rise to "what might almost be called a counter-reformational zeal in reasserting orthodox procedures" (46). And in 1995 Trouillot argued that the traditional positivist approach was so dominant in historical scholarship that it maintained a strong influence even on non-positivists and continues to inform the larger public's sense of history in the western world (*Silencing the Past* 5).

7. Here again historians disagree on the extent to which the suspicion toward oral sources has subsided in the last decades of the twentieth century. While Iggers claims that "oral history was well established by the 1980s" (153), Gwyn Prins nuanced this view by noting that if many historians may use oral history "as pleasant and helpful illustration," it is not commonly accepted as primary material for the study of "documented, modern societies" (120–21). Oral sources are thus used as "second best" when no written sources are available, and their main role is therefore, unsurprisingly, to "facilitate second-best histories about communities with poor sources" (121).

8. Consisting "solely of prominent scholars, historians, genealogists, lawyers, etc.," the Scholars Commission was formed in June 2000 to "make their best informed judgment on the evidence that is currently available on whether Thomas Jefferson fathered any of Sally Hemings' children" ("Scholars Commission"). Although it proclaimed itself an independent committee, it was sponsored by the Thomas Jefferson Heritage Society, a group composed of "concerned businessmen and women, historians, genealogists, scientists, and patriots," whose mission statement includes: "To stand always in opposition to those who would seek to undermine the integrity of Thomas Jefferson" ("Thomas Jefferson"). Made public in 2001 and published as a volume ten years later by Robert F. Turner, the arguments and conclusions of the commission firmly rejected the allegation, with the exception of a one-member, one-page minority report concluding that it is "somewhat more likely than not that Thomas Jefferson was the father of Eston Hemings," while remaining "agnostic as to the paternity of Sally Hemings's other children" (21).

9. Gordon-Reed acknowledges, however, that many black people would also reject the notion of a romantic or at least noncoerced intimate relationship between a slave

woman and her master. She raises the question of whether reciprocation could really be possible within the system of slavery and whether, given that "the slave system was inherently coercive," any sexual act could be understood as anything else than "non-consensual sex, in other words, rape" (109). While scholars like Spillers, Hartman, Jenny Sharpe, and Christina Sharpe have clearly answered these questions in the negative, and problematized the notion of "consent" within the legal and social context of slavery, Gordon-Reed contends such certainties are "true in the theoretical sense" but maintains that we cannot rule out such possibilities "in every situation, under every circumstance" throughout the three hundred years of the institution (109).

10. Trouillot identifies the popular reedition of C. L. R. James's *The Black Jacobins* in the early 1960s and the civil rights movement in the United States as the context that led to the emergence outside Haiti of a counter-discourse that finally identified the event as a revolution (*Silencing the Past* 104–5).

11. Of course, Cocoa and Miranda also follow limited scripts that restrict their view of their ancestor to her power and arguably make them blind to the limits of her agency as Bascombe's slave. As I show in the second part of the chapter, however, what distinguishes Miranda's narrative about Sapphira from George's is its dynamic character, as she is able to re-vision it.

12. Interestingly, Gordon-Reed also points out the possible influence of *Gone with the Wind* on some historians' approach to slaves when she suggests that the common notion of "what a slave sounded like" largely comes from Margaret Mitchell's literary transcription and David O. Selznick's oral rendering of what was supposed to be slave dialect in the novel and its film adaptation (19).

13. As Meisenhelder points out, Cocoa also follows white romantic scripts in her understanding of her relationship with George.

14. DNA tests were run in 1998 on male-line descendants of Sally Hemings's son Eston, of Thomas Jefferson's uncle Field Jefferson (Thomas Jefferson having no officially attested male-line descendants), of the Carr brothers (who were designated by some sources as more likely candidates), and of Thomas Woodson (whose family claimed they were Jefferson's descendants). The tests confirmed a genetic link between the descendants of Eston Hemings and those of Field Jefferson, but invalidated supposed links between the Hemingses and the Carrs, as well as between the Woodsons and the Jeffersons (Foster).

15. As Huggins points out, however, many African Americans, from Frederick Douglass to W. E. B. Du Bois, have also subscribed to this narrative in their faith in the nation's Manifest Destiny (xlvi).

16. Jefferson scholars have rejected Gordon-Reed's work on the grounds that she is not a professional historian and uses methods that come from the fringes of the historical discipline. Although Gordon-Reed holds a degree in history from Harvard, where she is currently a professor of history and law, her detractors often present her as "a lawyer" (Mayer 296). As a scholar, and perhaps as an African American woman, Gordon-Reed does not seem to belong to the guild. As Trouillot reminds us, archival power also "determines the difference between a historian, amateur or professional, and a charlatan" (*Silencing the Past* 52).

17. Derrida bases his rumination on specters on a reading of *Hamlet*, in the first scene of which Marcellus calls to Hamlet's friend Horatio to speak to the ghost in his capacity as "scholar." Derrida glosses the term as "a reader, an expert, a professor, an interpreter" (12).

18. While the narrative structure of *Mama Day*, as a dialogue, demonstrates that George and Cocoa have learned to listen to each other, their respective narratives do not really show it, but more often betray a lack of self-criticism that often verges on bad faith. This reveals the limits of the novel's narrative strategy: the novel cannot both tell the story as if it was happening (in order to delay the revelation of George's death, and of the ghostly character of his narrative, until the very end) and show how the protagonists have grown from an event (his death and their conversation beyond the grave) that precisely happens only at the end of the novel.

19. My reading thus runs against those that identify the ghosts in *Mama Day* as instances of the "supernatural" or "magical" quality of Willow Springs. Although most encounters with ghosts occur in locations typical of the gothic (the woods, a graveyard, an ancestral house), these places are not "haunted" in the sense usually associated with the genre. The protagonists' ghostly interlocutors are in fact clearly distinguished from the "haints" Dr. Buzzard thinks he sees in the woods in his frequent moonshine-induced fantasies (81). More generally, I do not read Miranda's power as pertaining to magic but rather as the result of her profound knowledge of nature—which she knows "how to get under, around, and beside" but knows better than to try to "get *over*" (262)—and her understanding of human psychology, coupled with a strong power of suggestion, for she knows the effectiveness of "disguis[ing] a little dose of nothing but mother-wit with a lot of hocus-pocus" (97). She is much more closely associated with Dr. Smithfield's mainland medicine than with Dr. Buzzard's hoodoo and mojo hands, as her outraged reaction at George's mention of the "little professional rivalry" (196) Dr. Buzzard claims to have with her clearly shows.

20. Meisenhelder points out that hens and eggs are "associated throughout the novel with female creative powers" and argues that George's violent reaction in the chicken coop is due to the fact he is "subconsciously afraid of what the chicken represents" (412).

21. Gordon's description of the affective impact of haunting can be said to parallel or duplicate the affective dimension of literature itself. In the way it offers an alternative or supplement to the "cold" and limited knowledge scientific disciplines provide, literature can be understood as the ghost of history or sociology. I am indebted to Teresa Goddu for this parallel.

22. While Gordon's discipline is sociology, the same question applies to history—and in fact she regularly borrows from Certeau's analysis of historical discourse and adapts it to sociology.

23. A prime example of such differing versions is the way Cocoa and George both relate the fight they have on the night of the hurricane. Both start with the words "Our worst fight ever. And it was all your fault" (230, 232). But of course their perspective on the incident and their respective responsibilities in it are very different.

24. Interestingly, Thandie Newton, who stars as Sally Hemings in *Jefferson in Paris*, also plays Beloved in Jonathan Demme's film adaptation.

3. *"You best remember them!": Repossessing the Spirit of Diaspora*

1. Marshall mentions the way her mother and her friends addressed each other as "'soully-gal'—soul: spirit; gal: the body, flesh, the visible self," by which they "gave one [term] as much weight and importance as the other. They had never heard of the mind/body split" ("From the Poets" 31).

2. As Dayan explains, in Haitian culture zombification results from the simultaneous and correlated weakening of the *ti bon anj* ("little good angel," a person's conscience and personality) and the *lwa* or *loa* (the possessing spirit). When the *ti bon anj* loses its force, so does the *lwa*, which depends on it for support. "Without the lwa, the ti bon anj in turn loses its necessary anchor: the ti bon anj will be free-floating, attaching itself to anything, or in its dislocation may be stolen by a sorcerer and turned into a zombi" (68).

3. A notable exception is Caroline A. Brown's recent *The Black Female Body in American Literature and Art*, which offers a reading of the novel in some ways similar to mine. Stelamaris Coser also associates the steps in Avey's "descent" with "the usual stages of spirit possession" (63), which she mentions in a footnote, but this point does not play any significant part in her reading of the novel. Elizabeth McNeil, on the other hand, reads Avey's initiation in light of the Gullah seeker's journey as described by Margaret Washington Creel, who studied Gullah cultures in the Sea Islands.

4. Of the few critics who refer to at least some apparitions in the novel as ghosts, only Brogan and Smith-Wright give them a particular place in their argument.

5. Double vision is also to be related to the West African notion of "seeing with a third eye," which Brenda Cooper associates with the ability to "capture the paradox of the unity of opposites" (1).

6. Giving it a prominent place in her analysis of Marshall's work, Eugenia DeLamotte actually refers to this technique as "double exposure." Cheryl Wall speaks of "triple exposure," in reference to the three primary locations in *Praisesong for the Widow*—Tatem, New York, and Carriacou—which often collide in Avey's perception.

7. The *lwa* or *loa* are the highest: they are spirits who, having reached a level of *konesans* unavailable to living men and women, can ride, that is, possess, the living. The *houngan* and *mambo*, respectively male and female leaders, initiate new devotees and facilitate the community's contact with the deities and ancestral spirits. The *hounsi*, or "spouses" of the *lwa*, are vodou servitors, generally women, who have been initiated (Olmos and Paravisini-Gebert 285–86).

8. This story, which recalls Mintah's imagined flight back to Africa and Sapphira's legendary walk across the Atlantic, is a major topos in African diaspora literature and culture. In her comments on her film *Daughters of the Dust*, in which Ibo Landing also figures prominently, Julie Dash notes that during her preparatory research she discovered that the story of the Ibos exists in each and every community of the Sea Islands. This, she explains, is due to the message of the story of the Ibos, which is "so strong, so powerful, so sustaining to the tradition of resistance, by any means possible, that every Gullah community embraces this myth" ("*Daughters*" 30). Interestingly, Dash's own version of the story in the film, as related by one of the protagonists, is closely borrowed from *Praisesong for the Widow*.

9. Cliff makes these critiques in much more explicit terms in her novels, ironi-

cally pointing out that sugar, which "was a necessity of western civilization—to the tea-drinkers of England and the coffee-drinkers on the Continent," depended on the slave system (*Abeng* 27) and mocking and denouncing the neocolonial American use of the Caribbean as a "sandbox" (*No Telephone* 187).

10. *Beloved* offers a most poignant example of the process Hartman describes here in Baby Suggs's clearing preaches, in which she calls the men, women, and children of the community—most of them former slaves—to "love their flesh" (88).

11. Vodou appears in various spellings, including "vaudou," "voudou," and "vodoun." Scholars in the field generally avoid the term "voodoo," which appeared during the American occupation of Haiti and is thus understood to have a pejorative connotation. The spelling "vodou" also suggests an African or diasporic origin, rather than a North American one, hence my choice of this spelling—like my preference for "zombi" rather than "zombie."

12. Hartman counts juba as one of the redressive practices she examines in *Scenes of Subjection*. This might explain the rejuvenating and revitalizing effect the dance has on Lebert.

13. Legba and Anancy, or Ananse, are both trickster figures originating from West Africa, but while Ananse is Ashanti, Legba is Fon, and Eshu is Yoruba (Pelton). Shanna Greene Benjamin interestingly argues for an alternative and complementary reading of Lebert as Anancy. Besides explaining Lebert's "gender-swapping qualities," this reading also tones down the strongly gendered identity of Legba, who is, at least in Gates's account, a phallic god. These two figures, Benjamin further notes, "are not mutually exclusive" but rather conflated in Lebert "so that together they will provide Avey with two related, albeit different, energies needed for her cultural reintegration" (54). While Legba's traditional attribute is a cane or crutch, the spider Anancy is often shown with needle and thread, objects that Lebert indeed uses in Avey's presence, and a motif that recurrently appears in *Praisesong for the Widow*.

14. *Feeding the Ghosts* evokes a similar scene when the *Zong* finally reaches land, as Mintah's body is washed and stroked by "softer hands" (133) than those that earlier force-fed her, while softer voices call her name, helping her reattach it to her slowly re-enlivened body. In "Black Atlantic, Queer Atlantic," Omise'eke Natasha Tinsley argues that relationships between "shipmates" on the Middle Passage can be read as queer, "not in the sense of a 'gay' or same-sex loving identity" but "in the sense of marking disruption to the violence of normative order and powerfully so: connecting in ways that commodified flesh was never supposed to, loving your own kind when your kind was supposed to cease to exist, forging interpersonal connections that counteract imperial desires for Africans' living deaths" (199). It is noteworthy that Rosalie's massage enables Avey to reconnect with her body both as a site of reproduction and as a site of erotic pleasure, and that her role interestingly shifts in this passage from a traditional one as maternal figure and culture bearer to a queer one.

15. In her theorization of diaspora as queering time and space (see n. 18 of chapter 1), Nadia Ellis identifies spirit possession as "a structure of diasporic belonging," insofar as "one belongs, under a spirit's possession, neither to oneself strictly, nor to any one particular moment in or place in time. Rather, for an eternal moment, a moment during which nothing but paradox reigns, a subject may be both *here* and *there*" (145).

16. In that respect, it is certainly no coincidence that Marshall made her protagonist a "middle-aged, middle-class black woman" (Baer 24).

17. In that sense, it is not only Avey, but the entire diaspora that suffers from "orphan consciousness." According to Ifekwunigwe, "an orphan consciousness emerges when one does not grow up with one's natal parents or kin—in this case 'Mama Africa.' In a metaphorical sense, one's image of that person can then only be an imaginary construction" (146). Just as orphans can never find their "true," original parents again, cultural orphans must reconstruct their own versions of cultural heritage.

18. To say that Africa is a phantom does not mean, however, that it is "mere phantasm": "It is *something*—not a mere trick of the imagination. It has its histories—and histories have their real, material and symbolic effects" (Hall, "Cultural Identity" 226). For a poignant articulation of this ambivalence, of the effects of "hav[ing] one's belonging lodged in a metaphor" (18), see Brand's *A Map to the Door of No Return.*

19. The fact that Avey seems to be Marshall's first fully African American protagonist makes this rhizomatic construction of her identity and these diasporic connections all the more important, in the absence of a more direct and explicit connection to the Caribbean.

20. Carissa Turner Smith makes a similar argument, basing her discussion of *Praisesong for the Widow* on a critique of Gilroy's inattention to gender in *The Black Atlantic.* Based on the premise that "place itself is static, rather than an ever-changing construction," Gilroy's account, Smith argues, overlooks "the agency and creativity of those who, by law or economics, have been forced to stay in one place" (719, 716).

21. For example, I find Lebert's justification at the Big Drum that he must salute his father's nation first, but will do "a turn or two out in the ring" for his mother "so she won't feel [he's] slighting her" (166), a little difficult to account for, even if, according to Erna Brodber, the kinship system in Carriacou is patrilineal (*Continent of Black Consciousness* 154).

22. Helmreich argues that Gilroy's efforts to contest the collapsing of nation into race and the conflation of cultural with biological heritage in narratives of nationalism and ethnic absolutism—a gesture that allows these narratives, notably British citizenship law, to "exclud[e] people from the 'national family' on the basis of 'racial origin'" (244)—actually recapitulate these very problems because Gilroy relies on the same ideas of kinship, nature, and territory.

23. I borrow the expression "native daughter" from an interview with Maryse Condé in which Marshall relates her own experience of "adoption" by the local community during her visits to Africa in the late 1970s and early 1980s. She explains: "There is an expression of Yoruba or Ibo origin 'Omowale' which roughly translates to mean 'a native daughter has returned.' This expression summarizes the experience of my physical return to Africa" (J. Williams 52). This is a point she also develops in her memoir *Triangular Road* (2008). This account starkly contrasts with Hartman's experience as she describes it in *Lose Your Mother*, published the same year as Marshall's memoir. Recounting a much more recent visit to West Africa, Hartman explains how upon arriving in Ghana and throughout her stay she was called "Orbuni," or stranger.

4. *"A ghost-life": Queering the Limits of Identity*

1. Many of the poems in *Claiming an Identity* also appear in the later collection *The Land of Look Behind*. Throughout this chapter I cite *Claiming an Identity* when referring to the poems that appear in both collections. I subsequently use the abbreviations *CI* and *LLB* in the parenthetical citations to refer to these two works.

2. Critics who have discussed Cliff's early work from a queer perspective have generally focused on the character of Harry/Harriet in *No Telephone to Heaven* and, to a lesser extent, on Clare and Zoe's relationship in *Abeng*. What is still lacking is a broader examination of Cliff's treatment of sexuality beyond these two novels, and indeed beyond single texts.

3. For critiques of and correctives to this "myopia" see E. Patrick Johnson and Mae G. Henderson's *Black Queer Studies*, Roderick A. Ferguson's *Aberrations in Black*, Siobhan B. Somerville's *Queering the Color Line*, and the 2002 special issue of *Modern Fiction Studies* Somerville edited on "Queer Fictions of Race."

4. See, for instance, Audre Lorde's *Zami: A New Spelling of My Name*, Wesley Crichlow's *Buller Men and Batty Bwoys*, Antonia MacDonald-Smythe's "*Macocotte*," and Gloria Wekker's account of "mati" in *The Politics of Passion*.

5. For an analysis of Morrison's ghosts as queer see Bennett.

6. As Paulina Palmer notes in *The Queer Uncanny*, many of the elements Sedgwick analyzes in *The Coherence of Gothic Conventions*, such as motifs of liminality, inside/outside, and live burial, reappear in other forms in *Epistemology of the Closet* (106).

7. In his discussion of Rhys's *Wide Sargasso Sea*, Brathwaite famously argued that "white Creoles in the English and French West Indies have separated themselves by too wide a gulf and have contributed too little culturally, as a group, to give credence to the notion that they can, given the present structure, meaningfully identify or be identified, with the spiritual world on this side of the Sargasso Sea" (*Contradictory Omens* 38). This statement launched a decades-long debate.

8. For Cliff, limiting the definition of Caribbean literature to writers who live in the Caribbean makes no sense, first because this would "diminish [Caribbean] literature enormously," as so many writers do indeed live outside the Caribbean, but also because "the Caribbean doesn't exist as an entity; it exists all over the world. It started in diaspora and it continues in diaspora" (Schwartz 597).

9. Several critics have noted that "'authentic' blackness is most often associated with the 'folk' or the working-class black." According to E. Patrick Johnson, "Much of this sentiment stems from the belief that black economic mobility necessarily breeds assimilationists and race traitors because of interracial mixing. Moreover, there is an assumption that educated blacks are much more likely to disavow their racial 'roots' than might their poor and illiterate brothers and sisters" (*Appropriating Blackness* 23). This view is notably confirmed, as we saw, in *Praisesong for the Widow*, although Marshall resists presenting this as a fatality.

10. The fact that Cliff was the partner of Adrienne Rich, a white American feminist, might be significant here.

11. Blanco and Peeren similarly note that, like other normative "categories of subjectification" (masculinity, heterosexuality), whiteness "can . . . be conceived as spec-

tral" in the sense that "it remains un(re)marked, transparent in its self-evidentiality" ("Spectral Subjectivities" 310).

12. This link is also attested in some nineteenth-century accounts about Nanny and the Maroons (J. Sharpe 9).

13. His reaction thus also echoes Jerome's irritated comment upon hearing about his daughter Marion's participation in the Poor People's March on Washington: her social and political commitment is incomprehensible to her father because, in his view, she does not belong with these people, having never "ha[d] to go without three square meals a day" (*Praisesong* 141).

14. Interestingly, Ginsberg speaks of the "specter of passing," which, she contends, "derives its power not from the number of instances of passing," which actually remains little documented, but "as a signification that embodies the anxieties and contradictions of a racially stratified society" (8).

15. "pass, v," defs. 43d and 43a, *OED Online*, Oxford University Press, December 2016.

16. As King points out, however, gender is the one category that seems to remain stable, as the description specifies that "these people" are "men and women" ("Re/Presenting Self" 597). The presence in the band of the transgender character Harry/Harriet could be seen as destabilizing binary gender here (a view King herself contests), but at this early point in the novel—though late point in the story—Harry/Harriet is named simply Harriet and we have no reason yet to see her as unconventionally gendered. But the fact that she is the only one in the band who does not swap uniforms and keeps the same false identity of the soldier her fatigue once belonged to suggests that her "passing" is in some way different from that of the other guerrillas.

17. King criticizes Cliff, among other Caribbean writers, for portraying trans characters as mere supports rather than "full human beings," as "caretakers" whose only function is to help the "conventionally gendered" protagonists in their quest before being "pushed back into the shadows" ("Re/Presenting Self" 594). Cliff's appraisal of her trans character, however, and the fact that it is rather Clare who ends up drowned in the shadows while Harriet's fate remains unknown, perhaps mitigates King's point.

18. In their introduction to the section on "Spectral Subjectivities: Gender, Sexuality, Race," Blanco and Peeren also point out Butler's spectral rhetoric, but read it with respect to her theorization of performativity.

19. Crichlow explains the differences in the treatment of male and female same-sex acts in the context of Trinidad by the fact that gender roles, though they are stereotypical for both, are more blurred for women, allowing some practices to go uncorrelated with sexual preference, while men's sexual identity is much more closely policed (53).

20. First published in a different version in *Small Axe* (2000), "Ecce Homo" also appears in Cliff's last collection of short stories *Everything Is Now* (2009). My references here are to the latter version.

21. Diana Davidson pertinently argues that by refraining from explicitly identifying Bill as AIDS-infected, Cliff forces us to question our own assumptions and the all-too-easy association of AIDS with nonheterosexual men. Similarly, by never identifying Bill and Jess as white, black, or other, the story "leads us to question how and why race matters" (236).

22. A notable exception is Lisa Walker's *Looking Like What You Are: Sexual Style, Race, and Lesbian Identity*, which examines *Abeng* alongside *Jane Eyre* and Rhys's postcolonial prequel *Wide Sargasso Sea.*

23. For a more detailed analysis of these scenes see Tinsley's *Thiefing Sugar.*

24. In her 1989 interview with Opal Palmer Adisa, she only vaguely explained that the diary contained "very intimate details" (273). We learn here, however, that Bill's desperate outcry, "And don't I have any rights?" (141) was a question Cliff herself asked her own parents. In her interview with Raiskin in 1991, she associated this event with her parents' discouraging attitude toward her desire to write, because in her family it was "considered almost taboo to be a writer. It was too revelatory" ("Art of History" 61). Indeed, the next thing she wrote was her dissertation—a very non-private kind of writing.

25. Cliff returns to this incident in the poem "And What Would It Be Like," published in her 2008 collection of nonfiction, *If I Could Write This in Fire.* Exploring the links between racist and heterosexist ideologies, the poem also echoes scenes from *Abeng* detailing Clare and Zoe's relationship.

26. Queer's real conceptual and political power to deconstruct binaries has been contested, however. Cathy J. Cohen argues that "in many instances, instead of destabilizing the assumed categories and binaries of sexual identity, queer politics has served to reinforce simple dichotomies between the heterosexual and everything 'queer'" (22).

27. For a detailed critique of "the closet as raceless paradigm" see Ross.

Afterword: Learning to Live with Ghosts

1. Several critics have used Derrida's redefinition of mourning in their reading of *Beloved* and of *Feeding the Ghosts.* See Craps; Durrant; Luckhurst, "'Impossible Mourning'"; and Weinstock, "Ten Minutes."

2. In this thought-provoking essay, which recently became part of his *Slaves of the State*, Childs reads *Beloved* not as a neo–slave narrative but as a "narrative of neoslavery" by drawing links between the antebellum and postbellum penal architectures (the slave ship, the plantation, the chain gang) and their extension into the modern prison complex, a "Middle Passage carceral model" that "now encages one out of every nine black men in the United States between the ages of twenty and twenty-nine" (274, 275).

3. The voice-over narrator in *Daughters of the Dust* is the unborn child of two of the protagonists. Sent by the "old souls" to help her father, a wounded man eager to forget and move North, come to terms with the rape of his wife, she leads him to reconnect with the history of his ancestors, a history of violence and oppression but also of resistance and resilience.

WORKS CITED

Abraham, Nicolas, and Maria Torok. *The Shell and the Kernel*. Vol. 1. Translated by Nicholas T. Rand. Chicago: University of Chicago Press, 1994.

Adisa, Opal Palmer. "Journey into Speech—a Writer between Two Worlds: An Interview with Michelle Cliff." *African American Review* 28.2 (Summer 1994): 273–81.

Ahluwalia, Pal. *Out of Africa: Post-structuralism's Colonial Roots*. Oxford: Routledge, 2010.

Alexander, M. Jacqui. "Not Just (Any) *Body* Can Be a Citizen: The Politics of Law, Sexuality and Postcoloniality in Trinidad and Tobago and the Bahamas." *Feminist Review* 48.1 (Autumn 1994): 5–23.

Anderson, Melanie R. *Spectrality in the Novels of Toni Morrison*. Knoxville: University of Tennessee Press, 2013.

Angelo, Bonnie. "The Pain of Being Black: An Interview with Toni Morrison." In Taylor-Guthrie, *Conversations with Toni Morrison*, 255–61.

Ansa, Tina McElroy. *Baby of the Family*. New York: Harcourt, 1989.

———. *The Hand I Fan With*. New York: Doubleday, 1996.

———. *Ugly Ways*. New York: Harcourt, 1993.

Armstrong, Tim. "Slavery, Insurance, and Sacrifice in the Black Atlantic." In *Sea Changes: Historicizing the Ocean*, edited by Bernhard Klein and Gesa Mackenthun, 167–86. New York: Routledge, 2004.

Auchter, Jessica. *The Politics of Haunting and Memory in International Relations*. London: Routledge, 2014.

Baer, Sylvia. "Holding onto the Vision: Sylvia Baer Interviews Paule Marshall." *Women's Review of Books* 8.10–11 (July 1991): 24–25.

Balutansky, Kathleen. "Anglophone and Francophone Fiction by Caribbean Women: Redefining 'Female Identity.'" In *A History of Literature in the Caribbean*, edited by A. James Arnold. Vol. 3, *Cross-Cultural Studies*, 267–82. Amsterdam: John Benjamins, 1997.

Bambara, Toni Cade. *The Salt Eaters*. New York: Random House, 1980.

Barnes, Fiona R. "Resisting Cultural Cannibalism: Oppositional Narratives in Michelle Cliff's *No Telephone to Heaven*." *Journal of the Midwest Modern Language Association* 25.1 (Spring 1992): 23–31.

Barnes, Steven. *Blood Brother*. New York: St. Martin's, 1996.

Baucom, Ian. "Specters of the Atlantic." *South Atlantic Quarterly* 100.1 (Winter 2001): 61–82.

———. *Specters of the Atlantic: Finance Capital, Slavery, and the Philosophy of History*. Durham, NC: Duke University Press, 2005.

Beaulieu, Elizabeth Ann. *Black Women Writers and the American Neo-Slave Narrative: Femininity Unfettered.* Westport, CT: Greenwood, 1999.

Bell, Bernard W. *The Afro-American Novel and Its Tradition.* Amherst: University of Massachusetts Press, 1987.

Beloved. Directed by Jonathan Demme. Touchstone Pictures, 1998. Film.

Benítez-Rojo, Antonio. *The Repeating Island: The Caribbean and the Postmodern Perspective.* Translated by James Maraniss. Durham, NC: Duke University Press, 1996.

Benjamin, Shanna Greene. "Weaving the Web of Reintegration: Locating Aunt Nancy in *Praisesong for the Widow.*" *MELUS* 30.1 (Spring 2005): 49–67.

Benjamin, Walter. "Theses on the Philosophy of History." In *Illuminations*, translated by Harry Zohn, edited by Hannah Arendt, 253–64. New York: Schocken, 1968.

Bennett, Andrew, and Nicholas Royle. "The Uncanny." In *Introduction to Literature, Criticism and Theory*, 36–43. London: Prentice, 1999.

Bennett, Juda. *Toni Morrison and the Queer Pleasure of Ghosts.* New York: SUNY Press, 2014.

Berger, James. "Trauma and Literary Theory." *Contemporary Literature* 38.3 (Autumn 1997): 569–82.

Bergland, Renée L. *The National Uncanny: Indian Ghosts and American Subjects.* Hanover, NH: University Press of New England, 2000.

Bernier, Celeste-Marie. "'The Slave Ship Imprint': Representing the Body, Memory, and History in Contemporary African American and Black British Painting, Photography, and Installation Art." *Callaloo* 37.4 (2014): 990–1022.

Binder, Wolfgang. "Uses of Memory: The Middle Passage in African American Literature." In *Slavery in the Americas*, edited by Wolfgang Binder, 539–64. Wurzburg: Konighausen & Neumann, 1993.

Blanco, María Del Pilar, and Esther Peeren. "Introduction: Conceptualizing Spectralities." In Blanco and Peeren, *Spectralities Reader*, 1–27.

———, eds. *Popular Ghosts: The Haunted Spaces of Everyday Culture.* New York: Continuum, 2010.

———, eds. *The Spectralities Reader: Ghosts and Haunting in Contemporary Cultural Theory.* New York: Bloomsbury, 2013.

———. "Spectral Subjectivities: Gender, Sexuality, Race / Introduction." In Blanco and Peeren, *Spectralities Reader*, 309–16.

Blazan, Sladja. "Introduction: Welcoming Ghosts." In *Ghosts, Stories, Histories: Ghost Stories and Alternative Histories*, edited by Sladja Blazan, 1–8. Newcastle, UK: Cambridge Scholars, 2007.

Boyd, Colleen E., and Coll Thrush, eds. *Phantom Past, Indigenous Presence: Native Ghosts in North American Culture and History.* Lincoln: University of Nebraska Press, 2011.

Brace, Jeffrey. *The Blind African Slave: Or Memoirs of Boyrereau Brinch, Nicknamed Jeffrey Brace.* Edited by Kari J. Winter. Madison: University of Wisconsin Press, 2004.

Brand, Dionne. *At the Full and Change of the Moon.* New York: Grove, 1999.

———. *A Map to the Door of No Return: Notes on Belonging.* Toronto: Vintage, 2002.

Brathwaite, Edward Kamau. *The Arrivants: A New World Trilogy.* London: Oxford University Press, 1973.

———. *Contradictory Omens: Cultural Diversity and Integration in the Caribbean.* Mona, Jamaica: Savacou, 1974.

———. "New Gods of the Middle Passage." *Caribbean Quarterly* 46.3/4 (September–December 2000): 12–58.

Brodber, Erna. *The Continent of Black Consciousness: On the History of the African Diaspora from Slavery to the Present Day.* London: New Beacon, 2003.

———. *Louisiana.* London: New Beacon, 1994.

Broeck, Sabine. "Enslavement as Regime of Western Modernity: Re-reading Gender Studies Epistemology through Black Feminist Critique." *Gender Forum* 22 (2008). http://genderforum.org/black-womens-writing-revisited-issue-22-2008/.

Brogan, Kathleen. *Cultural Haunting: Ghosts and Ethnicity in Recent American Literature.* Charlottesville: University Press of Virginia, 1998.

Brown, Caroline A. *The Black Female Body in American Literature and Art: Performing Identity.* New York: Routledge, 2012.

Brown, Vincent. "Social Death and Political Life in the Study of Slavery." *American Historical Review* 114.5 (December 2009): 1231–49.

Buse, Peter, and Andrew Stott, eds. *Ghosts: Deconstruction, Psychoanalysis, History.* Basingstoke, UK: Palgrave Macmillan, 1999.

———. "Introduction: A Future for Haunting." In Buse and Stott, *Ghosts*, 1–20.

Busia, Abena P. A. "What Is Your Nation? Reconnecting Africa and Her Diaspora through Paule Marshall's *Praisesong for the Widow.*" In *Changing Our Own Words: Essays on Criticism, Theory, and Writing by Black Women*, edited by Cheryl A. Wall, 96–211. London: Routledge, 1990.

Butler, Judith. *Bodies That Matter: On the Discursive Limits of "Sex."* New York: Routledge, 1993.

———. *Gender Trouble: Feminism and the Subversion of Identity.* 1990. New York: Routledge, 2008.

———. "Gender Trouble, Feminist Theory, and Psychoanalytic Discourse." In *Identities: Race, Class, Gender and Nationality*, edited by Linda Martín Alcoff and Eduardo Mendieta, 201–11. Malden, MA: Blackwell, 2003.

Caldwell, Gail. "Author Toni Morrison Discusses Her Latest Novel *Beloved.*" In Taylor-Guthrie, *Conversations with Toni Morrison*, 119–28.

Calixte, Shana L. "Things Which Aren't to Be Given Names: Afro-Caribbean and Diasporic Negotiations of Same Gender Desire and Sexual Relations." *Canadian Woman Studies* 24.2/3 (Winter/Spring 2005): 128–37.

Carpenter, Lynette, and Wendy K. Kolmar, eds. *Haunting the House of Fiction: Feminist Perspectives on Ghost Stories by American Women.* Knoxville: University of Tennessee Press, 1991.

———. Introduction to Carpenter and Kolmar, *Haunting the House of Fiction*, 1–25.

Carretta, Vincent. "Olaudah Equiano or Gustavus Vassa? New Light on an Eighteenth-Century Question of Identity." *Slavery & Abolition* 20.3 (December 1999): 96–105.

———. "Venture Smith, One of a Kind." In *Venture Smith and the Business of Slavery and Freedom*, edited by James Brewer Stewart and James O. Horton, 163–83. Amherst: University of Massachusetts Press, 2010.

Carsten, Janet, ed. *Ghosts of Memory: Essays on Remembrance and Relatedness.* Malden, MA: Blackwell, 2007.

Caruth, Cathy. *Unclaimed Experience: Trauma, Narrative, and History*. Baltimore: Johns Hopkins University Press, 1996.

Castle, Terry. *The Apparitional Lesbian: Female Homosexuality and Modern Culture*. New York: Columbia University Press, 1993.

Certeau, Michel de. "History: Science and Fiction." In *Heterologies: Discourse on the Other*, 199–224. Translated by Brian Massumi. Minneapolis: University of Minnesota Press, 1986.

———. *The Practice of Everyday Life*. 1984. Translated by Steven Rendall. Berkeley: University of California Press, 2011.

———. *The Writing of History*. Translated by Tom Conley. New York: Columbia University Press, 1988.

Chase-Riboud, Barbara. *The President's Daughter*. New York: Crown, 1994.

———. *Sally Hemings*. New York: Ballantine, 1979.

Chassot, Joanne. "'Voyage through death / to life upon these shores': The Living Dead of the Middle Passage." *Atlantic Studies* 12.1 (2015): 90–108.

Cheah, Pheng. *Spectral Nationality: Passages of Freedom from Kant to Postcolonial Literatures of Liberation*. New York: Columbia University Press, 2003.

Chesnutt, Charles W. *The Conjure Woman*. 1899. Ann Arbor: University of Michigan Press, 1969.

Childs, Dennis. *Slaves of the State: Black Incarceration from the Chain Gang to the Penitentiary*. Minneapolis: University of Minnesota Press, 2015.

———. "'You Ain't Seen Nothin' Yet': *Beloved*, the American Chain Gang, and the Middle Passage Remix." *American Quarterly* 61.2 (June 2009): 271–97.

Chin, Timothy S. "'Bullers' and 'Battymen': Contesting Homophobia in Black Popular Culture and Contemporary Caribbean Literature." *Callaloo* 20.1 (Winter 1997): 127–41.

Chireau, Yvonne P. *Black Magic: Religion and the African American Conjuring Tradition*. Berkeley: University of California Press, 2003.

Christian, Barbara. "Ritualistic Process and the Structure of Paule Marshall's *Praisesong for the Widow*." *Callaloo* 18 (Spring–Summer 1983): 74–84.

Clarkson, Thomas. *The History of the Rise, Progress and Accomplishment of the Abolition of the African Slave Trade by the British Parliament*. 1808. London: J. W. Parker, 1839.

Clawson, Jim. "Re-visioning Our History: An Interview with Michelle Cliff." *NIDUS*. 2002. https://web.archive.org/web/20040304022211/http://www.pitt.edu/~nidus/archives/spring2002/cliff1.html.

Clewell, Tammy. "From Destructive to Constructive Haunting in Toni Morrison's *Paradise*." *West Coast Line* 36.1 (2002): 130–42.

Cliff, Michelle. *Abeng*. New York: Plume, 1984.

———. "Bodies of Water." In *Bodies of Water*, 119–49. 1990. London: Plume, 1995.

———. "Caliban's Daughter: The Tempest and the Teapot." *Frontiers: A Journal of Women Studies* 12.2 (1991): 36–51.

———. *Claiming an Identity They Taught Me to Despise*. Watertown, MA: Persephone, 1980.

———. "Clare Savage as Crossroads Character." In *Caribbean Women Writers: Essays from the First International Conference*, edited by Selwyn R. Cudjoe, 263–68. Wellesley, MA: Calaloux, 1990.

———. "Ecce Homo." 2000. In *Everything Is Now*, 66–70. Minneapolis: University of Minnesota Press, 2009.

———. *Free Enterprise*. 1993. San Francisco: City Lights, 2004.

———. *If I Could Write This in Fire*. Minneapolis: University of Minnesota Press, 2008.

———. *Into the Interior*. Minneapolis: University of Minnesota Press, 2010.

———. *The Land of Look Behind*. Ithaca, NY: Firebrand, 1985.

———. *No Telephone to Heaven*. 1987. London: Methuen, 1989.

———. "Notes on Speechlessness." *Sinister Wisdom* 5 (Winter 1978): 5–9.

Cohen, Cathy J. "Punks, Bulldaggers, and Welfare Queens: The Radical Potential of Queer Politics." In Johnson and Henderson, *Black Queer Studies*, 21–51.

Collier, Eugenia. "The Closing of the Circle: Movement from Division to Wholeness in Paule Marshall's Fiction." In *Black Women Writers, 1950–1980: A Critical Evaluation*, edited by Mari Evans, 295–315. New York: Doubleday, 1984.

Condé, Maryse. *I, Tituba*. 1986. Translated by Richard Philcox. London: Faber, 2000.

Cooper, Brenda. *Magical Realism in West African Fiction: Seeing with a Third Eye*. London: Routledge, 1998.

Cooper, J. California. *Family*. New York: Anchor Books, 1991.

Coser, Stelamaris. *Bridging the Americas: The Literature of Paule Marshall, Toni Morrison, and Gayle Jones*. Philadelphia: Temple University Press, 1994.

Couser, G. Thomas. "Oppression and Repression: Personal and Collective Memory in Paule Marshall's *Praisesong for the Widow* and Leslie Marmon Silko's *Ceremony*." In *Memory and Cultural Politics: New Approaches to American Ethnic Literatures*, edited by Joseph T. Skerrett Jr., Amritjit Singh, and Robert E. Hogan, 106–20. Boston: Northeastern University Press, 1996.

Craps, Stef. *Postcolonial Witnessing: Trauma out of Bounds*. Basingstoke, UK: Palgrave Macmillan, 2013.

Crichlow, Wesley. *Buller Men and Batty Bwoys: Hidden Men in Toronto and Halifax Black Communities*. Toronto: University of Toronto Press, 2004.

Cugoano, Ottobah. *Thoughts and Sentiments on the Evil of Slavery*. 1787. Edited by Vincent Carretta. New York: Penguin, 1999.

Cummings, Ronald. "Queer Theory and Caribbean Writing." In *The Routledge Companion to Anglophone Caribbean Literature*, edited by Michael A. Bucknor and Alison Donnell, 323–31. London: Routledge, 2011.

Curtin, Philip D., ed. *Africa Remembered: Narratives by West Africans from the Era of the Slave Trade*. Madison: University of Wisconsin Press, 1967.

Dabney, Virginius. *The Jefferson Scandals: A Rebuttal*. New York: Dodd, 1981.

Dabydeen, David. *Turner: New and Selected Poems*. 1995. Leeds: Peepal Tree, 2003.

D'Aguiar, Fred. *Bloodlines*. 2000. London: Vintage, 2001.

———. *Feeding the Ghosts*. London: Vintage, 1998.

———. "The Last Essay about Slavery." In *The Age of Anxiety*, edited by Sarah Dunant and Roy Porter, 125–48. London: Virago, 1997.

———. *The Longest Memory*. London: Chatto & Windus, 1994.

Darling, Marsha. "In the Realm of Responsibility: A Conversation with Toni Morrison." *Women's Review of Books* 5.6 (March 1988): 5–6.

Dash, Julie. *Daughters of the Dust*. New York: Dutton, 1997.

———. *"Daughters of the Dust": The Making of an African American Woman's Film*. New York: New Press, 1992.

Daughters of the Dust. Directed by Julie Dash. Kino International, 1992. Film.
Davidson, Diana M. "Ghosting HIV/AIDS: Haunting Words and Apparitional Bodies in Michelle Cliff's 'Bodies of Water.'" In Weinstock, *Spectral America*, 221–44.
Davies, Carole Boyce. *Black Women, Writing and Identity: Migrations of the Subject*. London: Routledge, 1994.
Davis, Colin. *Haunted Subjects: Deconstruction, Psychoanalysis and the Return of the Dead*. New York: Palgrave Macmillan, 2007.
Davis, Kimberly Chabot. "'Postmodern Blackness': Toni Morrison's *Beloved* and the End of History." *Twentieth Century Literature* 44.2 (Summer 1998): 242–60.
Dawes, Kwame. *Requiem*. Leeds, UK: Peepal Tree, 1996.
Dayan, Joan. *Haiti, History, and the Gods*. Berkeley: University of California Press, 1998.
DeLamotte, Eugenia C. *Places of Silence, Journeys of Freedom: The Fiction of Paule Marshall*. Philadelphia: University of Pennsylvania Press, 1998.
Derrida, Jacques. *Specters of Marx: The State of the Debt, the Work of Mourning and the New International*. 1994. Translated by Peggy Kamuf. New York: Routledge, 2006.
Diouf, Sylviane A. *Servants of Allah: African Muslims Enslaved in the Americas*. New York: NYU Press, 1998.
Donnell, Alison. *Twentieth-Century Caribbean Literature: Critical Moments in Anglophone Literary History*. London: Routledge, 2006.
Due, Tananarive. *The Between*. New York: Harper, 1995.
———. *The Good House*. New York: Atria Books, 2003.
———. *Joplin's Ghost*. New York: Washington Square, 2005.
Dunbar, Paul Laurence. "We Wear the Mask." 1896. In *The Collected Poetry of Paul Laurence Dunbar*, edited by Joanne M. Braxton, 71. Charlottesville: University of Virginia Press, 1993.
Durrant, Sam. *Postcolonial Narrative and the Work of Mourning: J. M. Coetzee, Wilson Harris, and Toni Morrison*. Albany: SUNY Press, 2004.
Edmondson, Belinda. "Race, Privilege, and the Politics of (Re)Writing History: An Analysis of the Novels of Michelle Cliff." *Callaloo* 16.1 (Winter 1993): 180–91.
Edwards, Justin D. *Gothic Canada: Reading the Spectre of a National Literature*. Edmonton: University of Alberta, 2005.
———. *Gothic Passages: Racial Ambiguity and the American Gothic*. Iowa City: University of Iowa Press, 2003.
———. *Postcolonial Literature*. Basingstoke, UK: Palgrave Macmillan, 2008.
Eko, Ebele O. "Oral Tradition: The Bridge to Africa in Paule Marshall's *Praisesong for the Widow*." *Western Journal of Black Studies* 10.3 (Fall 1986): 143–47.
Elia, Nada. "'A Man Who Wants to Be a Woman': Queerness as/and Healing Practices in Michelle Cliff's *No Telephone to Heaven*." *Callaloo* 23.1 (Winter 2000): 352–65.
Ellis, Joseph J. *American Sphinx: The Character of Thomas Jefferson*. New York: Knopf, 1997.
———. "Jefferson: Post-DNA." *William and Mary Quarterly* 57.1 (January 2000): 125–38.
Ellis, Nadia. *Territories of the Soul: Queered Belonging in the Black Diaspora*. Durham, NC: Duke University Press, 2015.

Ellison, Ralph. *Invisible Man.* 1952. London: Penguin, 2001.
Equiano, Olaudah. *The Interesting Narrative and Other Writings.* 1789. Edited by Vincent Carretta. London: Penguin, 2003.
Erickson, Daniel. *Ghosts, Metaphor, and History in Toni Morrison's "Beloved" and Gabriel Garcia Marquez's "One Hundred Years of Solitude."* Basingstoke, UK: Palgrave Macmillan, 2009.
Eyerman, Ron. *Cultural Trauma: Slavery and the Formation of African American Identity.* Cambridge: Cambridge University Press, 2001.
Falconbridge, Alexander. *An Account of the Slave Trade on the Coast of Africa.* London: J. Phillips, 1788.
Fanon, Frantz. *Black Skin, White Masks.* Translated by Charles Lam Markmann. London: Pluto Press, 1986.
———. *The Wretched of the Earth.* Translated by Richard Philcox. New York: Grove, 2004.
Felix, Michelle Miesen. "Paule Marshall's Critique of Contemporary Neo-imperialisms through the Trope of Travel." Dissertation, Marquette University, 2011. E-Publi cations@Marquette. http://epublications.marquette.edu/dissertations_mu/121.
Ferguson, James. "Decomposing Modernity: History and Hierarchy after Development." In *Global Shadows: Africa in the Neoliberal World Order,* 176–93. Durham, NC: Duke University Press, 2006.
Ferguson, Roderick A. *Aberrations in Black: Toward a Queer of Color Critique.* Minneapolis: University of Minnesota Press, 2004.
Finley, Cheryl. "Committed to Memory: The Slave-Ship Icon and the Black-Atlantic Imagination." *Chicago Art Journal* 9 (Spring 1999): 2–21.
Foster, Eugene A. "Jefferson Fathered Slave's Last Child." *Nature* 396 (November 1998): 27–28.
Francis, Jacqueline. "The *Brooks* Slave Ship Icon: A 'Universal Symbol'?" *Slavery & Abolition* 30.2 (June 2009): 327–38.
Freud, Sigmund. "The Uncanny." In *Art and Literature,* vol. 14, Pelican Freud Library, translated by James Strachey, 335–76. Harmondsworth, UK: Penguin, 1985.
Frías, Maria. "'Building Bridges Back to the Past': An Interview with Fred D'Aguiar." *Callaloo* 25.2 (Spring 2002): 418–25.
Friedlander, Saul. "Trauma, Transference and 'Working through' in Writing the History of the *Shoah.*" *History and Memory* 4.1 (Spring–Summer 1992): 39–59.
Fuss, Diana. "Inside/Out." In *Inside/Out: Lesbian Theories, Gay Theories,* edited by Diana Fuss, 1–10. New York: Routledge, 1991.
Gamson, Joshua. "Must Identity Movements Self-Destruct? A Queer Dilemma." *Social Problems* 42.3 (August 1995): 390–407.
Garber, Marjorie B. *Shakespeare's Ghost Writers: Literature as Uncanny Causality.* New York: Methuen, 1987.
Gates, Henry Louis, Jr. *Figures in Black: Words, Signs, and the "Racial" Self.* New York: Oxford University Press, 1989.
———. *The Signifying Monkey: A Theory of African-American Literary Criticism.* New York: Oxford University Press, 1989.
Geggus, David. "The Bois Caïman Ceremony." *Journal of Caribbean History* 25.1 (January 1991): 41–57.

Gikandi, Simon. *Writing in Limbo: Modernism and Caribbean Literature*. Ithaca, NY: Cornell University Press, 1992.

Gilroy, Paul. *The Black Atlantic: Modernity and Double Consciousness*. Cambridge, MA: Harvard University Press, 1993.

———. *Small Acts: Thoughts on the Politics of Black Cultures*. London: Serpent's Tail, 1993.

Ginsberg, Elaine K. "Introduction: The Politics of Passing." In *Passing and the Fictions of Identity*, edited by Elaine K. Ginsberg, 1–18. Durham, NC: Duke University Press, 1996.

Glave, Thomas. "Introduction: Desire through the Archipelago." In Glave, *Our Caribbean*, 1–11.

———, ed. *Our Caribbean: A Gathering of Lesbian and Gay Writing from the Antilles*. Durham, NC: Duke University Press, 2008.

Glissant, Édouard. *Caribbean Discourse: Selected Essays*. Translated by J. Michael Dash. Charlottesville: University of Virginia Press, 1989.

———. *Poetics of Relation*. Translated by Betsy Wing. Ann Arbor: University of Michigan Press, 1997.

Goddu, Teresa A. *Gothic America: Narrative, History, and Nation*. New York: Columbia University Press, 1997.

Goldman, Marlene. *DisPossession: Haunting in Canadian Fiction*. Montreal: McGill–Queen's University Press, 2012.

Goodison, Lorna. "Nanny." In *I Am Becoming My Mother*, 44–45. London: New Beacon, 1986.

Gopinath, Gayatri. *Impossible Desires: Queer Diasporas and South Asian Public Cultures*. Durham, NC: Duke University Press, 2005.

Gordon, Avery F. *Ghostly Matters: Haunting and the Sociological Imagination*. 1997. Minneapolis: University of Minnesota Press, 2008.

Gordon-Reed, Annette. *Thomas Jefferson and Sally Hemings: An American Controversy*. 1997. Charlottesville: University of Virginia Press, 1999.

Gorn, Elliott J. "Black Spirits: The Ghostlore of Afro-American Slaves." *American Quarterly* 36.4 (Autumn 1984): 549–65.

Gossman, Lionel. "History and Literature: Reproduction or Signification." In *The Writing of History: Literary Form and Historical Understanding*, edited by Robert H. Canary and Henry Kozicki, 3–39. Madison: University of Wisconsin Press, 1978.

Gronniosaw, James Albert Ukawsaw. "A Narrative of the Most Remarkable Particulars in the Life of James Albert Ukawsaw Gronniosaw: An African Prince, as Related by Himself." 1772. In *Slave Narratives*, edited by William L. Andrews and Henry Louis Gates Jr., 1–34. New York: Literary Classics of the United States, 2000.

Gubar, Susan. *Racechanges: White Skin, Black Face in American Culture*. Oxford: Oxford University Press, 2000.

Halberstam, Judith. *The Queer Art of Failure*. Durham, NC: Duke University Press, 2011.

———. *Skin Shows: Gothic Horror and the Technology of Monsters*. Durham, NC: Duke University Press, 1995.

Haley, Alex. *Roots: The Saga of an American Family*. 1974. New York: Vanguard, 2004.

Hall, Stuart. "Cultural Identity and Diaspora." *Identity: Community, Culture, Difference*, edited by Jonathan Rutherford, 222–37. London: Laurence and Wishart, 1990.
———. "Ethnicity: Identity and Difference." In *Becoming National: A Reader*, edited by Geoff Eley and Ronald Grigor Suny, 339–49. Oxford: Oxford University Press, 1996.
———. "What Is This 'Black' in Black Popular Culture?" In *Stuart Hall: Critical Dialogues in Cultural Studies*, edited by David Morley and Kuan-Hsing Chen, 465–75. London: Routledge, 1996.
Handler, Jerome S. "Survivors of the Middle Passage: Life Histories of Enslaved Africans in British America." *Slavery & Abolition* 23.1 (April 2002): 25–56.
Harris, Wilson. *The Ghost of Memory*. London: Faber, 2006.
———. *The Guyana Quartet*. London: Faber, 1985.
———. "History, Fable and Myth in the Caribbean and Guianas." *Selected Essays of Wilson Harris*, edited by A. J. M. Bundy, 152–66. London: Routledge, 1999.
Hartman, Saidiya V. *Lose Your Mother: A Journey along the Atlantic Slave Route*. New York: Farrar, Straus and Giroux, 2008.
———. *Scenes of Subjection: Terror, Slavery, and Self-Making in Nineteenth-Century America*. New York: Oxford University Press, 1997.
———. "The Time of Slavery." *South Atlantic Quarterly* 101.4 (Fall 2002): 757–77.
———. "Venus in Two Acts." *Small Axe* 12.2 (June 2008): 1–14.
Haslett, Tim. "Hortense Spillers Interviewed by Tim Haslett for the Black Cultural Studies Web Site Collective in Ithaca, NY February 4, 1998." *Black Cultural Studies*. http://www.blackculturalstudies.net/spillers/spillers_intvw.html
Hayden, Robert E. "Middle Passage." 1962. In *Collected Poems*, edited by Frederick Glaysher, 48–54. New York: Liveright, 1985.
Hayes, Jarrod. "Queering Roots, Queering Diaspora." In *Rites of Return: Diaspora Poetics and the Politics of Memory*, edited by Nancy K. Miller and Marianne Hirsch, 72–87. New York: Columbia University Press, 2011.
Helmreich, Stefan. "Kinship, Nation, and Paul Gilroy's Concept of Diaspora." *Diaspora: A Journal of Transnational Studies* 2.2 (Fall 1992): 243–49.
Herskovits, Melville. *The Myth of the Negro Past*. 1941. Boston: Beacon, 1990.
Hesse, Barnor. "Forgotten Like a Bad Dream: Atlantic Slavery and the Ethics of Postcolonial Memory." In *Relocating Postcolonialism*, edited by David Theo Goldberg and Ato Quayson, 143–73. Oxford: Blackwell, 2002.
Hirsch, Marianne. *The Generation of Postmemory: Writing and Visual Culture after the Holocaust*. New York: Columbia University Press, 2012.
Hirsch, Marianne, and Nancy K. Miller. Introduction to *Rites of Return: Diaspora Poetics and the Politics of Memory*, edited by Nancy K. Miller and Marianne Hirsch, 1–20. New York: Columbia University Press, 2011.
Holland, Sharon Patricia. *Raising the Dead: Readings of Death and (Black) Subjectivity*. Durham, NC: Duke University Press, 2000.
Hopkinson, Nalo. *Brown Girl in the Ring*. New York: Warner Books, 1998.
Hoving, Isabel. "Michelle Cliff: The Unheard Music." In *The Routledge Companion to Anglophone Caribbean Literature*, edited by Michael A. Bucknor and Alison Donnell, 27–33. London: Routledge, 2011.
Huggins, Nathan Irvin. *Black Odyssey: The African-American Ordeal in Slavery*. 1977. New York: Vintage, 1990.

Hutcheon, Linda. *The Politics of Postmodernism*. 1989. London: Routledge, 2002.
Ifekwunigwe, Jayne O. "Diaspora's Daughters, Africa's Orphans? On Lineage, Authenticity and Mixed-Race 'Identity.'" In *Black British Feminism: A Reader*, edited by Heidi Mirza, 127–52. London: Routledge, 1997.
Iggers, Georg G. *Historiography in the Twentieth Century: From Scientific Objectivity to the Postmodern Challenge*. Middletown, CT: Wesleyan University Press, 1997.
Jacobs, Harriet A. *Incidents in the Life of a Slave Girl, Written by Herself*. 1861. Edited by Jean Fagan Yellin. Cambridge, MA: Harvard University Press, 2000.
Jagose, Annamarie. *Queer Theory: An Introduction*. New York: NYU Press, 1996.
Jefferson in Paris. Directed by James Ivory. Touchstone Pictures, 1995. Film.
Jessee, Sharon. "'Tell Me Your Earrings': Time and the Marvelous in Toni Morrison's *Beloved*." In *Memory and Cultural Politics: New Approaches to American Ethnic Literatures*, edited by Joseph T. Skerrett, Amritjit Singh Jr., and Robert E. Hogan, 198–211. Boston: Northeastern University Press, 1996.
Johnson, E. Patrick. *Appropriating Blackness: Performance and the Politics of Authenticity*. Durham, NC: Duke University Press, 2003.
———. "Introduction: Queering Black Studies / 'Quaring' Queer Studies." In Johnson and Henderson, *Black Queer Studies*, 1–17.
Johnson, E. Patrick, and Mae G. Henderson, eds. *Black Queer Studies: A Critical Anthology*. Durham, NC: Duke University Press, 2005.
Johnson, Erica L. *Caribbean Ghostwriting*. Madison, NJ: Fairleigh Dickinson University Press, 2009.
Joseph-Vilain, Mélanie, and Judith Misrahi-Barak, eds. *Postcolonial Ghosts / Fantômes post-coloniaux*. Montpellier: Presses universitaires de la Méditerrannée, 2009.
Kamau, Kwadwo Agymah. *Flickering Shadows*. Minneapolis: Coffee House, 1996.
Kaplan, Sara Clarke. "Our Founding (M)other: Erotic Love and Social Death in *Sally Hemings* and *The President's Daughter*." *Callaloo* 32.3 (Summer 2009): 773–91.
———. "Souls at the Crossroads, Africans on the Water: The Politics of Diasporic Melancholia." *Callaloo* 30.2 (Spring 2007): 511–26.
Kempadoo, Kamala. "Caribbean Sexuality: Mapping the Field." *Caribbean Review of Gender Studies* 3 (2009): 1–24.
Kenan, Randall. *Let the Dead Bury Their Dead*. New York: Harcourt, 1992.
———. *A Visitation of Spirits*. New York: Grove, 1989.
King, Rosamond S. "More Notes on the Invisibility of Caribbean Lesbians." 2005. In Glave, *Our Caribbean*, 191–96.
———. "Re/Presenting Self & Other: Trans Deliverance in Caribbean Texts." *Callaloo* 31.2 (Spring 2008): 581–99.
———. "Sex and Sexuality in English Caribbean Novels—a Survey from 1950." *Journal of West Indian Literature* 11.1 (November 2002): 24–38.
Klein, Herbert S. *The Atlantic Slave Trade*. Cambridge: Cambridge University Press, 1999.
———. *The Middle Passage: Comparative Studies in the Atlantic Slave Trade*. Princeton, NJ: Princeton University Press, 1978.
Kristeva, Julia. *Powers of Horror: An Essay on Abjection*. Translated by Leon S. Roudiez. New York: Columbia University Press, 1982.
LaCapra, Dominick. *History and Criticism*. Ithaca, NY: Cornell University Press, 1985.

———. *Writing History, Writing Trauma*. Baltimore: Johns Hopkins University Press, 2001.

Lewis, Jan, and Peter S. Onuf. "American Synecdoche: Thomas Jefferson as Image, Icon, Character, and Self." *American Historical Review* 103.1 (February 1998): 125–36.

Lorde, Audre. Foreword to *Wild Women in the Whirlwind: Afra-American Culture and the Contemporary Literary Renaissance*, edited by Joanne M. Braxton and Andrée Nicola McLaughlin, xi–xiv. New Brunswick, NJ: Rutgers University Press, 1990.

———. *Zami: A New Spelling of My Name*. Watertown, MA: Persephone, 1982.

Low, Gail. "The Memory of Slavery in Fred D'Aguiar's *Feeding the Ghosts*." In *Post-colonial Literatures: Expanding the Canon*, edited by Deborah Madsen, 104–19. London: Pluto, 1999.

Luckhurst, Roger. "The Contemporary London Gothic and the Limits of the 'Spectral Turn.'" *Textual Practice* 16.3 (2002): 527–46.

———. "'Impossible Mourning' in Toni Morrison's *Beloved* and Michèle Roberts's *Daughters of the House*." *Critique: Studies in Contemporary Fiction* 37.4 (Summer 1996): 243–60.

Lyotard, Jean-François. *The Postmodern Condition: A Report on Knowledge*. Translated by Geoff Bennington and Brian Massumi. Minneapolis: University of Minnesota Press, 1984.

MacDonald-Smythe, Antonia. "*Macocotte*: An Exploration of Same-Sex Friendship in Selected Caribbean Novels." In *Sex and the Citizen: Interrogating the Caribbean*, edited by Faith Smith, 224–40. Charlottesville: University of Virginia Press, 2011.

Maddern, Jo Frances, and Peter Adey, eds. *Spectro-Geographies*, special issue of *Cultural Geographies* 15.3 (2008): 291–402.

Mair, Lucille Mathurin. "Recollections of a Journey into a Rebel Past." In *Caribbean Women Writers: Essays from the First International Conference*, edited by Selwyn R. Cudjoe, 51–60. Wellesley, MA: Calaloux, 1990.

Major, Clarence. "The Slave Trade: View from the Middle Passage." *African American Review* 28.1 (Spring 1994): 11–22.

Malchow, Howard L. *Gothic Images of Race in Nineteenth-Century Britain*. Stanford, CA: Stanford University Press, 1996.

Malone, Dumas. *Jefferson the President: The First Term, 1801–1805*. Boston: Little, Brown, 1970.

Marshall, Paule. "From the Poets in the Kitchen." 1983. *Callaloo* 24.2 (Spring 2001): 627–33.

———. *Praisesong for the Widow*. New York: Plume, 1983.

———. "Shaping the World of My Art." 1973. In *Shaping Memories: Reflections of African American Writers*, edited by Joanne V. Gabin, 14–21. Jackson: University of Mississippi Press, 2009.

———. "To Da-Duh: In Memoriam." 1967. In *Reena and Other Stories*, 93–106. New York: Feminist Press, 1983.

———. *Triangular Road: A Memoir*. New York: Basic Civitas Books, 2008.

Matsuoka, Atsuko, and John Sorenson, eds. *Ghosts and Shadows: Construction of Identity and Community in an African Diaspora*. Toronto: University of Toronto Press, 2001.

Mayer, David N. "The Thomas Jefferson–Sally Hemings Myth and the Politicization of American History." In Turner, *Jefferson-Hemings Controversy*, 285–307.
Mbembe, Achille. "Life, Sovereignty, and Terror in the Fiction of Amos Tutuola." *Research in African Literatures* 34.4 (Winter 2003): 1–26.
Mbiti, John S. *African Religions and Philosophy*. 1969. London: Heinemann, 1990.
McCoubrey, John. "Turner's *Slave Ship*: Abolition, Ruskin, and Reception." *Word & Image* 14.4 (October–December 1998): 319–53.
McDowell, Deborah E. *"The Changing Same": Black Women's Literature, Criticism, and Theory*. Bloomington: Indiana University Press, 1995.
———. "Negotiating between Tenses: Witnessing Slavery after Freedom—*Dessa Rose*." In *Slavery and the Literary Imagination*, edited by Deborah E. McDowell and Arnold Rampersad, 144–63. Baltimore: Johns Hopkins University Press, 1989.
McDowell, Edwin. "Jefferson Liaison Is Disputed Again." *New York Times*, June 2, 1981, C7.
McGill, Lisa D. *Constructing Black Selves: Caribbean American Narratives and the Second Generation*. New York: NYU Press, 2005.
McKay, Nellie. "An Interview with Toni Morrison." In Taylor-Guthrie, *Conversations with Toni Morrison*, 188–217.
McNeil, Elizabeth. "The Gullah Seeker's Journey in Paule Marshall's *Praisesong for the Widow*." *MELUS* 34.1 (Spring 2009): 185–209.
Meisenhelder, Susan. "'The Whole Picture' in Gloria Naylor's *Mama Day*." *African American Review* 27.3 (Autumn 1993): 405–19.
Métraux, Alfred. *Voodoo in Haiti*. Translated by Hugo Charteris. New York: Oxford University Press, 1959.
Miller, Joseph C. *Way of Death: Merchant Capitalism and the Angolan Slave Trade, 1730–1830*. London: James Currey, 1988.
Mitchell, Mozella G. *Crucial Issues in Caribbean Religions*. New York: Peter Lang, 2006.
Mordecai, Pamela, and Betty Wilson, eds. *Her True-True Name: An Anthology of Women's Writing from the Caribbean*. Oxford: Heinemann, 1989.
Morrison, Toni. *Beloved*. 1987. New York: Plume, 1988.
———. "A Bench by the Road: *Beloved* by Toni Morrison." In *Toni Morrison: Conversations*, edited by Carolyn C. Denard, 44–50. Jackson: University Press of Mississippi, 2008.
———. *Jazz*. New York: Knopf, 1992.
———. "Nobel Lecture." 1993. *World Literature Today* 68.1 (Winter 1994): 5–8.
———. *Playing in the Dark: Whiteness and the Literary Imagination*. 1992. New York: Vintage, 1993.
———. "Rootedness: The Ancestor as Foundation." In *Black Women Writers, 1950–1980: A Critical Evaluation*, edited by Mari Evans, 339–45. New York: Doubleday, 1984.
———. "The Site of Memory." In *Out There: Marginalization and Contemporary Cultures*, edited by Russell Ferguson, Martha Gever, Trinh T. Minh-ha, and Cornel West, 299–326. Cambridge, MA: MIT Press, 1992.
———. *Song of Solomon*. New York: Knopf, 1977.
———. *Tar Baby*. New York: Knopf, 1981.
———. "Unspeakable Things Unspoken: The Afro-American Presence in American Literature." *Michigan Quarterly Review* 28.1 (Winter 1989): 1–34.

Murphy, Joseph M. *Working the Spirit: Ceremonies of the African Diaspora*. Boston: Beacon, 1994.

Naylor, Gloria. "A Conversation: Gloria Naylor and Toni Morrison." In Taylor-Guthrie, *Conversations with Toni Morrison*, 188–217.

———. *Mama Day*. New York: Vintage, 1988.

Neptune, Harvey. "Loving through Loss: Reading Saidiya Hartman's History of Black Hurt." *Anthurium: A Caribbean Studies Journal* 6.1 (2008). http://anthurium.miami.edu/volume_6/issue_1/neptune-loving.html.

Okri, Ben. *The Famished Road*. New York: Doubleday, 1991.

Olmos, Margarite Fernández, and Lizabeth Paravisini-Gebert. "Introduction: Religious Syncretism and Caribbean Culture." In *Sacred Possessions: Vodou, Santería, Obeah, and the Caribbean*, edited by Margarite Fernández Olmos and Lizabeth Paravisini-Gebert, 1–12. New Brunswick, NJ: Rutgers University Press, 2000.

Palmer, Paulina. *Lesbian Gothic: Transgressive Fictions*. London: Cassell, 1999.

———. *The Queer Uncanny: New Perspectives on the Gothic*. Cardiff: University of Wales Press, 2012.

Parham, Marisa. *Haunting and Displacement in African-American Literature and Culture*. New York: Routledge, 2009.

Parish, Peter J. *Slavery: History and Historians*. New York: Westview, 1989.

Parton, James. *Life of Thomas Jefferson, Third President of the United States*. Boston: James R. Osgood, 1874.

Passage du milieu. Directed by Guy Deslauriers. Kreol Productions, 2000. Film.

Patterson, Orlando. *Slavery and Social Death: A Comparative Study*. Cambridge, MA: Harvard University Press, 1982.

Pecic, Zoran. *Queer Narratives of the Caribbean Diaspora: Exploring Tactics*. Basingstoke, UK: Palgrave Macmillan, 2013.

Peeren, Esther. *The Spectral Metaphor: Living Ghosts and the Agency of Invisibility*. Basingstoke, UK: Palgrave Macmillan, 2014.

Pelton, Robert D. *The Trickster in West Africa: A Study of Mythic Irony and Sacred Delight*. Berkeley: University of California Press, 1980.

Perdigao, Lisa K., and Mark Pizzato. Introduction to *Death in American Texts and Performances: Corpses, Ghosts, and the Reanimated Dead*, edited by Lisa K. Perdigao and Mark Pizzato, 1–8. Farnham, UK: Ashgate, 2010.

Perry, Phyllis Alesia. *Stigmata*. New York: Hyperion, 1998.

Peterson, Nancy J. *Against Amnesia: Contemporary Women Writers and the Crises of Historical Memory*. Philadelphia: University of Pennsylvania Press, 2001.

Pettis, Joyce. *Toward Wholeness in Paule Marshall's Fiction*. Charlottesville: University Press of Virginia, 1995.

Philip, M. NourbeSe. *Zong!* Middletown, CT: Wesleyan University Press, 2008.

Phillips, Ulrich B. *American Negro Slavery: A Survey of the Supply, Employment and Control of Negro Labor as Determined by the Plantation Régime*. 1918. Baton Rouge: Louisiana State University Press, 1966.

Pollard, Cherise A. "Self-Evident Truths: Love, Complicity, and Critique in Barbara Chase Riboud's *Sally Hemings* and *The President's Daughter*." In *Monuments of the Black Atlantic: Slavery and Memory*, edited by Maria Diedrich and Joanne M. Braxton, 117–29. Münster: LIT, 2004.

Prins, Gwyn. "Oral History." In *New Perspectives on Historical Writing*, edited by Peter Burke, 120–56. Cambridge: Polity, 2001.

Punter, David. *Postcolonial Imaginings: Fictions of a New World Order*. Edinburgh: Edinburgh University Press, 2000.

Rabaté, Jean-Michel. *The Ghosts of Modernity*. Gainesville: University Press of Florida, 1996.

Raiskin, Judith. "The Art of History: An Interview with Michelle Cliff." *Kenyon Review* 15.1 (Winter 1993): 55–71.

———. "Inverts and Hybrids: Lesbian Rewritings of Sexual and Racial Identities." In *The Lesbian Postmodern*, edited by Laura Doan, 156–72. New York: Columbia University Press, 1994.

Rankine, Claudia. "The Condition of Black Life Is One of Mourning." *New York Times*, June 22, 2015. https://www.nytimes.com/2015/06/22/magazine/the-condition-of-black-life-is-one-of-mourning.html.

Rayner, Alice. *Ghosts: Death's Double and the Phenomena of Theatre*. Minneapolis: University of Minnesota Press, 2006.

Redding, Arthur. *Haints: American Ghosts, Millennial Passions, and Contemporary Gothic Fictions*. Tuscaloosa: University of Alabama Press, 2011.

Rediker, Marcus. *The Slave Ship: A Human History*. New York: Viking, 2007.

Reyes, Angelita. "Politics and Metaphors of Materialism in Paule Marshall's *Praisesong for the Widow* and Toni Morrison's *Tar Baby*." In *Politics and the Muse: Studies in the Politics of Recent American Literature*, edited by Adam J. Sorkin, 179–205. Bowling Green, KY: Bowling Green State University Popular Press, 1989.

Rhys, Jean. *Wide Sargasso Sea*. New York: Norton, 1966.

Rich, Adrienne. "When We Dead Awaken: Writing as Re-Vision." *College English* 34.1 (1972): 18–30.

Roach, Joseph. *Cities of the Dead: Circum-Atlantic Performance*. New York: Columbia University Press, 1996.

Robinson-Walcott, Kim. "Claiming an Identity We Thought They Despised: Contemporary White West Indian Writers and Their Negotiation of Race." *Small Axe* 7.2 (September 2003): 93–110.

Rody, Caroline. *The Daughter's Return: African-American and Caribbean Women's Fictions of History*. Oxford: Oxford University Press, 2001.

Rogers, Susan. "Embodying Cultural Memory in Paule Marshall's *Praisesong for the Widow*." *African American Review* 34.1 (Spring 2000): 77–93.

Rohy, Valerie. "Displacing Desire: Passing, Nostalgia, and *Giovanni's Room*." In *Passing and the Fictions of Identity*, edited by Elaine K. Ginsberg, 218–33. Durham, NC: Duke University Press, 1996.

Ronell, Avital. *Dictations: On Haunted Writing*. Lincoln: University of Nebraska Press, 1993.

Rose, Jacqueline. *States of Fantasy*. Oxford: Oxford University Press, 1998.

Ross, Marlon B. "Beyond the Closet as Raceless Paradigm." In Johnson and Henderson, *Black Queer Studies*, 161–89.

Rowell, Charles H. "An Interview with Gloria Naylor." *Callaloo* 20.1 (Winter 1997): 179–92.

Royle, Nicholas. "The Phantom Review." *Textual Practice* 11.2 (Summer 1997): 386–98.

———. *The Uncanny: An Introduction*. Manchester: Manchester University Press, 2003.

Rupprecht, Anita. "'A Limited Sort of Property': History, Memory and the Slave Ship *Zong*." *Slavery & Abolition* 29.2 (June 2008): 265–77.

Rushdy, Ashraf H. A. "Neo-Slave Narrative." In *The Oxford Companion to African American Literature*, edited by William L. Andrews, Trudier Harris, and Frances Smith Foster, 533–35. New York: Oxford University Press, 1997.

———. *Neo-Slave Narratives: Studies in the Social Logic of a Literary Form*. New York: Oxford University Press, 1999.

———. *Remembering Generations: Race and Family in Contemporary African American Fiction*. Chapel Hill: University of North Carolina Press, 2001.

Ruskin, John. *Modern Painters*. 1843. Vol. 1. New York: Wiley, 1853.

Russell, Heather. *Legba's Crossing: Narratology in the African Atlantic*. Athens: University of Georgia Press, 2009.

Sale, Maggie. "Call and Response as Critical Method: African-American Oral Traditions and *Beloved*." *African American Review* 26.1 (Spring 1992): 41–50.

Sally Hemings: An American Scandal. Directed by Charles Haid. CBS, 2000. Film.

Sandiford, Keith A. "Paule Marshall's *Praisesong for the Widow*: The Reluctant Heiress, or Whose Life Is It Anyway?" *Black American Literature Forum* 20.4 (Winter 1986): 371–92.

Savoy, Eric. "The Rise of American Gothic." In *The Cambridge Companion to Gothic Fiction*, edited by Jerrold E. Hogle, 167–88. Cambridge: Cambridge University Press, 2002.

"The Scholars Commission on the Jefferson-Hemings Issue." *Thomas Jefferson Heritage Society*, May 26, 2000. https://www.tjheritage.org/the-scholars-commission.

Schuler, Monica. "Enslavement, the Slave Voyage, and Astral and Aquatic Journeys." In *Africa and the Americas: Interconnections during the Slave Trade*, edited by Hosé C. Curto and Renée Soulodre-LaFrance, 185–213. Trenton, NJ: Africa World Press, 2005.

Schwartz, Meryl F. "An Interview with Michelle Cliff." *Contemporary Literature* 34.4 (Winter 1993): 595–619.

Scott, David. *Refashioning Futures: Criticism after Postcoloniality*. Princeton, NJ: Princeton University Press, 1999.

Sedgwick, Eve Kosofsky. *The Coherence of Gothic Conventions*. New York: Methuen, 1986.

———. *Epistemology of the Closet*. Berkeley: University of California Press, 1990.

———. *Tendencies*. Durham, NC: Duke University Press, 1994.

Sharpe, Christina. *In the Wake: On Blackness and Being*. Durham, NC: Duke University Press, 2016.

———. *Monstrous Intimacies: Making Post-Slavery Subjects*. Durham, NC: Duke University Press, 2010.

Sharpe, Jenny. *Ghosts of Slavery: A Literary Archaeology of Black Women's Lives*. Minneapolis: University of Minnesota Press, 2003.

Sherman, Charlotte Watson. *One Dark Body*. London: Women's Press, 1993.

Shugart, Helene A. "Crossing Over: Hybridity and Hegemony in the Popular Media." *Communication and Critical/Cultural Studies* 4.2 (June 2007): 115–41.

Silvera, Makeda. "Man Royals and Sodomites: Some Thoughts on the Invisibility of Afro-Caribbean Lesbians." 1992. In Glave, *Our Caribbean*, 344–54.

Smallwood, Stephanie E. *Saltwater Slavery: A Middle Passage from Africa to American Diaspora*. Cambridge, MA: Harvard University Press, 2007.

Smith, Carissa Turner. "Women's Spiritual Geographies of the African Diaspora: Paule Marshall's *Praisesong for the Widow*." *African American Review* 42.3/4 (Fall–Winter 2008): 715–29.

Smith, Jennifer J. "Birthed and Buried: Matrilineal History in Michelle Cliff's *No Telephone to Heaven*." *Meridians: Feminism, Race, Transnationalism* 9.1 (2009): 141–62.

Smith, Linda Tuhiwai. *Decolonizing Methodologies: Research and Indigenous Peoples*. London: Zed Books, 1999.

Smith, Venture. "A Narrative of the Life and Adventures of Venture . . . Related by Himself." 1798. In *Five Black Lives: The Autobiographies of Venture Smith, James Mars, William Grimes, the Rev. G. W. Offley, and James L. Smith*, edited by Arna Bontemps, 1–34. Middletown, CT: Wesleyan University Press, 1971.

Smith-Wright, Geraldine. "In Spite of the Klan: Ghosts in the Fiction of Black Women Writers." In Carpenter and Kolmar, *Haunting the House of Fiction*, 142–65.

Sollors, Werner. "African Americans since 1900." In *The Cambridge Companion to Modern American Culture*, edited by Christopher Bigsby, 153–73. Cambridge: Cambridge University Press, 2006.

Somerville, Siobhan B., ed. *Queer Fictions of Race*. Special issue of *Modern Fiction Studies* 48.4 (Winter 2002): 787–1076.

———. *Queering the Color Line: Race and the Invention of Homosexuality in American Culture*. Durham, NC: Duke University Press, 2000.

Sommer, Doris. *Proceed with Caution, When Engaged by Minority Writing in the Americas*. Cambridge, MA: Harvard University Press, 1999.

Spillers, Hortense J. "Mama's Baby, Papa's Maybe: An American Grammar Book." *Diacritics* 17.2 (Summer 1987): 65–81.

Spivak, Gayatri C., and Sneja Gunew. "Questions of Multiculturalism." In *The Cultural Studies Reader*, edited by Simon During, 193–202. London: Routledge, 1993.

Stitt, Jocelyn Fenton. "Gendered Legacies of Romantic Nationalism in the Works of Michelle Cliff." *Small Axe* 11.3 (October 2007): 52–72.

Stone-Mediatore, Shari. *Reading across Borders: Storytelling and Knowledges of Resistance*. New York: Palgrave Macmillan, 2003.

Stuckey, Sterling. *Slave Culture: Nationalist Theory and the Foundations of Black America*. New York: Oxford University Press, 1987.

Sword, Helen. *Ghostwriting Modernism*. Ithaca, NY: Cornell University Press, 2002.

Taussig, Michael. *Shamanism, Colonialism, and the Wild Man: A Study in Terror and Healing*. Chicago: University of Chicago Press, 1987.

Taylor-Guthrie, Danille, ed. *Conversations with Toni Morrison*. Jackson: University Press of Mississippi, 1994.

Thomas, H. Nigel. *Spirits in the Dark*. Concord, ON: House of Anansi, 1993.

"Thomas Jefferson Heritage Society." *Thomas Jefferson Heritage Society*, n.d. http://www.tjheritage.org.

Thompson, Robert Farris. *Flash of the Spirit: African and Afro-American Art and Philosophy*. New York: Vintage, 1984.

Thurston, Luke. *Literary Ghosts from the Victorians to Modernism: The Haunting Interval*. New York: Routledge, 2012.

Tiffin, Helen. "Post-Colonialism, Post-Modernism and the Rehabilitation of Post-Colonial History." *Journal of Commonwealth Literature* 23.1 (March 1988): 169–81.

Tinsley, Omise'eke Natasha. "Black Atlantic, Queer Atlantic: Queer Imaginings of the Middle Passage." *GLQ: A Journal of Lesbian and Gay Studies* 14.2–3 (2008): 191–215.

———. *Thiefing Sugar: Eroticism between Women in Caribbean Literature*. Durham, NC: Duke University Press, 2010.

Toews, John E. "Historiography as Exorcism: Conjuring up 'Foreign' Worlds and Historicizing Subjects in the Context of the Multiculturalism Debate." *Theory and Society* 27.4 (August 1998): 535–64.

Trouillot, Michel-Rolph. "Silencing the Past: Layers of Meaning in the Haitian Revolution." In *Between History and Histories: The Making of Silences and Commemorations*, edited by Gavin Smith and Gerald Sider, 31–61. Toronto: University of Toronto Press, 1997.

———. *Silencing the Past: Power and the Production of History*. Boston: Beacon, 1995.

Turner, Robert F., ed. *The Jefferson-Hemings Controversy: Report of the Scholars Commission*. Durham, NC: Carolina Academic Press, 2011.

Unsworth, Barry. *Sacred Hunger*. New York: Norton, 1992.

Walcott, Derek. *Omeros*. New York: Farrar, Straus and Giroux, 1990.

———. "The Sea Is History." 1979. In *Selected Poems*, edited by Edward Baugh, 123–25. London: Faber, 2007.

Wald, Gayle. *Crossing the Line: Racial Passing in Twentieth-Century U.S. Literature and Culture*. Durham, NC: Duke University Press, 2000.

Walker, Lisa. *Looking Like What You Are: Sexual Style, Race, and Lesbian Identity*. New York: NYU Press, 2001.

Walker, Margaret. *Jubilee*. Boston: Houghton Mifflin, 1966.

Walker, Sheila. *Ceremonial Spirit Possession in Africa and Afro-America: Forms, Meanings, and Functional Significance for Individuals and Social Groups*. Leiden: Brill, 1972.

Wall, Cheryl A. *Worrying the Line: Black Women Writers, Lineage, and Literary Tradition*. Chapel Hill: University of North Carolina Press, 2005.

Wallace, Michele. *Invisibility Blues: From Pop to Theory*. London: Verso, 2008.

Walvin, James. *The* Zong*: A Massacre, the Law and the End of Slavery*. New Haven, CT: Yale University Press, 2011.

Webster, Jane. "The *Zong* in the Context of the Eighteenth-Century Slave Trade." *Journal of Legal History* 28.3 (December 2007): 285–98.

Weinstock, Jeffrey Andrew. "Introduction: The Spectral Turn." In Weinstock, *Spectral America*, 3–17.

———, ed. *Spectral America: Phantoms and the National Imagination*. Madison: University of Wisconsin Press, 2004.

———. "Ten Minutes for Seven Letters: Reading *Beloved*'s Epitaph." *Arizona Quarterly* 61.3 (Autumn 2005): 129 52.

Wekker, Gloria. *The Politics of Passion: Women's Sexual Culture in the Afro-Surinamese Diaspora*. New York: Columbia University Press, 2006.

White, Deborah Gray. *Ar'n't I a Woman? Female Slaves in the Plantation South*. 1985. New York: Norton, 1999.

White, Hayden. *The Content of the Form: Narrative Discourse and Historic Representation*. Baltimore: Johns Hopkins University Press, 1987.

Whooley, Owen. "Objectivity and Its Discontents: Knowledge Advocacy in the Sally Hemings Controversy." *Social Forces* 86.4 (June 2008): 1367–89.

Wideman, John Edgar. *The Cattle Killing*. Boston: Houghton Mifflin, 1996.

Wiegman, Robyn. *American Anatomies: Theorizing Race and Gender*. Durham, NC: Duke University Press, 1996.

Williams, John. "Return of a Native Daughter: An Interview with Paule Marshall and Maryse Condé." *Sage* 3.2 (Fall 1986): 52–53.

Williams, Lawson. "Homophobia and Gay Rights Activism in Jamaica." 2000. In Glave, *Our Caribbean*, 382–87.

Williams, Sherley Anne. *Dessa Rose*. New York: Morrow, 1986.

Winsbro, Bonnie. *Supernatural Forces: Belief, Difference, and Power in Contemporary Works by Ethnic Women*. Amherst: University of Massachusetts Press, 1993.

Wiredu, Kwasi. "Toward Decolonizing African Philosophy and Religion." *African Studies Quarterly* 1.4 (1998): 17–46.

Wolfreys, Julian. *Victorian Hauntings: Spectrality, Gothic, the Uncanny and Literature*. Basingstoke, UK: Palgrave, 2002.

Wood, Marcus. *Blind Memory: Visual Representations of Slavery in England and America, 1780–1865*. New York: Routledge, 2000.

———. "Imaging the Unspeakable and Speaking the Unimaginable: The 'Description' of the Slave Ship *Brookes* and the Visual Interpretation of the Middle Passage." *Lumen: Selected Proceedings from the Canadian Society for Eighteenth-Century Studies* 16 (1997): 211–45.

Woodson, Byron W., Sr. *A President in the Family: Thomas Jefferson, Sally Hemings, and Thomas Woodson*. Westport, CT: Praeger, 2001.

Young, Al. *Seduction by Light*. New York: Delta, 1988.

Young, Hershini Bhana. *Haunting Capital: Memory, Text and the Black Diasporic Body*. Hanover, NH: University Press of New England, 2006.

Young, Jason R. *Rituals of Resistance: African Atlantic Religion in Kongo and the Lowcountry South in the Era of Slavery*. Baton Rouge: LSU Press, 2007.

Young, Robert J. C. *White Mythologies: Writing History and the West*. 1990. London: Routledge, 2004.

Zamora, Lois Parkinson. "Magical Romance / Magical Realism: Ghosts in U.S. and Latin American Fiction." In *Magical Realism: Theory, History, Community*, edited by Lois Parkinson Zamora and Wendy B. Faris, 497–550. Durham, NC: Duke University Press, 2005.

CREDITS

Grateful acknowledgment is made to the following for permission to reprint previously published material:

Universitätsverlag Winter GmbH: "The Ghost as Alternative Epistemology in the Works of Toni Morrison, Gloria Naylor, and Michelle Cliff," by Joanne Chassot, in *"Forever Young"? The Changing Images of America*, European Views of the United States 4, ed. Philip Coleman and Stephen Matterson (Heidelberg: Universitätsverlag Winter, 2012), 183–96.

McFarland & Company Inc. (Box 611, Jefferson, NC 28640, www.mcfarlandpub.com): "Black Women's Ghostly Re-visions of History," by Joanne Chassot, in *Afterimages of Slavery: Essays on Appearances in Recent American Films, Literature, Television and Other Media*, ed. Marlene D. Allen and Seretha D. Williams, © 2012 Marlene D. Allen and Seretha D. Williams.

Taylor & Francis Ltd. (www.tandfonline.com): "'Voyage through death / to life upon these shores': The Living Dead of the Middle Passage," by Joanne Chassot, *Atlantic Studies* 12, no. 1 (January 2, 2015): 90–108, reprinted here with modifications as chapter 1, "'Voyage through death / to life upon these shores': Representing the Middle Passage."

Liveright Publishing Corporation: "Middle Passage," © 1962, 1966 by Robert Hayden, from *Collected Poems of Robert Hayden* by Robert Hayden, edited by Frederick Glaysher.

BSN Press: "'Dusky Sally': La femme esclave entre histoire et fiction," by Joanne Chassot, *A Contrario*, vol. 14 (2010), 78–91, translated by Joanne Chassot from the French and reprinted with modifications as chapter 2, "Dusky Sallys: Re-Visioning the Silences of History."

The Michelle Cliff Trust, Diana Horowitz, Trustee, c/o Faith Childs Literary Agency Inc., 111 John Street, Suite 1260, New York, NY 10038: *Claiming an Identity They Taught Me to Despise* © 1980 by Michelle Cliff, and *The Land of Look Behind* © 1985 by Michelle Cliff. There can be no usage of these works without express permission to do so.

Lorna Goodison, "Nanny," from *I Am Becoming My Mother* (London: New Beacon Books, 1986), © 1986 by Lorna Goodison.

INDEX

Note: Page numbers with "n" indicate notes.